D0567020

Economics Does Not Lie

Economics Does Not Lie

A Defense of the Free Market in a Time of Crisis

Guy Sorman

Translated by Alexis Cornel

ENCOUNTER BOOKS
NEW YORK · LONDON

First American edition published in 2009 by Encounter Books, an activity of Encounter for Culture and Education, Inc.,a nonprofit, tax exempt corporation. Encounter Books website address: www.encounterbooks.com

Manufactured in the United States and printed on acid-free paper. The paper used in this publication meets the minimum requirements of ANSI/NISO Z39.48 1992 (R 1997) *(Permanence of Paper)*.

FIRST AMERICAN EDITION

LIBRARY OF CONGRESS CATALOGING-IN-PUBLICATION DATA

Sorman, Guy.
    Economics does not lie : a defense of the free market in a time of crisis / by Guy Sorman.
      p. cm.
    Includes bibliographical references and index.
    ISBN-13: 978-1-59403-254-7 (hbk. : alk. paper)
    ISBN-10: 1-59403-254-8 (hbk. : alk. paper)
    1. Free enterprise. 2. Free trade. 3. Economic policy.
4. Economics. I. Title.
HB95.S67 2009
330.12'2—dc22

2009006924

Table of Contents

Introduction

ECONOMICS IS A SCIENCE, whose purpose is to distinguish between good and bad policies. In a time of economic turmoil, it is essential to recall that economics as a discipline is based on real knowledge. Under the pressure of public opinion and media hysteria, political leaders tend to act like know-nothings. But to proceed as if economics were not a science is a sure recipe for disaster. Because the world economy has entered a period of slowing growth, it is important as well to remember that economic life is cyclical by definition. Economic cycles are the result of innovation. Innovations—whether technical, financial, or managerial—generate growth, but not all innovations are successful. We learn by trial and error, as the economy selects the useful innovations and rejects the useless ones. This process inevitably has its ups and downs. It would be nice to escape economic cycles, but there is no way to have growth without innovation, innovation without risk, or risk without economic cycles. Cycles and downturns are thus not the enemies of economic progress; the enemy of human development is bad economic policies.

During the course of the twentieth century alone, bad economic policies ravaged entire nations, producing more victims than any epidemic. The collectivization of land—in Russia during the thirties, in China during the fifties, in Tanzania during the sixties—starved hundreds of millions of peasants. The uncontrolled creation of currency produced runaway inflation that destabilized Germany during the twenties and facilitated the rise of Nazism. In 2007, hyperinflation devastated Zimbabwe. The nationalization of enterprises and the expulsion of entrepreneurs ruined Argentina during the forties and Egypt during the fifties. India's licensing regime froze the country's development from 1949 to 1991.

Good economic policies, by contrast, allowed for the reconstruction of Western Europe after World War II in less than thirty years, followed by that of Eastern Europe beginning in 1990. Over the two last decades until the 2008 crisis, good economics lifted 800 million people out of mass poverty, particularly in India and in China. In civilizations once thought to be stagnant—Japan, Korea, Turkey—good economic strategies have engendered prosperity. For the last ten years in Africa, more rational economic management has been gradually rescuing from poverty the thirteen nations that French economist François Bourguignon calls the "African G13."

As they become more prosperous, people live longer, their freedom of choice increases, and their freedoms expand. Modern economic history teaches that access to natural resources is not absolutely essential for progress, as many still believed during the 1960s, and it also shows that there is no civilization unfit for development, as was commonly supposed until as late as the 1980s. Growth does not even require democracy; under anarchy, however, economic development is impossible.

All that matters for development are good economic decisions. This is a very recent finding. Though economics as a science arose in Great Britain and in France at the end of the eighteenth century, only beginning in the 1960s did it cross the threshold of true rationality. If progress is essential to the meaning of science, as philosopher Karl Popper believed, then economics in the twentieth century has demonstrated extraordinary scientific progress. In an earlier day, intuition, observation, opinion, and conviction enjoyed equal status; theories were vague and hardly verifiable. It is significant that during the 1960s, one could still teach economics at prestigious universities without using equations. Today, economics is inconceivable without algorithms. Back in the seventies, French economist and statesman Raymond Barre deplored the conquest of economics by mathematicians, at the expense of history and culture. It is true that computers, which make it possible to work with formerly incalculable statistical quantities, tend to reduce, sometimes excessively, the science of economics to mathematical models inaccessible to the uninitiated. Still, these models are not built from abstractions but rather are based on statistics that describe observed reality. And like all sciences, economics is rooted in the permanent confrontation between theoretical models and concrete experimentation: A model as such does not make good economics.

Since 1990, experience has verified theoretical models and the science of economics has been revolutionized. The preceding period was characterized by the rivalry between two economic systems: state socialism and market capitalism, East and West. Both models seemed to represent valid, if imperfect, examples of economic organization. Faced with this alternative, nations hesitated and economists were divided. Advocates on both sides attributed the obvious defects of each system not to the model itself but to management errors external to it. When the Soviet Union crumbled, the model that it embodied was eliminated—or, more precisely, the Soviet Union crumbled because the socialist economic system proved unviable.

Now there exists only one economic system: free-market capitalism, informed by classical liberal economic theory. Some regret this state of affairs, but no one can deny it. Thus economics now focuses exclusively on this model, aiming to understand it better, to improve it, and to extend its application. As Alan Greenspan writes in his memoir, *The Age of Turbulence,* it is quite extraordinary that such a complex and counterintuitive economic organization as the free market, based on self-regulation, has gained such wide acceptance. Mankind tends to prefer ostensibly better-organized systems, ruled from the top down. This explains people's continuing ambivalence toward market forces, adds Greenspan.

The socialist critique, not unlike Sovietology, now belongs to the history of ideas, and hardly at all to the science of economics. One can now say that a consensus exists among economists as to the superior efficiency of market economies. Such a consensus annoys idealists and ideologues, who dream of a world more just, more spiritual, or more green. Because the contemporary situation disappoints them, such voices tend to deny to economics the status of science. True, it is not an exact science; it is a human science. Still, the history of the exact sciences teaches that exactness is never more than relative, evolving from one theory to the next, each one approximating a reality that eludes our complete grasp.

Thus, in 2007, a new kind of financial crisis generated by "derivatives"—a major financial innovation—has created a new kind of disequilibrium that calls for new solutions. Since the beginning of this crisis, the global consensus among world leaders and economists has been to repair the free-market economy, not replace it. Some incline toward strictly free-market solutions: Let the market clean up the mess and select the winners and the losers. Others prefer state intervention to save financial institutions—but they are not statists, and they do not advocate replacing the free-market economy with a centrally planned one; the state should only act as an insurer of the system. The still-open debate between both schools is not ideological but pragmatic: Which is the quickest way to restart the normal pace of the free economy?

One might ask: Is not the science of economics political from the outset? Yes, but all the sciences are deeply conditioned by philosophical preferences. The historian Thomas Kuhn has shown that scientists must always situate themselves within preestablished paradigms and can only look in directions where they already hope to find something. Economics is no different. Within the free-market model, however, there is an immense field of investigation, since the functioning of the market is far from automatic. Is the market imperfect because it is too free, or because it is not free enough? What political, legal, judicial, regulatory, monetary, social, fiscal, and international institutions are essential to the market's optimal functioning? Where does one draw the (fluid) line between market and state?

The role of economists in this debate is to propose the soundest possible solutions, while realizing that markets and states are motivated by particular interests: Profit-seeking by some will always collide with power-seeking by others. It is the economist's job to analyze both and to denounce their excesses.

Berkeley professor Gérard Debreu, who won the 1983 Nobel Prize in Economics, has observed that the only thing economists cannot do is predict. This is not quite true: Economists *can* predict that a bad policy will necessarily lead to a catastrophe. Avinash Dixit, a development economist at Princeton, is quite willing to explain that, if one wants to arrive at a certain point, one should not go in a certain direction. Economists say no more than this; people remain free to go in one direction or another. The science of economics says only that those intent on concrete results must not adopt means inconsistent with the ends they seek. Just as the success of modern medicine consists mainly in the prevention of risks, contemporary economic science attempts to avoid collective poverty. An economist cannot guarantee the prosperity of each individual any more than a doctor can heal every patient. But today Rimbaud would no longer write "economics is a horror"; for the mass of mankind, it has become a source of hope. The following inquiry attempts to retrace the theoretical steps behind this immense progress and explore their practical applications.

The Capitalist Break

Is it not the case that economic progress has always outpaced political progress? During the Middle Ages, the expansion of commerce preceded the creation of city-states; after World War II, the European Common Market was the forerunner of a politically unified Europe (which has still not been achieved); in 1991, the Soviet economy collapsed before the Communist Party realized the fact and dissolved its empire; contemporary governments talk and behave as if they controlled the choices of businesses, when in fact firms operate in a global economy; and we still speak of the Third World (an expression coined by Alfred Sauvy in 1952), even though many poor countries have adopted free-market economic policies and are now experiencing growth similar to that of rich countries.

Authoritarian governments still attempt to control information in the market, but since the U.S. government privatized the Internet, the World Wide Web has become independent of all authority. In 1989, the Berlin Wall fell, and in 1995, the Internet was liberated; thus the world changed economic systems. Every economy, to one degree or another, is now necessarily capitalist and global—that is, determined primarily by the rules of the market and operating across national borders. Governments are reluctant to adapt to the new rules, which do not eliminate the necessity of the rule of law but profoundly modify the available means of intervention. Political power recedes, and economic power advances; the distinction between the two roles remains, but the boundary has shifted. There are losers and winners, but this is not a zero-sum game, for the globalized world has been in a cycle of regular growth. Because global wealth is increasing, the losses are only relative.

The theory of this free-market revolution was elaborated before the revolution happened. How was it possible for economists such as Milton Friedman (monetarism), Gérard Debreu (optimal markets), Robert Lucas (rational anticipation), George Stigler (deregulation), and Edmund Phelps (the harmful character of inflation) to predict, as early as the 1960s and 1970s, which economic policies would be widely accepted in the years after 1980? For what might appear to be a prophetic gift, one may discern two rational explanations.

First, simple theoretical analysis made it possible to foresee the dysfunctions of centralized, planned, statist, and inflationary economies. The inefficiency of the anti-market system was well established, but it was impossible to know when—or whether— it would come to an end. The theorists cited above, and others of the same schools, prepared an alternative model, assuming that the statist system might break down. Second, when attempts to restart economies by so-called Keynesian interventions failed, governments turned naturally toward the only "alternative utopia" (Friedrich Hayek's expression) that was available: economic freedom. Its effectiveness, as demonstrated in the Anglo-Saxon world during the early 1980s, rallied the whole planet, from Paris to Beijing, from New Delhi to Brasilia and Moscow. For there is only one good economic system: the one that works.

The Minimal State Is Indispensable

For those who do not know what the free market is, to say that it has won the battle of facts will sound like a provocation or an aberration. But facts are facts, and the power of the market is undeniable, once one is clear on its definition. As the Hungarian economist János Kornai has explained, there are only two known and tested economic systems: the socialist system and the market system. They are founded on opposing principles. In the socialist system, property is public, competition is eliminated, and production is planned; this is a "planned" or "dictated" order, to use Hayek's expression. In the market system, property is private, internal and external competition is the rule, and production is determined by the initiatives of an active minority, the entrepreneurs (a term coined by Jean-Baptiste Say in the 1820s); here, order is "spontaneous." The victory of the market system since the 1980s has been marked by the disappearance of the socialist system and its transformation into a capitalist economy. Everywhere, the public sector has given way to privatization; currency has escaped state control, to be governed by independent central banks; competition has been stimulated by the deregulation of markets and the opening of borders; and taxation has become less progressive, so as to retain entrepreneurs within a national territory, where they can create new jobs.

But is not China an exception to this general trend? Certainly, according to the rhetoric of its leaders. But in practice, the whole country is moving toward a capitalist system. We will show that the Chinese case represents a transition from a rural to an industrial society, not a general model distinct from the free-market system. In any case, India and Brazil, the other emerging powers, have clearly joined the movement toward free-market democracy, and in this sense they are ahead of China on a predictable path.

Simultaneously with this worldwide liberalizing trend, it has become clearer that states or international organizations—in effect, superstates—are essential for the proper functioning of markets. The most absolutist of free-market advocates now recognize that the state must be a guarantor of rules, for reasons intrinsic to the market. Not all economic actors dispose of the same information. Since information is asymmetric (to use economist George Akerlof's term), an arbiter must create transparency. In complex economies, particularly financial markets, as the French economist Jean Tirole has observed, informational intermediaries like the ratings agencies spring up to dispense information. These private institutions allow economic actors to make relatively well-informed decisions in the labyrinth of globalized finance. The credibility of these intermediaries stems from the fact that they risk their reputations and their money. If the information they offer is false, the intermediary is discredited. It is nevertheless the case that financial crises, such as the Enron scandal in 2001 or the subprime and credit crisis that began in 2007, can reveal the imperfection of private sources of information. There is no last resort in this context other than the state, the ultimate insurer when the market fails: The state also puts its reputation and its funds on the line, though this is not to say that it is absolutely trustworthy. Modern free-market theory thus recognizes the essential role of good public institutions in ensuring that transactions in national and international markets lead to lasting economic development.

Modern states perform another essential function in free-market economies, which some purists are less willing to admit: the establishment of collective responsibility. Friction is inevitable between this function and the state's guarantee of the market. Libertarian thinkers might see the state as the ultimate guarantor of public services, but they prefer that the private sector actually manage education, social services, sanitation, and security. Those who are less libertarian refuse to dissociate the state's guarantee of services from its actual management of them. The arbitration of this conflict has become a main focus of politics in contemporary democracies, and even in the absence of democracy. The business of politics has come down to moving the boundary of public policy toward the market or toward the state, toward solidarity or toward entrepreneurship—but all now within a free-market system.

Does this mean that we have reached an "end of history" in economics, to borrow a phrase made famous by Francis Fukuyama, by way of Hegel? In one sense, perhaps yes: Economic science will never rediscover the virtues of hyperinflation or industrial nationalization. But if we understand the end of history in economics to mean the complete realization, in practice, of the findings of economic science, then it has not arrived. The free market still has enemies and critics, ranging from those who dream of a world more just, more spiritual, or transformed in some other utopian way to those who simply seek to defend their own narrow material interests to those legitimate researchers who try to look beyond the market. And we must not overlook ignorance: Economic principles aren't widely understood among the public or even among lawmakers. The indisputable fact that the world has experienced a long period of growth as global trade has expanded remains strangely unknown. Doubtless the news is too good.

In the future, the threat to the beneficial influence of economic science will come less from tired socialist-revolutionary rhetoric than from new dangers, such as terrorism and epidemics. Terrorism is partly a consequence of globalization: Young, uprooted people unable to adapt to a dynamic, capitalist world invent new global ideologies and seek to put them into practice with global weapons. Globalization can also accelerate the proliferation of deadly illnesses. The AIDS epidemic was the first global attack by a mutant virus; SARS, avian flu, or some unknown illness could follow, surging from uncontrolled Chinese, Indian, or African backwaters and following the massive migrations of a global economy. Terrorism and epidemics could both unleash political upheavals that would undermine the market order itself.

Then there is the fear of ecological disturbances, which could result in incoherent policies that would not necessarily diminish risks to the environment but might prevent development and thus harm the interests of the poorest peoples. To take one example, prohibiting genetically modified organisms—which, evidence suggests, pose no threat whatsoever to the environment—will hurt the productivity of farming at a time when global demand for food is sure to grow.

Another danger is inseparable from the very nature of economic systems: Growth is cyclical. Despite the present anxiety about a deep recession, the progress of economic science now allows governments and economic actors to understand crises and manage them better. The Great Depression probably could not happen again, since the political mistakes that aggravated it, such as protectionism and the evaporation of credit, are not as likely to be repeated in the future: The Federal Reserve, the European Central Bank, and the Bank of England have demonstrated as much in the current mortgage crisis by supporting the banking system. But occasional crises are inevitable, bound up as they are with innovation—and when the new drives out the old through creative destruction and forces sometimes painful adaptations, we find these upheavals harder to bear, as we have grown more accustomed to perpetual growth.

Similarly, free trade means that some people will lose their jobs, as we all know; foreign competition can wipe out entire companies or even entire industries. We all know it because, as Friedman argued, layoffs and closings receive disproportionate media coverage. Meanwhile, no one talks about the ongoing reduction in prices for consumers and investors, scattered among a huge number of beneficiaries. That helps explain why politicians are prone to deride free trade and voters are too often ready to agree.

If it seeks to help the losers in the free market, government should not back away from either free trade or creative destruction to start subsidizing doomed and obsolete activities, a protectionist course that guarantees only economic decline. Instead, it should help the losers change jobs more easily by improving educational opportunities and by facilitating new investment, which creates more employment. The essential task of democratic governments and opinion makers, when a society is confronting economic cycles and political pressure, is to secure and protect the system that has served humanity so well, not to change it for the worse on the pretext of its imperfection.

Still, this lesson is doubtless one of the hardest to translate into language that public opinion will accept. The best of all possible economic systems is indeed imperfect. Whatever truths are uncovered by economic science, the free market is finally only a reflection of human nature, itself hardly perfectible.

PART 1

The New Economy

Since the 1980s, modern economies have become denationalized—removed from state control—and dematerialized. Frontiers no longer form the frame of reference for entrepreneurs or consumers; national governments develop alongside the economy but tend no longer to determine its choices or its rhythms; all kinds of services wind up added to the production of traditional material goods. These are global tendencies—so much so that the old notion of national growth rates becomes less significant than that of the worldwide trend analyzed by Edward Prescott: We all progress together—from Paris to Beijing to New York to New Delhi—or together we stagnate. The balance sheet for this ever-globalizing economy is positive for humanity, argues Jagdish Bhagwati, because it has enabled immense populations to lift themselves out of misery.

This evolution partly results from technical progress. Even more, it is the happy consequence of an improved comprehension of the engines of growth. Entrepreneurs won't start businesses, savers won't save, and consumers won't consume unless they can take a long view and have confidence in stable and predictable institutions. True money (as described by Kenneth Rogoff), free trade, the durability of contracts (as illustrated by Avner Greif), solid banking, guaranteed property rights, honest states, legitimate international organizations (as defended by François Bourguignon)—these constitute the good institutions necessary for sustained development. When cyclical recessions occur, as in 2008, the priority for rational governments should be to maintain such institutions and to resist giving way to political passion or magical interventions.

How are good institutions born? Can they take root in any civilization? The experience of the past thirty years shows that the institutions essential to a good economy are compatible with the most diverse cultures—it is not necessary, despite what many still believe, to change mind-sets before starting the process of economic development. But it is essential, according to Jean Tirole, to employ a good pedagogy to show people that certain objective conditions are prerequisites to this development. These can be described and taught: One must understand good economics in order to practice it.

Is democracy absolutely essential for development? Dani Rodrik and Daron Acemoglu observe that while capitalism can do without democracy, democracy cannot exist without capitalism.

CHAPTER ONE

Natural Growth

WHY TRAVEL THE WORLD to meet economists? Isn't everything they know available in their publications? Such questions occur to me as I wait for Edward Prescott in his office at the Federal Reserve Bank of Minneapolis in mid-August 2007. But Prescott's works are expressed in the language of mathematics; he addresses himself to his peers, not to the public. Upon receiving the Nobel Prize in 2004, Prescott declared that economists must educate the public to prevent politicians from lapsing into error or demagogy. But good economists are not necessarily great teachers. A researcher is rarely a public intellectual, and the economists who do address the general public are not always the most legitimate. There are also well-known economists who, bolstered by a Nobel Prize, speak publicly about things outside their realm of expertise, profiting from a glory acquired elsewhere. As Jean Tirole has observed, one has to be a bit schizophrenic to be a serious researcher and at the same time address the general public. The mind of the researcher tends toward nuance and complexity, whereas public communication requires simplification and exaggeration. But by speaking directly with Prescott and other

17

economic thinkers of the same caliber, one may better understand what their research is really about, what their real findings are, and what they have to teach us.

According to Prescott, the average growth rate of the United States from 1890 to the present is 2 percent per capita. This trend, which may be considered natural or spontaneous, reflects the constant progress of economic efficiency in the world's leading country—that is, the country at the forefront of economic innovation. Economists have measured this growth by "smoothing out" the accidental events along the way, such as business cycles and depressions. Over the same period, the average return rate of invested capital was 4 percent. Keep those two numbers in mind: 2 percent and 4 percent. In Prescott's view, the leading country defines the global trend because innovations necessarily spread in all directions fairly rapidly. In the leading country, a short-term trend may be affected by exterior shocks, such as a rise in oil prices, or by internal chaos caused by the appearance of a new product or by errors in economic policy. Outside the leading country, it is possible to surpass the trend momentarily—say, in a time of reconstruction, as in postwar Europe, or during a takeoff phase, as in India or China. But in the long run, the trend of the leading country cannot be surpassed without a change in leadership. Before the United States, Great Britain and Germany were the leaders; after the United States, Prescott expects the European Union to take the lead, but this is only a hypothesis. In the meantime, a developed economy that grows at a rate of less than 2 percent would be underperforming: It would be in a virtual crisis. Such a crisis, according to Prescott, always results from bad economic policy.

The 2-percent trend reflects observable and unarguable statistics. But the human benefits of growth are, in fact, far greater. The growth trend does not measure the decline in the death rate or the increase in life expectancy; these are real consequences of growth, but they do not show up in economic data. Nor do the statistics account for the improvement in our daily comfort.

William Nordhaus of Yale calculated the rate of increase of artificial light, from which almost all humanity now benefits at a very low cost; this rate has been much greater than 2 percent. Electric lighting, once a luxury, is now available to all, yet economic data do not account for this improvement. The trend thus undervalues the real benefits of growth, and its perturbations are less significant than the trend itself. Paradoxically, Prescott notes, economists pay the most attention to the perturbations. Crises are more fascinating than spontaneous growth, given the fear (or hope, for some) that these crises will eventually overturn the market economy. Prescott says that this won't happen—unless we forget the direct relation between growth and the quantity of labor.

The Labor Factor

The "Prescott model" seems quite simple: Growth results from the combination of capital, labor, and efficiency. This third factor, the most difficult to evaluate, has to do with the relation between institutions and productivity. It is the origin of differences in growth rates among nations. Among developed countries, it is easy to compare efficiency because means of production are similar. If one measures the productivity of the automobile industry in the United States, Japan, and France, the discrepancies are modest because innovation circulates and imitation is almost instantaneous. In this group of homogeneous nations, the amount of invested capital is also comparable. Thus it is the quantity of labor alone, Prescott argues, that explains the real differences in growth.

Prescott has shown that after World War II, in a period of reconstruction, the Europeans and the Japanese worked more than the Americans but did so less efficiently; their labor surplus allowed growth to catch up, followed by efficiency. For a quarter-century, the Europeans and the Japanese have been as efficient as the Americans, with small differences: France is more efficient than the United States (by 10 percent) and Japan slightly less (by 10 percent). But these small gaps in efficiency are not enough to explain the gaps in growth. The slower growth in continental Europe in comparison with the United States since the 1980s is due to a reverse in the labor equation between America and other developed countries: With comparable efficiency, Americans now work more and become wealthier, whereas others work less and grow relatively poorer. Let us be precise about what Prescott means by "quantity of labor": His model only takes into account productive labor subject to taxation. Labor "under the table" is deducted, as is uncompensated and untaxed household labor. In each nation, the quantity of taxed labor is affected by vacations, the length of the workweek, the age of entry into the labor market, the retirement age, and unemployment. Thus one is comparing homogeneous data.

Beginning with this simple definition of the amount of work, for every 100 hours worked in the United States, workers put in 75 hours in Germany, 68 in France, and 64 in Italy. For the record, in 1970, the French and the Germans worked 105 hours for every 100 hours worked in the United States. The productivity of a Frenchman in 1970 was measured at 74 on a scale where 100 represented the productivity of an American worker; by working more than the Americans, but with less efficiency, the productivity of a Frenchman was measured at 77 to the U.S. worker's 100. Today, a Frenchman, in 68 hours of work with an efficiency of 110 (to the U.S. worker's 100), produces on a scale of 74. In total, productivity per person in the United States is measured on average at 40 percent above productivity in Western Europe; with close to the same efficiency, this difference between businesses on the two sides of the Atlantic can only be explained by the quantity of labor. In other words, there is no way for the French and the Germans to catch up with the American standard of living except to work more.

It remains to be understood why, since the 1980s, Americans have "chosen" collectively to work more, whereas Europeans have made the opposite choice. Who chooses—and how? No one knows who chooses, but everything happens as if there had been a choice. What motivates this choice, or this appearance of choice? The answer, according to Prescott, leaves no room for doubt: taxation.

Taxes on Labor

In 1980, Americans and Europeans worked the same amount; the level of taxes on labor (income and payroll taxes) was identical in Europe and in the United States. Now that Americans produce, per capita, 40 percent more than Europeans, we find that taxes in Europe, on average, confiscate 60 percent of earnings; in the United States, the average taken away is 40 percent. What is measured here is a marginal, not an average, rate, which affects the quantity of additional labor. Because an American, by working more, keeps 60 percent of what he earns, as opposed to 40 percent in Europe, Prescott concludes that fiscal pressure suffices to explain Europeans' implicit choice to work less.

There are many other reasons—psychological, social, legal—for this collective choice; but the preference for leisure, the rigidity of the labor market, and unemployment are *consequences* of nonwork, not the cause. Prescott's model shows that on the basis of statistical data and comparisons over time, simulations can measure the impact of taxation on work. These simulations produce theoretical results that one may then compare with reality. Within a few decimals, the manipulation of taxation alone, in fact, determines the choice of whether to work or not. The other factors behind nonworking, though not negligible, are not necessary to the demonstration.

In France's case, Prescott's model indicates that a reduction of taxes on labor from 60 percent to 40 percent would give rise to an increase in labor time of 6.6 percent, in turn increasing buying power by 19 percent over a worker's life. Over the long term, an increase in labor time produces cumulative growth. The extra growth generated by the reduction of taxes, by creating new employees, reduces unemployment: It is not unemployment that slows growth or reduces the quantity of work, but the opposite.

Prescott's theory is far from unanimously accepted. It is provocative and, like all theories, falsifiable. Still, considered empirically, the American experience seems to confirm it. Beginning in the 1980s, in the United States, fiscal pressure decreased, in particular for couples. On average, a working spouse could retain 80 percent of his or her earnings—a strong incentive to seek a second salary. Coinciding with this reduction in taxes on labor, the rate of women participating in the American labor market has greatly increased since the 1980s. American growth seems therefore to have accelerated, thanks to the decrease in taxes and the simultaneous increase in working hours. One great surprise of modern economics, in Prescott's view, is the flexibility of work. Salaries respond to positive and negative incentives, revealing reserves of unexploited growth in each nation.

How to Reduce Taxes on Labor

To understand what follows—the logic of reducing taxes on labor—a brief detour by way of what is called the supply-side theory of economics is necessary. It was not an American but a Frenchman who, early in the nineteenth century, observed that the motor of the economy was not the consumer but the producer: "Production," wrote Jean-Baptiste Say, "creates its own markets." This determination of growth by supply is easy to understand, almost trivial: If no business asked you to buy a cellular phone, you would not seek to buy one, because you would feel no need for a telephone that did not exist.

This primacy of supply was contested by John Maynard Keynes, who attributed the crisis of 1930 to a lack of demand. It was necessary, Keynes argued, to revive consumption to get out of the crisis. This idea—to increase buying power to increase overall growth—could not fail to seduce, but it has unfortunately failed each time it has been applied, particularly after the economic crisis of 1973 in the West. When supply is lacking, an increase in buying power merely translates into a price increase.

According to the logic of supply, which Prescott emphasizes, only an increase in the quantity of labor—in supply—leads to an increase in production; the new growth thus induced allows the state to tax at a lower rate but on a greater accrued total wealth. The state benefits from this growth as much as the workers. This hypothesis was popularized by the American economist Arthur Laffer, who became known in the early 1980s because of a bell curve that bears his name. The "Laffer curve" suggests that, at a rate of taxation above 50 percent, tax revenues for the state actually diminish, because growth slows; on the other hand, the lowering of rates augments tax revenues, since it stimulates growth. The theory of the Laffer curve, "mathematically approximate, but intuitively correct," says Prescott, has exercised considerable influence in the United States, beginning with the presidency of Ronald Reagan; it justified a steady decrease of the level of taxation, which has coincided with vigorous economic growth. Is this a coincidence? One could argue the point indefinitely. The fact is that the rest of the world has followed the U.S. by reducing maximum tax rates. Even the Europeans have embraced Laffer. Is this because Laffer's curve is true, Prescott wonders? More likely, states, which in the world economy are in fiscal competition with one another, had no choice: High taxes make entrepreneurs flee to more advantageous environments.

If one believes Prescott and Laffer, it would be possible and desirable to reduce taxes without ruining public finances. But in Europe, where taxes on labor finance social welfare programs, the reduction of the highest tax rates alone would not suffice to lighten taxation on labor. To be significant, a reduction would require a different means of financing the social safety net and retirement benefits—a transition from mandated contributions to optional investment. Obviously, the more individuals take responsibility for their risks, the more taxes can decrease.

But how does one determine the optimum that guarantees individuals against greater risks without placing both social solidarity and public finances in peril? This optimum is calculable: In the case of the United States, Prescott shows that with a rate of return on invested capital at about 4 percent per year, it is necessary to invest 8.7 percent of one's salary to receive, at the age of sixty-three, for twenty years, a retirement equivalent to one's final salary. Such privatized retirement funding would allow taxes on labor to fall from 40 percent to 27 percent. Privatized retirement would therefore be less expensive (8.7 percent invested, compared with 13 percent of revenue saved from taxation) to the employee, for an equivalent benefit, because the decrease in taxes would bring about an increase in the quantity of labor and an acceleration of growth. More pragmatically than these mathematical models might suggest, Prescott recommends that employees have the choice between privatized and publicly funded retirement. Under any hypothesis, Prescott's model of dynamic growth, with which almost all economists now agree, does leave open other realistic options to governments seeking full employment and growth. One can seek to evade reality, but one cannot, by evasive speeches or by short-term interventions, obtain concrete and measurable results. Economics, Prescott concludes, obeys laws, not the discretionary power of governments.

There is something worse than evasion, however. Public intervention at the wrong time, which often starts with a poorly interpreted natural business cycle, can plunge the economy into a depression.

How States Cause Depressions

Prescott's scientific authority is founded upon a mathematical model that allows one to predict and analyze depressions quite accurately. Unlike most earlier models, which took snapshots of the situation, Prescott's model is dynamic: It deals with the long term and anticipates the behavior of economic agents. Prescott is therefore one of the architects (Robert Lucas is another) of the scientific revolution of the 1980s that transformed economic policymaking. Previous creators of models and of the policies that applied them believed that entrepreneurs or consumers modified their behavior in response to signals given to them by the state. But in a dynamic model, economic agents are assumed to know that these signals are only signals, not real changes. Thus, they undermine the policies by anticipating the artificial effects that governments expect.

It follows from Prescott's dynamic model that expressions such as "stimulate the economy" or "slow down overheating" make no sense and are merely political or journalistic metaphors. In reality, the economy can only follow real and lasting incentives, not speeches about "stimulating" or "overheating." This implies neither the disappearance of states nor governmental passivity, Prescott argues; indeed, the market economy cannot function without a good state. But the proper role of the state is to maintain the long-term growth trend, not to intervene at every moment. The permanence of this trend will depend, most of all, on the stability and the quality of institutions: the independence of the central bank, a predictable and noninflationary management of money, viable and not-too-onerous judicial institutions, free trade, bankruptcy laws that facilitate industrial renewal, and stable fiscal and social laws that do not create obstacles to the market's proper functioning. It's plenty, Prescott notes, to keep governments busy full-time.

What to do when growth slows? According to Prescott, doing nothing can prove to be expedient. Innovation creates cycles that purge the economy of outdated techniques and products, replacing them with new products or lower prices. In developed countries, the cycle of innovation repeats itself regularly about every forty-two months, though recently the cycle has shown a lengthening trend. These cycles spread out from the leading economy because innovations today are diffused almost instantaneously. Inevitably, these ruptures spark protest from their victims, who in democratic societies are free to exert political pressure on governments. But thanks to a better understanding of the operation of cycles, governments tend not to intervene as much as they once did—or at least they intervene more judiciously by facilitating the retraining of workers affected by innovation. It has not always been this way: An analysis of the depressions of the twentieth century shows how government intervention can transform a natural cycle into a major crisis, even to the point of causing a profound rupture in the growth trend.

Let us consider, with Prescott, a few of the great crises in economic history: the United States' situation in the 1930s, France's and Germany's during the same era, and Japan's stagnation in the last ten years. In the American case, Prescott holds Franklin Roosevelt's New Deal responsible for the severity and the length of the crisis. In 1932, Roosevelt flew to the aid of the distressed sectors by prohibiting competition and price reductions; unproductive businesses were put on public life support, which impeded their replacement by more innovative activities. After 1936, when Roosevelt received his second mandate, salaries and taxes increased, which prevented all investment and innovation. This freezing of the American economy (in fact inaugurated by Herbert Hoover, Roosevelt's predecessor, who had blocked free trade) pushed it toward a sort of soft socialism, marked more by the sharing of poverty than by the creation of new wealth. This New Deal, paradoxically, established Roosevelt's long popularity, even though it buried the American economy until rearmament put everyone back to work.

Prescott is no revisionist—the new scientific consensus among economists holds Roosevelt's policies responsible for the length of the crisis of 1930. Economists are equally in agreement about the French depression of the 1930s: Leon Blum's socialist government in fact prolonged the crisis by reducing the workweek while increasing salaries—a strategic error that the free-market economist Jacques Rueff condemned in his day. But, as with the New Deal, Blum's decisions responded to political and social demands that were legitimate in the short term, even though they violated economic principles.

Would it have been better for the well-being of the American or the French people to let the market work, allowing a more rapid escape from the crisis, or was it better to give priority to an interventionist social policy, thus prolonging the crisis? The question is relevant to any government confronted with an economic cycle. But what would be incoherent today would be to carry out an anti-crisis policy that is now known, beyond dispute, only to make the crisis worse. Are the Western governments acting in an incoherent fashion since the U.S. subprime-mortgage crisis began in 2007? The answer is probably yes. The rational decision would have been to let bankrupt banks disappear. Within a short period, months probably, the market would have eliminated bad banks and bad debts. New banks would have emerged. Simultaneously, nonintervention in the real-estate market would have restored true real-estate prices, and transactions would then have resumed on a new, sustainable basis.

But the U.S. government, followed by European governments, chose another path—or, more precisely, followed two contradictory strategies: Some banks in some countries were going to be deemed too big to fail. Which ones, though, was anybody's guess. Moreover, when governments took over certain banks in certain countries, it became impossible to predict whether they would behave as private shareholders or use their political clout to subsidize investments deemed necessary to implement social justice or to protect the environment. Those uncertainties have potentially created a long-term global stagnation. A free-market strategy could have brought a more severe recession, but a shorter one, followed by a quicker rebound.

The provisional lesson of the current crisis is ambiguous. On the one hand, governments did not repeat the dramatic mistakes of the 1930s. They have learned from economic science. On the other hand, they did not follow a perfectly coherent, scientific strategy—not when public opinion in democracies demanded instant action. In the end, the economists in their ivory towers can only suggest what theoretically would have been best. In this spirit, Prescott circulated the following petition in January 2009:

> Notwithstanding reports that all economists are now Keynesians and that we all support a big increase in the burden of government, we the undersigned do not believe that more government spending is a way to improve economic performance. More government spending by Hoover and Roosevelt did not pull the U.S. economy out of the Great Depression in the 1930s. More government spending also did not solve Japan's "lost decade" in the 1990s. As such, it is a triumph of hope over experience to believe that more government spending will help the United States today. To improve the economy, policy makers should focus on reforms that remove impediments to work, saving investment, and production. Lower tax rates and a reduction of the burden of government are the best ways to use fiscal policy to boost growth.

Hundreds of leading U.S. economists signed the petition. History will prove that they remained true to their science.

CHAPTER TWO

The Institutions of Wealth

HERE IS A PUZZLE: Why are some nations so rich and others so poor, and why have the rich been rich and the poor been poor for such a long time? In what circumstances did Western Europe take off, beginning in the thirteenth century, while other civilizations stagnated? For a contemporary economist, the point is not to understand poverty, since this always has been the common lot of humanity. It makes sense, rather, to inquire into the causes of Western progress, and then to consider the possible conditions for replicating this progress. For two centuries, from Adam Smith to Karl Marx and from Frédéric Bastiat to Max Weber, many causes have been proposed: climate, geography, feudalism, culture, religion, politics. Everyone seeks the light that would illuminate the miracle of growth. For a country to develop, was it necessary to have major ports, as did the Italians and the Dutch? Or was it necessary to destroy feudalism, as the Japanese did? Or to be Protestant, as in Germany, or Confucian, as in Korea? But Switzerland is not a maritime nation, nor is Italy Protestant—and Singapore is tropical. For every hypothesis, there is a counter-example.

This theoretical quest is not without practical consequences, since theories are influential; they frame political debates and ultimately determine the choices of governments and of international institutions concerned with development. In Washington, the World Bank, since its creation in 1944, has always based its loans on the dominant doctrine of the moment, changing policies according to various explanations of development and the solutions derived from these explanations. During the 1960s, for instance, it was necessary to finance "infrastructure" to spur development. Such projects have since rusted away. During the 1980s, the privatization of the public sector and the balancing of public expenses seemed to be the elixir. It was administered without great success. Next it seemed that good government, with elected leaders and uncorrupt administrations—if such could be imposed from outside—would be the key to development. Then the Chinese case turned this reasoning upside down. Is international aid a solution? Its partisans claim that aid is insufficient and that if it were increased, development would follow. Others reply that no country has ever developed thanks to foreign aid. Then a new hypothesis, the very latest, sprang up: Development is a matter of institutions.

Wealth Comes from Long Ago

Foreign aid, it seems, is useless. Good government? No point. Good economic policy? Hardly more promising, if nations are not blessed with the institutions essential to development. And what are these ideal institutions? The rule of law, real judicial institutions, banks and businesses independent of political pressure, and respect for promises and contracts. It is now thought that the existence of such institutions, in varied forms adapted to local cultures, is the foundation of all development. But this presupposes—as almost all economists now admit—that there is no form of development other than the Western model.

The modern economy of Europe was born with its institutions—or, to be more precise, these institutions were born in Europe, where historically they preceded the state. Banks and mercantile guilds appeared in Italy in the thirteenth century, when there was not yet a state or a stable political power. In the United States, the colonials created commercial and financial institutions because they had had practical experience with them in Great Britain, in Germany, or in the Low Countries. Outside Europe, the Japanese imported these institutions in the nineteenth century; Korea, Singapore, Thailand, and Indonesia followed suit in the twentieth century; and all these countries developed successfully. India inherited these institutions from the British, and the Chinese copied the West. Remaining on the sidelines are those countries that are both poor and without institutions. Why do they reject these institutions?

Two pioneers propose two contradictory explanations. For Avner Greif, a professor at Stanford University who was educated in Israel and the United States, culture—particularly religious values—determines the choice of good institutions. For Daron Acemoglu, an Armenian from Turkey and a professor at MIT, the legacies of colonization and the class struggle can lead to good or bad institutions. According to both hypotheses, history weighs heavily on development. Wealth as well as poverty comes from long ago, Greif argues.

Greif situates the historical and geographic origin of development in the Mediterranean region in the twelfth century. Within the international commercial network linking the great Italian cities—Genoa and Venice—with the Eastern Mediterranean and central Asia, a medieval economic revolution occurred, and this revolution was the matrix of future European prosperity; it took shape six centuries before the Industrial Revolution in Great Britain grabbed the baton and gave modernity its present form. Before industry, there was the trade that made possible the accumulation of capital and the birth of a society of bourgeois entrepreneurs.

At the end of this economic revolution, why did Italian cities become masters of the game, gaining the upper hand and keeping it while their Oriental partners sank into poverty? Based on the archives of the two major actors in this Mediterranean commerce, the Genoese and the North Africans known as Maghrebis, Greif has shown that the enduring strength of the former came from their capacity to create most of the modern economic institutions that we still find today: banks, bills of exchange, letters of credit, and joint-stock companies. As for the Maghrebis, they were a people of Jewish religion and Arab culture, traders originating in Baghdad who settled in the Maghreb before choosing Cairo as a base. Their migrations were determined by changes in the Muslim dynasties to which they were subject.

The Genoese and the Maghrebis alike were skillful businessmen; both peoples were energetic and prosperous. But their bases differed. Maghrebi networks were grounded in the family, communal solidarity, and personal engagements. Such bonds are fragile by nature: If they are broken, there is no legal means to restore them. In Genoa, on the other hand, business took place between individuals, not communities. Each person committed himself by written contract and borrowed not by pleading his lineage but by producing real guarantees. The great Genoese ventures were not familial but corporate: Joint-stock companies assumed the risks. With the Maghrebis, the economic risks remained confined to families, which limited ambitions. To establish the rule of law, the Genoese created a political power that was relatively weak and suited to their needs: the city-state, which would become the Italian model and then spread across Europe before the appearance of the great states of the modern age. This Genoese model would stand the test of time; the other would disappear. The Maghrebis have long since melted into the Jewish communities of the Arab world, while the Genoese have become Italians. Why, then, did the Maghrebis fail to adopt the good institutions of the Genoese? In Greif's view, the institutions contradicted their values, their conception of the world, and their faith.

Individualism: The Foundation of Prosperity

In the Christian and individualist society of Genoa, families were of limited size, nuclear. This is the European tradition, anchored in the Greco-Roman past and reinforced by Christianity; here, sin and redemption are personal matters. Individuals are bound not by blood but by good contracts, beginning with the contract of marriage, which, at least in principle, is unforced. The opposite is the case in the East, particularly in the Arab world from which the Maghrebi Jews came.

Among the Maghrebis, the individual had no existence outside the community. Whoever deserted the community lost his personal and economic credit; thus one could undertake nothing apart from the family. And what of women? They had no rights, but rather belonged to their husbands and to their families. The status of women, as Greif observes, would suffice to distinguish the Occidental world, Christian and individualist, from the communitarian Orient.

This is how, in the West, culture may be seen as leading to the rule of law, to contracts, credit, and corporations. In Greif's view, one can understand all Western institutions, including the state, as substitutes erected in the place of the communitarian or tribal family, with the rational and constructed bond between individuals replacing the bond of blood. In the East—among Maghrebis in their day, and now the Muslim Arabs—these institutions had no raison d'être; the religious culture opposed them. The Jewish Maghrebis saw themselves, in effect, as a people collectively responsible before God. Not the individual Jew but the Jewish people was chosen by God. Likewise, in Islam, the Muslim believer is responsible for his actions, but he is also in solidarity with the righteous conduct of his community. Islam is as communitarian as the Jewish Maghrebis were.

The classification of societies as individualist or communitarian brings Greif from the thirteenth century to the present day. If the Arab Middle East is not developing, is this because it knows nothing of the institutions necessary to development? Alternatively, its values might dissuade it from adopting these institutions—a bad choice, from an economic standpoint. America's uphill battle to export capitalism and democracy, argues Greif, thus becomes predictable: One cannot impose social norms from the outside. Is poverty, then, an inevitable fate for the Arab world because of its communitarian tradition? Greif is cautious here, since the contemporary world is full of economic surprises that no economist foresaw. Moreover, let us not forget that non-Arab Muslim nations like Indonesia, Turkey, and Bangladesh are growing. Arabs represent only 20 percent of world Muslims.

Interests Determine History

Daron Acemoglu agrees with Greif that poverty is rooted in history, but he sees its origins as more political than religious. To demonstrate this point, his research focuses on the colonization of America and on the conditions for the emergence of Western democracy. Like Greif, Acemoglu represents the ambition of a new generation of economists ready to absorb the social sciences, both political and historical. Political science, he explains, is anything but scientific; it does not help us understand why some countries are democratic and others are not, or why some democracies are stable and others unstable. Historians, meanwhile, do not explain. They are satisfied to describe the movements of actors, but they do not grasp motives and they predict nothing. Only economists, Acemoglu believes, have the mathematical tools necessary to describe, understand, and predict collective behavior. (Historians reply that economists pick and choose, among complex events, those that fit their reductive theories—and here they have a point.)

Acemoglu holds that the pursuit of material interests is what motivates individuals: The quest for a better life or for its preservation is the engine of human societies. To be sure, other motivations exist, related to passion or ideology, but they are not essential to the construction of models of collective behavior. A model based on the sole criterion of material interest suffices to describe the movement of societies because individuals act as if they were economically rational. The fact that some individuals may not be rational, or that there are other intervening factors, does nothing to change this collective model. For Acemoglu, ideas do not rule the world. Interests alone drive history. Economics acts as the infrastructure, ideology the superstructure.

Acemoglu's model is deliberately simplistic. Political regimes are either democratic or not, and democracies are either durable or unstable. The nuances within democratic regimes are less significant, he says, than the distinction between democracies and nondemocracies. Similarly, the distinctions between dictatorships and tyrannies are less significant than the fact that both belong in the category of nondemocracies.

To build his model, Acemoglu has recourse to Ockham's razor. William of Ockham, an English logician of the thirteenth century, thought it useless to encumber reasoning with secondary considerations. Following this principle, every society's dynamics can be trimmed by Ockham's razor to an opposition between the people and the elites. In democracies, the people decide, while in nondemocracies, the elite does. Each group seeks to optimize its material interests. Thus elites oppose democracy when they have everything to lose by it, while the people, when they are in power, tend to confiscate the property of the rich and to enact a redistributive fiscal policy. Western history shows that people accommodate themselves to nondemocracy in stable societies that are not growing because injustices in these circumstances are bearable. However, in periods of growth—following the Industrial Revolution, for instance—a different balance of power and different demands come into play. People become more sensitive to injustices and demand a larger share of the benefits of development. Why would the elites grant these benefits to the people? They grant them when the cost of democracy appears less than the cost of resistance to democracy—repression or potential revolution. This calculation determines whether democracy comes to be. It also explains why democracies founded by elites stand the test of time better than democracies that result from popular revolts.

The most surprising feature of this theoretical model is that it seems to work; it helps to describe and understand actual history. Consider, with Acemoglu, the history of Great Britain in the nineteenth century. Until 1832, a rich landed aristocracy led it. Beginning in 1832, the number of eligible voters doubled from 400,000 men to 800,000, or 14 percent of the population. In 1867, another reform again doubled the electorate, to 2.5 million. In 1884, there was another doubling. In 1918, suffrage became universal for men, and in 1928, the right to vote was extended to women. Each of these democratic reforms, Acemoglu maintains, was the direct consequence of an economic choice that elites made as they confronted popular discontent. At the source of this discontent, one always finds economic growth, with the people demanding, at each step, a larger share of profits. Revolt threatens the social order. The elites calculate that a political concession will cost them less than repression. A little democracy makes it possible to buy social peace and to enlist manpower in industry, as well as in war.

As an opposing example, Acemoglu proposes Argentina's experience. Democracy is unstable there, he argues, because the elites feel no economic need to buy social peace. The Argentinean elites are heirs of the colonizers, who had no ambition to develop a modern economy but were content to extract rent from an all-but-virgin land. This situation still obtains in the cultivation of soybeans. The landowners employ little labor; their revenues, generated by exporting to China or Korea, are insulated from the agitation that prevails in the cities. As a result, democracy in Argentina is merely a popular demand for redistribution, wholly unrelated to production. This bifurcation between production and distribution, economics and politics, can only be unstable, varying with the balance of power between elites and people. This accounts for the volatility of democracy and for the unsteadiness of economic development in Argentina. It is impossible to understand the contemporary institutions and manner of development of former colonies, Acemoglu concludes, without recalling the history of their colonization. Beyond the case of Argentina, this theory makes it possible to understand why, in Latin America, popular demands for redistribution take precedence over demands for growth.

The ultimate illustration of Acemoglu's theory is Singapore. A one-party system rules there, uncontested by the people, because the people and the elites share economic profits equitably and the elites arise from the people. Economic logic suffices to explain this stable despotism.

Democracy as superstructure and economics as infrastructure: Is this the resurrection of Marxism? Acemoglu rejects this affiliation. His distinction between elites and people does not mirror the Marxist opposition between bourgeoisie and proletariat, in his view. Nor does he share Marx's catastrophic analysis of the ultimate crisis of capitalism. Acemoglu's explanatory keys are materialist, like Marx's, but unlike Marx, he derives no prophecy from this materialism. He simply concludes that a democracy will never be stable unless it is based on the economic necessity of sharing between elites and the people. But is democracy therefore essential for development?

Democracy as Reducer of Crises

It would be nice if democracy and development were interdependent, Dani Rodrik writes, but they are not. And it is impossible to prove a correlation between the two. Like Acemoglu, Rodrik is Turkish. Acemoglu is Sephardic and teaches at MIT; Rodrik is Armenian and teaches at Harvard's Kennedy School of Government. Both are rising stars in the science of economics.

What, then, of the correlation between democracy and growth? Chile, under Pinochet's dictatorship, developed faster than its democratic Latin American neighbors. Authoritarian China, for the moment, is outdoing liberal India. Japan took off under an authoritarian regime, as did Korea. Imperial Germany, at the end of the nineteenth century, progressed as fast as republican France and parliamentary Great Britain.

Although the relationship between democracy and growth is at best uncertain, Rodrik refutes those who believe that despotism is essential to the launching of economic progress. It is commonly held that authoritarian regimes were responsible for building economic power in the Soviet Union in its day, among the Asian Tigers during the 1960s, and in contemporary China. Is strong government not essential for concentrating investments and controlling salaries? But this correlation is not an explanation. Democratic countries such as India, Brazil, South Africa, and Mauritius have also taken off. And many authoritarian regimes, such as North Korea and the Congo, keep people in poverty. The economic argument in favor of despotism is therefore nothing but an ideological choice, with no historical validation. In a joint study with Stanford economist Romain Wacziarg, Rodrik showed that over the last twenty years, democracy in Eastern Europe, sub-Saharan Africa, and Latin America was not at all harmful to growth in these places. It is as if economies and democracy evolve on two separate planes.

Must one conclude that democracy has no economic impact? Rodrik points out some unconventional consequences of democracy. The best-known is redistribution. From South Korea to South Africa, democracy redistributes the results of development in a more egalitarian manner than occurs in nondemocratic regimes. On the other side, authoritarian China, though in the midst of development, is a good example of nonredistribution.

It is harder to understand why, in a democratic regime, a government might not manage to implement beneficial economic reforms. Rodrik bases his investigations on African countries that tried in the 1980s to implement effective policies under what came to be known as the "Washington consensus." This collection of free-market measures called for the opening of borders to business in order to lower consumer prices and encourage local enterprises to become involved in productive competition. These measures would have benefited the majority. But just who would have benefited? One cannot say, since it is impossible to predict who the winners will be in a growing economy. The politician, as Rodrik says, cannot shake the hand of tomorrow's winner because he does not know him. But the losers *are* known: bureaucrats, monopolies, and rent-holders. In this asymmetrical game, the status quo will win, since the losers are certain and known to themselves, while winners can be neither known nor organized. This "tyranny of the status quo" (Milton Friedman's expression) in a democratic regime, observed in Africa, also illuminates the difficulty of reform in Western Europe. For a reform to be accepted, it is not enough for it to be justified, because the effect of reform is asymmetrical.

Rodrik contributes a final and important note to this theory of democracy: Democracy makes it possible to overcome crises. During the financial crisis that shook Asia in 1998, the democratic governments of South Korea and Taiwan quickly brought their countries out of the slump, while authoritarian Indonesia aggravated the panic before slipping into revolution. Democracy makes it possible, in effect, to negotiate the new distribution of responsibilities among concerned partners—businessmen, unions, bureaucrats—that is necessary for the resolution of a crisis. In nondemocratic regimes, such a negotiation is impossible. Along the same lines, in the scenario of a crisis affecting Chinese growth, it is impossible to predict how the government would redistribute losses; until 2008, it redistributed only benefits—which is much easier.

The probability of crises cannot be ignored, and it is a fact that democracies often survive economic crises, while dictatorships rarely do. This is no doubt the real economic argument in favor of democracy. Democracy may be useless for growth, but it overcomes the jolts of crises and helps reduce uncertainty.

Democracy in America as a Growth Engine

This uncertain relation between economic growth and democracy, as Acemoglu and Rodrik describe it, does not seem to apply to the U.S. experience. In the unique case of America, where democracy preceded growth, one could argue that democracy jump-started the capitalist economy. How could one otherwise explain the fact that since 1820, years before Tocqueville visited America, income per person in the U.S. had already outpaced that of Western Europe? There were no more natural resources in the U.S. than in Europe, Americans were not more educated than Europeans, foreign trade was limited, and population was low. Could slavery be an explanation? On this controversial question, historians and economists tend to agree that the exploitation of slaves favored the rent-seeking Southern aristocracy but did not lead to economic growth. Slavery was not the basis for capitalist development, which began mostly in the free states. In the most democratic states, the emerging entrepreneurs tried to satisfy the new mass consumers: Standardization has been the American answer to an egalitarian demand for goods. And while population was relatively low in these democratic states, standardization required mechanization, another truly American breakthrough.

Thus one can argue that modern American capitalism, based on standardization and mechanization, was born from the democratic nature of North American society. The absence of an aristocracy was an economic godsend. In Europe, as in the American South and in Latin America, the local aristocracy demanded exquisite tailor-made products: Skilled workers were abundant in those aristocratic societies, but standardization and mechanization had to wait. When European entrepreneurs visited the

U.S. for the first time in large numbers at the 1904 St. Louis World's Fair, the technical advances of American industry surprised them. They could not grasp that democracy had given to the American economy a half-century advance that would not be easy to catch up with.

Today, the democratic characteristics of American society still give an edge to the U.S. economy. Most entrepreneurs will spontaneously target the masses and not the few. Products and services will thus be less expensive in the U.S. than in less democratic countries. Some American inventions are uniquely American. Before reaching the rest of the world, they have been inspired by the "wisdom of the crowd," an American concept of excellence. Google is a representative product of this belief in the wisdom of the crowd. In Western Europe, a research engine on the Internet would have been tailored by experts for experts, like any traditional encyclopedia. Google's ranking system, by contrast, is based on popularity: The more a site is visited, the higher the rank it attains. Wikipedia, another American breakthrough, has been inspired by a similar cultural principle: Wikipedia's articles are written by an "enlightened crowd." Jimmy Wales, its founder, relies on the "spontaneous community"—his own words—formed by Wikipedia's contributors and readers. Wales intervenes with a light hand only to regulate excess. Wikipedia, like Google, can be seen as an economic outgrowth of the American faith in the democratic idea, as were the Model T Ford and McDonald's in their day.

Intangible Capital

Having come to view institutions as key to the wealth of nations, the World Bank has attempted to quantify their economic value. Institutions form a kind of intangible capital. The World Bank's research shows that the rule of law represents 57 percent of a nation's capital, and education 36 percent. The rule-of-law figure derives from the judgment of various organizations that measure investor risks. Switzerland finds itself at the top, with a rating of 99.5 out of 100; the United States comes in at 91.8; and Nigeria is rated 5.8. The Organization for Economic Cooperation and Development (OECD) average is 90, compared with 28 for sub-Saharan Africa. The natural resources long believed to determine prosperity amount to only 1–3 percent of a nation's capital.

If one adds the intangible capital of institutions and education to natural capital, it is possible to calculate real capital per capita, the common assets that are the foundation of a nation's growth. Real capital averages $440,000 per capita in the OECD countries, of which $10,000 is natural capital, $70,000 is material capital (businesses, infrastructure, real estate), and $354,000 is intangible capital. Switzerland, by this measure, comes in first, with a virtual capital wealth of $640,000 per capita, while Nigeria measures only $2,748, despite its petroleum resources. Some countries, such as the Congo, are assigned a negative capital. Because their institutions destroy their natural resources, their inhabitants will become poorer and poorer. These differences in the capital of nations shed light on differences in income. It makes more sense for a worker in the United States to exploit a capital of $418,000 per person than for a Mexican to exploit a domestic capital of $62,000 per person (of which $6,000 comes from petroleum). Even if workers make comparable efforts in their respective countries, the return is not the same. This differentiation by the virtual capital of nations explains how a migrant Mexican who finds his way to the United States will, by his labor, produce seven times more than if he had stayed in Mexico and increase his income accordingly. The wealth of nations resides, above all, in their intangible capital.

This notion resolves a number of classic puzzles in economics, such as the decline of Argentina. Are not Argentineans industrious, educated, open to the world, and endowed with considerable natural resources for the production of energy and agricultural products? Then how have they gone from being the world's fifth-leading economic power at the beginning of the twentieth century to sitting in the middle of the pack, with a mediocre per-capita income of $16,000—and remained stagnant for the last twenty-five years? The explanation is the erosion of Argentinean nonmaterial capital. The constant degradation of political and financial institutions and the capricious, unpredictable nature of the Argentinean state have, by reducing nonmaterial capital, undermined the country's productivity, thus diminishing investment and the return on investment.

Should we conclude from this hypothesis that nothing matters more than the state? Our answer will be cautious, as is often the case in economics. It is true that the market cannot function without a policeman to guarantee the honesty of transactions. When the economy is of modest size and transactions remain limited to the neighborhood, partners know one another and the policeman is not necessary. At the next level—as with the Maghrebis studied by Greif—the community is adequate to guarantee contracts. But as soon as one ventures into larger concerns—as with the Genoese—a neutral state is necessary to ensure the successful outcome of transactions among strangers. The more an economy develops, the more it requires an independent public power.

But there is another side to this: Government is costly. The cost of the state, financed by taxes, is fixed. It thus weighs more heavily on small enterprises than on large ones, impeding their growth. On the other hand, where there is no state, costs for small enterprises are small. In certain circumstances, entrepreneurs may choose between appealing to the state, at a high fixed cost, or getting by without it. This was long the case in Sicily, where a merchant could have his contract guaranteed by the Mafia—remunerated according to need—or by the state. Entrepreneurs chose between public protection at a high fixed cost or private protection at a low but variable cost. This situation remains common in many countries where the informal economy is important, such as Brazil—the informal entrepreneur does not pay the state but also does not benefit from its protection. Non-state arbitration can be profitable in the short term, but it limits growth and prevents dealings with faraway and unknown agents. Finally, between these two extremes—the state at a fixed cost and the Mafia on demand—no economy belongs wholly to one camp or the other. Thus the Mafia has not disappeared from developed countries. In Japan, for example, the yakuzas appear to be less onerous and more effective in enforcing certain contracts than the state. In the developed world, where the state is costly, a great number of transactions among individuals and within firms remain informal, not guaranteed by the government but based on trust. Trust is the final element of intangible capital, but it is difficult to measure. Certain thinkers, such as Francis Fukuyama, attempt to explain all development by the level of trust existing in a society. But does trust originate wholly in culture, as Fukuyama claims? One would expect trust to be proportional to the degree that the state serves as the ultimate guarantor in the case of a violation of contract.

This conception of institutions as guarantors of development has led to a new consensus or paradigm in the science of economics: There is no market economy without a guarantor, and the best guarantor is the state. But the guarantee should be the least onerous one possible; that is, the lower the cost, the more the economy will prosper. How can the cost of the state be adjusted to the service it provides? This cost cannot be determined absolutely. Usually it results from a balance of forces and of interests in conflict. Modern political economy is the attempt to determine as accurately as possible this just cost.

CHAPTER THREE

Real Money

MEDICINE IS NOT THE ONLY science that saves lives; economics does, too. Take inflation. Until the 1980s, this social illness afflicted whole nations. In Europe, a rise in prices of about 10 percent a year was enough to stop growth and ruin the most fragile businesses. For those who owned capital, speculation became more profitable than the creation of new jobs. High interest rates discouraged investment, and the decline of salaries relative to rising prices impoverished retired persons and those with lower salaries. Yet there were certain charlatans—there are bad economists, just as there are incompetent doctors—who justified inflation. They asked: Are rising prices not a stimulant? Do they not energize the patient and encourage him to consume by borrowing? Do they not encourage the entrepreneur to look to the future? This fictional economics, a legacy of Keynesian metaphors, had no empirical basis. In a few random cases, inflation and development had coincided for a moment, no more than that. Just as a patient can get well despite the doctor, nations can survive incompetent economists.

45

There have also been more serious cases of what is called hyperinflation, in which prices rise every day and money is worth no more than the paper it is printed on. Hyperinflation not only destroys growth; it crushes society. The resulting disorder is so intolerable that affected populations have sought salvation in the arms of dictators. Napoleon, Hitler, Mao Zedong, and the caudillos of Latin America were born of hyperinflation, even if this was not the only cause of their rise. There is no better way to destroy a society than to corrupt its currency, Lenin said. Few democracies have survived hyperinflation; no economy has been improved by it.

Chicago's Victory Against Inflation

These unhappy experiences now seem far in the past. With a few exceptions in Africa (Zimbabwe in particular), today's world benefits from stable monetary systems and predictable prices. Just as with epidemic disease—smallpox, poliomyelitis—we tend to forget that severe inflation ever happened and that it took great effort to prevail over it.

The victory against inflation belongs, above all, to a school of thought led by Milton Friedman at the University of Chicago. It was Friedman who, during the 1960s, isolated the bacteria of inflation in a sort of Pasteurian revolution in economics: Inflation, he demonstrated, was not the result of a rise in prices, but rather the reverse. Price controls, as applied by European governments, could not halt inflation. Friedman explained that rising prices always come from states' printing too much money and that inflation is nothing but the result of governmental prodigality. A government's creation of money without value can in no way encourage consumption or investment; in the long run, it never stimulates demand.

In 1965, Robert Lucas (also at the University of Chicago) explained why. His theory of "rational anticipation" showed that economic actors know that inflation does not really create buying power but is only a monetary illusion. Consumers therefore see through the supposed stimulation and do not modify their behavior, contrary to what governments expect. This rational anticipation explains why inflationary stimulation seldom works, as would soon be illustrated by the failure of Keynesian policies during the 1970s, when they were tried on a grand scale in Western economies for the first time. If the theory of rational anticipation needs proof, consider Argentina. Each time a government pursuing popularity "creates" buying power by pumping money into the economy, merchants demand payment in American dollars, anticipating the devaluation of the national currency.

The creation of money serves only to finance public spending by imposing an invisible tax on the people. This rise in prices weighs on the poorest without their knowing it. The state benefits, as do privileged individuals who live off nonnational currencies such as dollars or gold. To defeat inflation, Friedman showed, it is sufficient to eliminate the public deficit and to avoid putting more money into circulation than is necessary.

Friedman also suggested having different currencies compete so that their rates would no longer be determined artificially by the states that issue them. This convertibility according to flexible exchange rates, he thought, would settle currencies at the right prices. Failing this, people could rid themselves of the "false" money generated by their state and substitute a currency of truer value. According to this monetarist theory, it is also better for money to escape the control of governments by being entrusted to independent banks—thus protecting politicians from the temptation of inflation. It was left to Columbia University's Edmund Phelps to complete the work of Friedman and Lucas by demonstrating during the early 1960s that inflation ruined employment. Friedman, Lucas, and Phelps thus exploded the myth that creating money and manipulating interest rates could regulate growth and unemployment.

The monetarist theory, which owes as much to common sense as to science, was long contested, and it remains somewhat contested, but for the wrong reasons. The beneficiaries of inflation—that is, the government and its clientele—are not about to renounce willingly the privilege of minting money. This resistance on the part of the defenders of inflation has always been more partisan than scientific. The politicians who claimed that growth could be based on inflation were effectively abandoned around 1990, but the idea of regulating growth through the money supply endures as a myth.

But what about inflation provoked by external shocks like rising prices for imported oil or food? These price hikes do not lead to inflation as long as money remains under control. A rise in the price of oil, for example, redistributes wealth between producers and consumers. If consumers buy less oil, the price of oil will go down. Or consumers can choose to pay more for oil and less for other goods, the price of which will then go down. Therefore, an oil shock will generate global inflation only when governments create more money to absorb the shock, an approach that ultimately results in more trouble. Nothing is more vital in a time of increasing prices for energy or food than maintaining monetary stability and resisting the temptation of inflation. Only by keeping money stable and predictable will investment restart and pull the economy out of its slump. Such a rigorous policy, which the European Central Bank has implemented under the guidance of Jean-Claude Trichet, is not always well understood by the public and by political leaders in search of nonexistent quick-fixes to economic problems. This is one reason why a better knowledge of the rules of economics would benefit all nations. Governments and central banks would be more likely to make the right choices, which would shorten crises.

Good Advice from the International Monetary Fund

Kenneth Rogoff claims that development, which is happening everywhere today except in some parts of Africa, can also be explained by the triumph of the science of economics and the theories of the Chicago school. A disciple of Friedman and chief economist at the International Monetary Fund (IMF) from 2001 to 2005, Rogoff had the job of persuading those governments most inclined to inflation to get with the monetarist program.

The IMF today has two functions: that of technical advisor, which is widely accepted, and that of bank for nations at risk, which is often controversial. As a bank run by the member states of the United Nations, the IMF has often made political loans, hoping to save existing regimes and not expecting reimbursement. "These bad loans have enabled leaders to defer reforms essential to development, while blaming the IMF for problems that were their own fault," says Rogoff. But hypocrisy and incompetence have never prevented prodigal tyrants of poor countries from receiving the support of artists, religious leaders, and sometimes heads of state for the cancellation of debts—debts that have much to do with the corruption of the leaders, who have appropriated funds. Rogoff also notes that these oft-decried debts are never honored by poor countries. Every year, in the form of gifts or new loans, they receive larger sums than what the interest on the debts would amount to. For rich countries, however, the cancellation of the debt costs little and provides a clear conscience, sustaining the idea that debt is the cause of poverty. Even more unfortunate, Rogoff emphasizes, is the fact that "the cancellation of debts perpetuates the practice of embezzlement and frees governments from the pressure to create institutions that would encourage a better use of loans and grants."

One function of the IMF, according to a former director, Michel Camdessus, is to serve as a scapegoat for incompetent heads of state. It happens that the IMF is now left with hardly any resources or clients. Will the 2008 crisis give new life to the IMF? Its bureaucrats, led by the French socialist Dominique Strauss-Kahn, have perceived a window of opportunity and have restarted their loans to indebted nations. However, the same loans could be granted by other banks; the IMF remains redundant even in a time of global credit contraction. If the IMF were a business, it would logically be expected to disappear, having finished its work. Since it is a bureaucracy, however, it perpetuates itself by reinventing other, nonessential functions. While there may be some logic in the IMF's survival as a source of advice, it is shocking that it should maintain the same number of employees, 10,000 international functionaries, most of whom have nothing left to do!

As for its past record, the near-universal creation of independent central banks, run in a professional manner and inspired by American or German models, is one of the IMF's great achievements. These central banks have stabilized the currency of many poor countries, which is fortunate, as nothing causes instability so much as bad money, especially for the poor. Since 2004, the average worldwide inflation rate has fallen to 3.5 percent a year, an unprecedentedly low level. The stabilization and predictability of currencies could explain the new growth in the years before 2009—not negligible, at 5 percent a year—of countries without natural resources or industry in Africa and the Middle East. Even during a period of global stagnation, it appears that poor countries can survive, thanks to the stability of their currency. During previous crises, hyperinflation ravaged these countries; monetary discipline is proving more useful during a downturn than during a period of growth. The stabilization of the economic landscape has helped restore confidence in the future, which stimulates trade and investment rather than speculation and the flight of capital.

"Even an independent central bank is not sufficient," Rogoff adds. "The free circulation of capital is also an indispensable contribution to wisdom." No central banker could resist the demands of the local government if the globalization of capital did not render these pressures useless. The end of inflation thus results in the happy conjunction of the science of economics, the founding of good institutions, and globalization, which makes inflation impossible in open economies. In setting up competition among currencies, globalization guarantees price stability and, in fact, drives prices down. Today, for instance, Chinese imports, less expensive than domestic products, contribute to the stabilization of prices in the Western world. Savings by the Chinese and other nations that bank more than they consume and invest, like Japan and Taiwan, may contribute to global price stabilization as well. When global savings remain above global consumption, Alan Greenspan observes, prices will fall and interest rates will remain low. These exceptional circumstances, which are not guaranteed to last forever, together with the independence and better management of national currencies, explain why prices were stable, investments were easy, and the global economy grew during the early 2000s. Thanks to this globalization, prices stabilized in France, a country long addicted to inflation, even before the National Bank of France became independent in 1986. Thanks to external competition, French inflation disappeared even before the creation of the euro and of the European Central Bank (ECB) in Frankfurt.

The Uncertain Euro

What was the point of creating the ECB, whose primary objective was to fight inflation, once there was no more inflation— and when Great Britain, without the euro, also had no inflation? The ECB, Rogoff argues, is above all a political project, "a noble experiment," a symbol of Europe's irreversible unification. Would its existence prevent a falling back into inflation if the statist temptation reappeared? No, according to Rogoff: It is globalization more than the ECB that guarantees price stability. So what is the point of the euro? In the end, the ambition is to compete with the dollar—a legitimate, if uncertain, goal, Rogoff believes.

There is no doubt that Americans derive a substantial advantage from the fact that the dollar is the only universally recognized reserve currency. The tendency to accumulate dollars, the desire of non-Americans to hold them, allows the United States to borrow and invest at much lower rates than any other country in the world. In 2009, President Obama's $1-trillion stimulus plan would not have been conceivable without the Chinese, Japanese, and Saudis relentlessly buying U.S. Treasury bills at near zero interest. No other government on the planet, if tempted by a similar public spending spree, could take on so much debt without bankruptcy. The global attraction of American currency has allowed the various U.S. administrations since 1945 to finance wars or stimulus plans without many qualms: Yes, it will be necessary to repay the debt, but this will be done with the foreign depositors' own money, a legal Ponzi scheme. What if the foreigners suddenly keep their money or begin to go for euros? The U.S. Treasury would be as bankrupt as Argentina. Will it happen? It never has, but it is impossible to say more.

From time to time, the proposal for a new gold standard reappears. Initially promoted by the French economist Jacques Rueff in the 1960s, this would be the real threat to the U.S. dollar's supremacy. Absent a new gold standard, the U.S. dollar reigns supreme as the only currency reserve that nations feel comfortable keeping. Rogoff estimates that this advantage over Europe provides an additional 1 percent annual growth. Given that the annual growth rate of rich countries averages about 2 percent annually, the dollar's advantage would amount to half this growth. The European ambition to replace the dollar by the euro is therefore understandable.

The European error, explains Rogoff, is to believe that to have the equivalent of the dollar it is enough to create the euro.

Not so. Unlike the euro, the dollar, with its long history, has become predictable. The principles by which the Federal Reserve Board will continue to regulate it are known in advance. On the other hand, it is too early to foresee the future regulation of the euro, insofar as the ECB is still contested by certain European governments. Every political attack on the ECB tarnishes the euro's future and dilutes the advantage that Europeans might derive from it. The strength of the dollar also has to do with the fact that the American financial market is relatively well organized: Rates have been low there because the market works better than in Europe, where the complexity of national regulations and the absence of a unified financial market make transactions slower and more costly. In 2008, despite the banks' mismanagement of mortgage credit and Bernie Madoff's notorious Ponzi scheme, the flow of foreign money toward the United States has remained stable. The resilience of the U.S. financial market has demonstrated that it can overcome its own errors, though not without help from the Federal Reserve, itself part of the system. To finance investments in Europe at low rates, Rogoff says, a single and simple financial market would do better, even without the euro, than a euro-based system with complex rules. The euro can in no way make up for a lack of liberalized markets.

Another charge is leveled against the euro: A "strong" euro relative to the U.S. dollar would be harmful to European growth. But Rogoff objects that one does not know the correct value of a currency on the foreign-exchange markets. When the euro was worth 80 cents in 2002 (compared with $1.35 in 2009), some said that it was too weak, with no further justification than one hears today. In fact, the euro rose against the dollar because the dollar fell against Asian currencies. Rather than asking ourselves what the right exchange rate would be, we should evaluate the impact of these rates on the actual economy. This impact is, in fact, weak—almost nothing. In 2008, Germany exported more with a strong euro, while France exported less with the same strong euro; the cause of French decline thus was not the euro but a loss of the comparative advantages of French products. As an example covering a longer period, Rogoff points out that in thirty years, the value of the Japanese yen has increased three-fold, while Japan at the same time increased its exports by the same factor. This means that the value of a currency is only a modest factor in exports, particularly for complex products and services.

Exchange rates and economies move on different planes. Within a given domestic economy, however, the movement of exchange rates indeed produces winners and losers. Changes redistribute profits among businesses as a function of their greater or lesser dependence on the exchange rates. When the euro rises, the cost of importing oil falls, but Airbus increases in value. To blame the strong euro and the ECB for supposedly harming growth is thus misguided; the real fault lies, rather, with the lack of competitiveness of businesses and with the excessive regulation of markets.

It is equally groundless, Rogoff believes, to accuse the ECB, as many European governments do, of favoring the fight against inflation over growth. Since globalization has essentially contained inflation, the bank determines its rates in view of parameters such as growth, social stability, and the demands of European governments. Attacks against the ECB are only vestiges of archaic theories, a screen for particular interests, or proof of economic ignorance. Take your pick.

Rogoff concedes that certain central banks—though not the one in Frankfurt—are so obsessed with inflation that they set excessively high exchange rates, to the point of stifling investment. This is the case in Brazil, for example, where for historical reasons the popular memory is haunted by the nightmare of hyperinflation. The right inflation rate, Rogoff maintains, is not necessarily zero, as Milton Friedman would have wished. Zero can serve as a political goal to help convince the public and economic actors that times have changed, but in practice, Rogoff recommends a pragmatic approach, as long as a modest rise in prices does no harm to real development. The zealots of zero inflation harm their own cause, Rogoff believes. Their excesses are eagerly answered by demagogues, such as the economist Joseph Stiglitz, who go so far as to condemn all fiscal and budgetary discipline. One extreme matches the other—but with a key difference: The zealots of budgetary discipline exaggerate, but their opponents offer no proof. It is impossible for Stiglitz, Rogoff notes, to produce a single example of a country in which a rejection of globalization and of the convertibility of currencies led to economic development. Stiglitz's stance against globalization has no economic basis, though he won the Nobel Prize in Economics; the reason his public positions often contradict his scientific research goes beyond economics.

The Art of Failure: The Argentine Disaster

A certain art is also necessary in implementing economic policy. To succeed in implementing a good monetary policy, it is not enough to recognize its virtue, as there are some who profit from hyperinflation and who retain the political means to wreck reform. Argentina's recent experience reflects this kind of contradiction, between a country's general, long-term interest—which requires the creation of a new, stable currency—and the political mafias that often rule it.

During the 1990s, Argentina was close to coming out of a long slump. A new president, Carlos Menem, and his finance minister, the economist Domingo Cavallo, understood that the country's economy had been stagnant for fifty years because of a lack of predictable institutions, in particular that of a reliable currency. The rich lived off of American dollars and did not bring home the profits that they made in foreign markets from agricultural exports. The poor depended on the local currency, the peso, and fared worse and worse. Between these two groups, the middle class saved in dollars, which they deposited in Argentine banks. The peso was so unpredictable that prices were quoted in dollars. It would have been possible for Argentina to adopt the dollar as its national currency; Cavallo considered this strategy, but then gave up the idea, fearful not only of a chauvinist reaction but also because the fluctuation of the dollar would have made it impossible for Argentina to control the price of its trading with Europe or Japan. Cavallo opted for a solution that seemed ingenious but proved fatal: He pegged the value of the peso to the American dollar, guaranteed by dollar reserves. The Argentineans could use either currency. Out of this equivalence, Cavallo expected the peso's gradual return to legitimacy. In his envisioned second phase, which never happened, the peso would become Argentina's standard currency, convertible and floating, at rates set by the international exchange markets. There was little trust in the new peso, though, and Argentineans continued to state their long-term contracts (mortgages, for example) in dollars, while using the peso only for short-term transactions.

It was also in dollars that the Argentine central bank took on debts to guarantee the peso's parity. Was the peso valued too highly against the dollar? This was the main criticism addressed to Cavallo. Imports invaded the country, and exports became difficult. But the expensive peso, Cavallo believed, would motivate entrepreneurs to export more sophisticated products, with more value added. This virtuous cycle might have taken hold if the experiment had lasted. Unfortunately, the Argentine state was irresponsible and schizophrenic. On the one hand, Cavallo succeeded in stabilizing the money supply; on the other, the president of the republic was spending public funds with both hands. In the Peronist tradition from which Carlos Menem came, politics consisted of buying votes with public money. The closer that elections approached, the more his government spent, especially on public works in provinces, where such spending could ensure loyalty. The Argentine banks made loans to provincial governments without evaluating the risks involved. The external financial world was uneasy, remembering that in the past the

Argentine state had already gone bankrupt; loans made to the country thus became increasingly onerous. Cavallo found himself in a position he had not anticipated. Should he have renounced the peso-dollar linkage? But then all his efforts to provide his country with a legitimate currency would have crumbled. Moreover, since the Argentine debt was priced in dollars, if he devalued the peso, the country would be incapable of repaying and would again find itself bankrupt.

Menem's successors in 2001 chose to declare bankruptcy, rather than to repay debts, and to devaluation they added the stratagem called "pesofication": Dollars deposited in Argentine banks were considered "new" pesos, with a value set at 33 percent of the old currency. In effect, all the owners of accounts in pesos who had put their trust in the new money lost two-thirds of their property.

But what a boon for debtors! Their debt fell by two-thirds. This pesofication would profoundly redistribute wealth among the Argentineans: It was the equivalent of an economic coup d'état, and some have since wondered whether it wasn't premeditated. It so happened that the debtors included large businesses and local governments, who were immediately freed from paying their old debts, reconverted from dollars to revalued pesos. The victims included the lenders: All those foreigners who had invested in Argentina or made loans to Argentineans lost two-thirds of the value of their credit. In Argentina, the small savers, retired citizens who had put their assets in dollars for their old age, were the most harmed by the monetary conversion. Already unequal, Argentine society became still more so following this manipulation.

The Argentine state's refusal to repay its international debts and the confiscation of two-thirds of the assets of domestic creditors ruined what little legitimacy Argentine institutions had, casting a cloud over the country's future. The most significant consequence was a slowing down of domestic and foreign investment. A renewal of confidence in Argentine currency would take years, and growth would suffer accordingly. What growth remained would depend on the export of raw materials. By a stroke of luck, the spectacular growth in demand for soybeans on the world market saved Argentina from mass poverty in the short term. But without stable, predictable institutions, independent of political whims, Argentina cannot avoid a long decline.

It is even more unfortunate that this monetary disaster gave rise to no serious analysis within the country, except among economists. Political passions have again prevailed: The mafias behind the monetary coup, supported by the media that profited from it, have shifted blame and incriminated Cavallo, now the scapegoat of Argentine politics. Since Cavallo had appealed to the theory of the free market to justify his attempt to provide his country with a sound currency, didn't the disaster prove that the free market couldn't work in Argentina? In reality, authentic free-market reform would have required the creation of independent political and economic institutions, the opposite of what was done. But political battles in Argentina appeal more often to nationalist passions than to quiet reflection. As a result, Argentina's Peronist leaders (the governments of Nestor and of Cristina Kirchner, in charge since 2004) have brought back the old system: a return of inflation, starting in 2007; a breakdown of infrastructure because of the lack of investment, stagnant since 1975; spurts of growth linked to soybean export rates; and persistent unemployment in the absence of industrial investment. In the neighboring countries of Chile, Uruguay, and Brazil, leftist governments have recognized that without sound money, the economy will not function well. But in Argentina, political leaders behaved as if the universal laws of economics did not apply.

The Yuan: A Political Currency

And then there is China. Should we worry that the Beijing government has accumulated a trillion U.S. dollars (as of 2008)? Chinese leaders continue to hoard their gains from, above all, commerce in North American markets. These profits are invested in short-term U.S. Treasury bonds at low, but very secure, interest rates. If Chinese leaders withdrew their assets, the dollar would collapse. Who would suffer? Americans would have to restrict their buying as interest rates rose; but the Chinese would suffer more, since their prosperity depends on American consumers. In the next phase, the lower dollar would make American products more competitive on world markets and Chinese products less attractive; the result would be a new commercial equilibrium unfavorable to the Chinese, whose exports are attractive thanks to their low prices, not their irreplaceable quality. All in all, it would be better for the Chinese to invest more of their profits domestically. Kenneth Rogoff has often tried to explain this to Chinese leaders, but without success. Nor has he been able to persuade them to make their money convertible and allow the market to set the true value of the yuan.

Is the yuan overvalued, as many Americans, who see their stores "invaded" by cheap Chinese products, claim? Protests against the "weak" yuan come from relatively unsophisticated manufacturers in the United States, such as those in the basic electronics and textile industries, who compete with Chinese imports. The yuan is thus just a convenient scapegoat for the decline in the U.S. of certain outdated businesses. These protests against the weak yuan are of the same nature as the criticisms of the strong euro. In rebutting such familiar complaints, Rogoff claims that the yuan may actually be overvalued. Chinese savers, he explains, can put their money only in national banks, which pay only meager interest. In the event of the opening of Chinese financial markets, these savers would be expected to invest their resources in more favorable instruments. That could lead to a collapse of the yuan. Is it not the fear of such a future that causes Chinese leaders to prefer hoarding dollars?

Why would China's leaders refuse to make the yuan convertible like other currencies? Is it because control of the yuan allows them to lower the value of Chinese products artificially? Rogoff will have none of this, since a convertible yuan might fall lower than a regulated one. The true motive of this regulation, he argues, is political: Because the yuan is not convertible, the Chinese cannot freely invest their savings, exchange their money for other currencies, or circulate their capital assets without authorization. It is through the yuan that the people remain under the Communist Party's domination. This Chinese currency, because it is a political currency, is not attractive, and so in no way threatens the preference for the American dollar. In this way, Chinese leaders confine themselves within an economic model that is profitable in the short term for their urban elite, but without flexibility. If the world market slows down, the Chinese economy will be at risk of crashing, with incalculable domestic and foreign consequences.

If there is a threat to the United States, to China, and to the global economy, Rogoff concludes, it does not come from the Chinese accumulation of dollars. Nor is the U.S. trade deficit a risk factor: Since it is compensated for by financial investment in the United States, it may be a source of uncertainty, but it is not a time bomb. But China is indeed a threat, and its political and economic future is uncertain.

The Danger of Ignorance

For ten years, until the 2008 crisis, the global economy was in a growth cycle without historical precedent. In 2007, global growth was about 5 percent, whereas a relatively modest annual growth rate of 2.5 percent is sufficient to double income over a generation. Such growth has never happened in the past in such a continuous, sustained, and nearly universal manner. The main reason was the adoption by states of good institutions, namely true currency and free trade. This mechanism would not function without global commerce. The periodic mini-crises and short cycles that fascinate journalists and politicians had only a slight influence on this worldwide growth; on the other hand, an interruption of commerce would halt this widespread development.

What might cause such an interruption, Rogoff asks? War? The planet is by no means free of conflicts, but on a historical scale, these can be seen as local and contained, without major effects on international commerce. Only a major geopolitical upheaval would spoil growth for good. What about an unforeseen ecological threat—a natural catastrophe, or a bad economic policy intended to prevent a theoretical environmental threat?

Nor can one exclude the possibility an interruption of innovation. Rogoff does not share the optimism of the theorists of the "new economics," who envision uninterrupted innovation and infinite growth. In the past, Rogoff reminds us, growth has always been set in motion by innovation: the steam engine, electricity, communications, and now information technology. These great leaps forward in innovation have always operated in successive cycles, punctuated by crises. Could we, in our present cycle, have been carried away by the illusion of its infinity? Beyond the current credit crunch, the slowing down of innovation could explain the 2008 downturn. Rogoff considers the possibility. But the supreme risk is not so much the completion of an innovation cycle as the abandonment of all the knowledge gathered by economists. Unfortunately, we can see that in moments of crisis, magical thinking often returns and sweeps away acquired understanding. All that the science of economics has to teach us could be negated by panic and demagogy.

The Original Monetarist

Anna Schwartz must be the oldest active revolutionary on earth. Born in 1915 in New York, she can still be found nearly every day at her office in the National Bureau of Economic Research on Fifth Avenue, where she has been relentlessly gathering data since 1941. And as her experience proves, data can transform the world. During the 1960s, with Milton Friedman, she researched and wrote *A Monetary History of the United States,* a book that changed forever our knowledge of economics and the way governments operate. Schwartz spent ten years of detective work on the project, which helped found the monetarist theory of economics. "Not only by gathering new data, but by coming up with new ways to measure information, we were able to demonstrate the link between the quantity of money generated by the banks, inflation, and the business cycle," she explains.

Before the monetarist revolution, most economists believed that the quantity of money circulating in the economy had no influence on prices or on growth. History, Friedman and Schwartz argued, showed otherwise. Every time the Federal Reserve (and the central banks before it) created an excess of money, either by keeping interest rates too low or by injecting liquidity into banks, prices inflated. At first, the easy money might seem to increase consumers' purchasing power. But the increase would be only apparent, since sellers tended to raise the prices of their goods to absorb the extra funds. Investors would then start speculating on short-term bets—whether tulips in the seventeenth century or subprime mortgages more recently—seeking to beat the expected inflation. Eventually, such "manias," as Schwartz calls them, would begin replacing long-term investment, destroying entrepreneurship and harming economic growth.

By contrast, by taking away excess liquidity, the central bank can cause the sudden collapse of speculative excess. It can also hurt healthy recovery or growth by constricting the money supply. There is now a near-consensus among professional economists that a lack of liquidity caused the Great Depression. During the severe economic downturn of 1930, the Fed did nothing as a first group of banks failed. Other depositors became alarmed that they would lose their money if their banks failed too, leading to further bank runs, propelling a frightening downward economic spiral.

To encourage steady growth while avoiding the pitfalls of inflation, speculation, and recession, the monetarists recommended establishing predictability in the value of currency—steadily expanding or contracting the money supply to answer the needs of the economy. "At first, central bankers and governments did not accept our theory," says Schwartz. Margaret Thatcher was the first to understand that the monetarists were right; she followed the new monetarist rules when she came to power in 1979, which tamed inflation and reinvigorated the British economy. The U.S. soon followed during the early 1980s, led by Paul Volcker, a Friedmanite then at the head of the Federal Reserve who, with Ronald Reagan's tough-minded support, ended raging inflation, though not without considerable short-term pain. "It was a strenuous experience," Schwartz remembers. As Volcker tightened the money supply, making credit harder to come by, unemployment spiked to around 10 percent; many businesses failed. But starting in 1983, the inflation beast defeated, a new era of vigorous growth got under way, based on innovation and long-term investment.

This lesson of the recent past seems all but forgotten, Schwartz says. Instead of staying the monetarist course, Volcker's successor as Fed chairman, Alan Greenspan, too often preferred to *manage* the economy—a fatal conceit, a monetarist would say. Greenspan wanted to avoid recessions at all costs. By keeping interest rates at historic lows, his easy money fueled manias: first the Internet bubble and then, even more catastrophically, the recently burst mortgage bubble. "A too-easy monetary policy induces people to acquire whatever is the object of desire in a mania period," Schwartz notes.

Greenspan's successor as Fed chairman, Ben Bernanke, has followed the same path in confronting the current economic crisis, Schwartz charges. Instead of the steady course that the monetarists recommend, the Fed and the Treasury "try to break news on a daily basis and they look for immediate gratification," she says. "Bernanke is looking for sensations, with new developments every day."

Yet isn't Bernanke a disciple of Friedman and Schwartz? He publicly refers to them as his mentors; thanks to their scientific breakthrough, he famously declared, "the Great Depression will not happen again." Bernanke is right about the past, Schwartz says, "but he is fighting the wrong war today—the present crisis has nothing to do with a lack of liquidity." President Obama's economic stimulus is similarly irrelevant, she believes, since the crisis also has nothing to do with either a lack of demand or a lack of investment. The credit crunch, which is the actual cause of the recession, comes only from a lack of trust, argues Schwartz. Lenders aren't lending because they don't know who is solvent, and they can't know who is solvent because portfolios remain full of mortgage-backed securities and other toxic assets.

In order to rekindle the credit market, the banks must get rid of those toxic assets. That's why Schwartz supported, in principle, the Bush administration's first proposal for responding to the crisis, to buy bad assets from banks—though not, she emphasizes, while pricing those assets so generously as to prop up failed institutions. The administration abandoned its plan when it came to seem too complicated to price the assets. Bernanke and then–Treasury secretary Henry Paulson subsequently shifted to recapitalizing the banks directly. "Doing so is shifting from trying to save the banking system to trying to save bankers, which is not the same thing," Schwartz says. "Ultimately, though, firms that made wrong decisions should fail. The market works better when wrong decisions are punished and good decisions make you rich."

What about "systemic risk"—much heard about these days to justify the government's massive intervention in the economy in recent months? Schwartz considers this an excuse for bankers to save their skins after making so many disastrously bad decisions. "The worst thing for a government to do, though, is to act without principles, to make ad hoc decisions, to do something one day and another thing tomorrow," she says. The market will respond positively only after the government begins to follow a steady and predictable course. To prove her point, Schwartz points out that nothing the government has done since the subprime meltdown has really thawed the credit market.

Schwartz indicts Bernanke for fighting the wrong war. Could one turn the same accusation against her? Should we worry about inflation when some believe deflation to be the real enemy? "The risk of deflation is very much exaggerated," she answers. Inflation seems to her "unavoidable": The Federal Reserve is creating money with little restraint, while Treasury expenditures remain far in excess of revenue. The inflation spigot is thus wide open. To beat the coming inflation, a "new Paul Volcker will be needed at the head of the Federal Reserve."

Who listens to her these days? "I'm not a media person," she tells me. She rarely grants interviews, which distract her from her current research: a survey of government intervention in setting foreign exchange rates between 1962 and 1985. Never before have these data been put together to show what works and what doesn't. In her mid-nineties, she remains a trendsetter.

CHAPTER FOUR

Good Globalization

HERE IS SOMETHING TROUBLING: Most famous economists are found in the United States, yet they are far from all being Americans. In fact, in every discipline, American universities, research centers, and businesses recruit the best on the world market, and they know how to keep them. Should working conditions, remuneration, or the intellectual environment at one institution no longer satisfy a renowned researcher, another institution will be ready to hire him. This competitive pressure also affects the person in question, motivating him to remain at the peak of his profession, lest he lose his privileges and prestige. Many in Europe would not welcome these constraints, though others gladly embrace them: It is striking how many European researchers and teachers cross over to the other side of the Atlantic without making much of it. This migration is visible in the centers of excellence that are the great universities, such as Columbia, Yale, Harvard, and Stanford; at Harvard, a third of the economists come from Europe.

Jagdish Bhagwati comes from even farther away—from Gujarat, in northern India—though he arrived at Columbia by way of Cambridge University in England. Given that he is recognized as the leading economist and advocate of globalization, isn't he embarrassed to have abandoned his country just as it was taking off and most in need of his talents? Bhagwati is not troubled by this. "We tend to overestimate the negative effect of the brain drain," he says. On the surface, this "drain" deprives a nation of talent, but it also gives rise to communities in exile; these diasporas gather knowledge and create networks. India benefits from this, as do Korea and China. Their diasporas store knowledge that contributes to the economic success of the originating nations. All globalization, including the globalization of people, is good for the progress of humanity, Bhagwati concludes.

Economics Is Not an Ideology

Given Bhagwati's reputation as an apologist for globalization, we might wonder if his conduct is altogether scientific. Does his work derive mainly from ideological enthusiasm? Bhagwati protests that economics is a science, one that proceeds in the same way as all other sciences—the economist constructs hypotheses, which he then compares with social reality. The real world, not personal preferences, either validates or sweeps away these hypotheses. As in all sciences, economic models are imperfect and verification is never more than approximate. Nevertheless, Bhagwati continues, the theory of free trade, initially proposed by the Scotsman Adam Smith at the end of the eighteenth century, has repeatedly received empirical verification. Smith was the first to envision the possibility that, through trade, two partners could make each other rich—contradicting mercantilist theory, which held that each could profit only at the other's expense. Two and a half centuries later, in a regime of generalized trade, it is a known fact that all nations that participate grow rich together. It is no longer even necessary to explain by what mechanisms this enrichment comes about, since the positive results are so well measured and proven.

A negative proof of this free-trade theory is provided by the history of countries that have preferred self-sufficiency to commerce, such as the USSR, India, China until the 1980s, and today North Korea; never has the refusal of trade led to lasting development. This is a relatively recent finding. In the 1970s, some economists still advocated self-sufficiency as a mode of development. This popular idea spread from the USSR to Argentina via India and Egypt. What disasters! The experience of nations has come to the rescue of theory. It is enough to draw up a table with two columns, one dedicated to the countries that chose free trade (South Korea, Japan, China, Malaysia) and the other to those that refused it (China and India before 1990, the USSR, Argentina), to discover that the first group soared and the second stagnated.

But is reality enough to convince everyone? Bhagwati has spent an entire university life explaining and defending globalization, since it is still not universally accepted. Among his adversaries, Bhagwati distinguishes the ideologues from those who are simply ignorant. Ideologues, with whom an authentic debate is impossible, discern dark forces lurking behind globalization: capitalism, multinationals, Americans, market forces, and free-market ideas. In the face of the ideologue, Bhagwati concedes, the economist is disarmed: He sets forth facts, while his opponent produces myths. Myths can be more persuasive than facts. The economist reasons globally, in terms of anonymous masses and statistics; the ideologue counters by emphasizing a pathetic individual case, which mobilizes the imagination better than numbers do. Therefore, Bhagwati prefers to address the ignorant, those whom the facts might convince, when he defends each supposed weak point of globalization.

Globalization and Lower Wages

We will not take up here the battery of arguments in favor of globalization found in Bhagwati's works. We will consider only the two criticisms most frequently addressed to him: that globalization reduces salaries and that it destroys the environment.

Isn't one logical consequence of globalization a decrease in wages in rich countries, caused by the importation of goods produced cheaply elsewhere? In practice, though, average wages in the countries that import the most show no tendency to decrease. Bhagwati explains this apparent paradox. For an imported product from China, he notes, wages account for only a modest part of the price, about 10 percent. Competition is not a major factor in wages. Furthermore, a job eliminated in the wake of globalization or outsourcing will usually wind up replaced by another job. This new job is generally more skilled and more remunerative, since globalization draws all economies upward. Thanks to the growth that it engenders, globalization also creates new markets in developing countries that are open to the sophisticated products coming from rich countries. America sells some Boeing aircraft to China, generating better-paying jobs than those that China takes from America. Globalization gives rise to a virtuous economic cycle.

Behind the concern that globalization will lead to lower wages, Bhagwati discerns the return of the specter of the "yellow peril." In the 1930s and again in the 1980s, the West saw itself as being invaded by cheap products coming from Japan. It was thought that Japan was about to destroy watchmaking, textiles, and the automobile industry in the West, but nothing came of it—all trading partners progressed together toward more complex and more diversified products. This common error of perspective on globalization stems from our fixed point of view on a dynamic process. The error turns up even among economists: One of the best known, the American Paul Samuelson, predicted in the 1950s that generalized trade would finally wear itself out and that eventually, everyone would produce the same things at the same prices.

Samuelson had not taken into account the fact that the dynamic of globalization would ceaselessly create new needs and new demands. He had not considered that the differences among nations, which are the foundation of free trade, would deepen as much as they would erode. The original basis of trade lay in the natural conditions that determined the comparative advantages of different nations. This is no longer the case. Natural conditions and even wages no longer make much of a difference; other, less material factors, such as local cultures, have become more important. As proof of a permanent differentiation despite globalization, Bhagwati cites the example of Japan. The Japanese have remained artisans of genius, as seen in the ongoing perfection of their manufacturing processes. This perfection requires time and precision. But in areas where it is necessary to be responsive, as in the handling of financial markets, for example, the Japanese are remarkably absent, much to the delight of the Americans, who dominate careers in finance. East-West trade is based upon differences and complementarities among cultures more than on wage differences.

Yet it remains true that some wages do decrease in Western countries exposed to globalization, particularly for jobs in industrial production and local services. Bhagwati does not deny these measurable facts. But globalization, he argues, has nothing to do with it. Since the Industrial Revolution, every innovation has resulted in an initial decrease in remuneration in those activities that are affected by the gains in productivity made during periods of transition from one mode of production to another, or from one sector to another. Wages thus go down before rebounding in better-paying jobs (this is known as a "J" curve). Globalization is not the cause of this curve, though it may sometimes accelerate it. However, as Bhagwati admits, what is true on a global scale (the surge after the dip in the J) is only an average.

The J curve does not describe the painful situation of a particular worker.

Bhagwati thus invites us—and this is important—to distinguish clearly between globalization, which is good for worldwide growth, and its harmful side effects, which we must consider separately. If, because of ideology, ignorance, or self-interest, a government puts in place protectionist measures to preserve wages in an exposed sector, a general economic decline will follow that will reduce all wages. This type of misfortune has befallen those countries that allow themselves to be tempted by self-sufficiency. On the other hand, it is up to states and social actors to deal with the difficult transitions that affect jobs overwhelmed by technical progress or by globalization. As a globalist, Bhagwati is neither Pollyannaish nor passive. He does not believe that markets solve all problems.

Globalization and Environmental Destruction

Because of the very development it stimulates, globalization pollutes pristine nature, and this degradation will be all the more brutal in economies just taking off, such as in China, Brazil, or India. At this stage, countries rely on primitive methods, such as deforestation and coal-based energy, to fire their economies. Along with these depredations, however, economic growth produces a middle class that is more sensitive to the condition of the environment, as well as media and nongovernmental organizations that denounce excesses. The more the economy develops, the more domestic and international political pressures rise because of the increasing scarcity of resources and the awakening of social consciousness to environmental costs. Modes of production are then found that are more respectful of the balance of nature. It has been observed—and this is an empirical fact—that when income reaches $5,000 per capita, behavior toward the environment changes, and more efficient energy sources begin to replace the pure and simple exploitation of nature. Globalization by itself does not destroy nature, but by introducing development into vast nations that had previously been impoverished, it offers a new choice between environmental stewardship and economic development. A new economic discipline emerges, focused on a new question: The economy or the environment?

What price should we put on nature? To a Brazilian entrepreneur who wants to plant the soybeans that Chinese consumers demand, the Amazon rain forest is worth nothing; it can be cleared at no cost. But an ecologist in São Paulo or in New York would put an infinite price on the forest. How can we arbitrate between these two positions? At present, economists do not know: The worth of the forest escapes all objective evaluation. The question becomes still more complex if we include certain far-off risks, such as a hypothetical global warming, in the value of the environment. Is it rational to deforest the Amazon region to plant soybeans when we know the price of soybeans but not that of the forest, and even less the negative effects of deforestation on climate change? Someday, economists will know how to respond rationally to this question. In the meantime, practical forces determine transactions: Initially, development has its way, and then it becomes less brutal as public opinion grows more concerned. Economists, as Bhagwati observes, are content to describe the real world, to the despair of those fond of absolutes. Economists never talk about absolutes.

Cultural Exceptionalism

Globalization contributes to growth everywhere, but shouldn't exceptions to the policy of free trade be made in certain areas, especially agriculture and culture? Agricultural products are a locus of contention between free traders and protectionists. Sophistic arguments by "experts," panics about health, concern for the independence of the food supply, and local interests have managed, until now, to keep European and North American agriculture outside the scope of globalization. But the bill for these fine sentiments and these bad reasons is costly, and it is paid twice: once by taxpayers and consumers in rich countries, and again by the poor countries, whose exports are rejected. In the protected areas—Europe, the United States, Japan, Korea—who are the beneficiaries of protectionism? Tiny minorities, lobbies that know how to manage their image and hide their advantages behind grand speeches. And who are the losers? There are too many to count: the taxpayer who finances the subsidies, the consumer who pays extra for his food without knowing it, the African or Brazilian peasant who cannot export. Almost all the countries of sub-Saharan Africa are victims of European and American protectionism, particularly for cotton and sugar. Agricultural protectionism, argues Bhagwati, slows down technological progress, since it is no longer necessary for competitors to win over markets; it destroys the spirit of enterprise because there is no use for it in a protected sector; it deprives nations of the comparative advantages that they would gain from trading. The effect is similar to what all forms of protectionism produce: Growth slows in the North as well as in the South.

Bhagwati's attitude toward this controversial subject is less radical and more subtle than that of hard-core advocates of the free market. They attack the fortress of protectionism head-on—and in vain. Bhagwati prefers to distinguish between assistance to farmers and obstacles to trade. It is the prerogative of a democratic government, in his view, to protect a given category of the population. But it is in the general interest that this choice not interfere with free trade and globalization. Bhagwati does not object to a state's subsidizing farmers as individuals, in other words, as long as obstacles to free trade are lifted. Protectionist policy in Europe and in the United States is, in principle, tending in this direction: from the product to the producer. But how can we distinguish between assistance to people and assistance to their products? Such difficult decisions are the business of the court of the World Trade Organization. Bhagwati is encouraged that the government of Brazil succeeded in obtaining a judgment against the United States, in 2006, for cotton subsidies, and against Europe, in 2007, for sugar subsidies. Justice in this area is imperfect, and the judges politicized. Still, the offending nations respect the court's decisions to avoid retaliatory tariffs. This is a first step toward the establishment of internationally recognized economic law.

There is no good globalization without good institutions. World trade cannot function without institutions any more than domestic markets can organize themselves without the rule of law. These institutions are in their infancy, but they are progressing. Bhagwati attributes the aggressive opposition of antiglobalists to the World Trade Organization to ignorance, since the WTO is introducing many of the very rules that the antiglobalists demand.

Does culture deserve the same favorable treatment as agriculture? The notion of a "cultural exception," so dear to the French—and to the South Koreans—is incomprehensible in the United States. It is not that the Americans manifest bad faith in this matter but simply that their experience does not allow them to understand why it would be necessary to defend a cultural identity, since their own identity results from an assimilation of all cultures of the world. Bhagwati discourages hardening our positions in an endless philosophical debate: If a government wants to support the national production of films, so be it! But again, this should be done without harming free trade. In any case, the battle for national cultural quotas, long carried out by France and South Korea, seems to have lost meaning in the era of the Internet. Globalization is no longer a choice but a fact. This fact generates both anxiety and growth. Neither can be denied, but Bhagwati insists that they be treated separately.

A Justified Anxiety

Bhagwati admits that globalization has a destabilizing impact—and may henceforth continue to destabilize all economic activities. In Adam Smith's day, comparative advantages were clear: Climate, communications, and know-how were stable factors. A tropical orange-grower could be sure that Great Britain would never produce oranges. This situation no longer prevails; now almost anything can happen in a market formerly assumed to be sheltered from faraway competition. True, differences remain; the earth is not flat. Natural protections, geography, culture, politics, and knowledge isolate markets, but only a little. No profits are secure, and globalization speeds up the destruction of local businesses. The Austrian economist Joseph Schumpeter explained a half-century ago that this is a "creative destruction" because it leads to new activities that are more profitable than the old. But it is still destruction. It is therefore up to governments to raise the level of education so as to facilitate transitions from one job to another; globalization's ultimate constraint is to require people and markets to be flexible.

Americans accept this more readily than Europeans do. Superior adaptation to globalization produces in the United States a growth rate that surpasses that of Europe. Bhagwati explains this by a difference in the way work is understood on the two continents. The American work ethic motivates a person to accept all kinds of work, whereas in Europe work means status, as well as a paying job. An American easily changes jobs, while a European will not easily accept a change in status.

This difference between the continents sheds light on the European passion for supporting industrial champions that globalization has left behind. Is it always a mistake to run to the aid of national champions? Bhagwati notes that there is not a single example on record in which the protection given to a business incapable of standing up to international competition succeeded, in the end, either in saving the business or in securing the nation's economic progress. The failure of national industrial champions is particularly clear when it comes to businesses whose markets extend beyond the borders of the protecting state. The situation is different in the case of a champion that stays at home; the rejection of competition then represents a tax on domestic consumers, who must pay more for an inferior product in the name of the interest that the business supposedly embodies.

Consider a case of protectionism applied in the name of the national interest, one that remains significant in the annals of economics. In the 1980s, to encourage the development of Tierra del Fuego, the Argentine government created an industrial zone there for the assembly of electronic devices, with tax advantages at home and a customs barrier against external competition. Businesses moved to Ushuaia, the capital of Tierra del Fuego, to assemble televisions. These cost four times the global price, so it became profitable to import televisions in order to take them apart and reassemble them on site. This adventure was a money maker for ten years for a handful of entrepreneurs and a few thousand workers. The bill was paid by the Argentine consumer, who had to buy these televisions; by taxpayers, who subsidized the televisions; and by the potential employees of businesses that were never created elsewhere, since resources had been captured by Tierra del Fuego. It is also arguable that poor Argentineans were deprived of drinking water, of education, and of medical care because of the diversion of public funds from helping the neediest to aiding the national champions in Tierra del Fuego.

Examples like this are found everywhere, in countries rich and poor. They may not be as ridiculous as the Argentine case, but the same method of analysis should apply: that of the overall balance sheet, not only of the visible benefits. Only the overall balance sheet makes it possible to get beyond immediate appearances. Despite the well-attested inefficiency of national champions, protectionist instincts persist, but their logic is political—the quest for popularity, the fear of revolts—rather than economic. In 1830, the French economist Frédéric Bastiat imagined, in a well-known pamphlet, a protest of candle merchants against the disloyal competition of the sun. "There will always be candle merchants to complain about the sun," he concluded.

Can One Be Antiglobalist?

However moderate he may be, Bhagwati passes for a market ideologue, even in the United States—"a free-trade zealot," according to Harvard economist Dani Rodrik. Among economists, including Americans, there is no dearth of vehement critics of globalization. It cannot be denied, Rodrik says, that globalization stirs up societies, redistributes power, and creates new inequalities (he should say instead that it replaces old inequalities with new ones). It would be wrong, he concludes, for the World Trade Organization to divest states of the power to defend themselves against the invasion of foreign products, all in the name of the ideology of globalization.

Yes to globalization, but without excessive zeal: That sums up the antiglobalist criticisms advanced in the United States by economists like Rodrik and Joseph Stiglitz. Because they are economists, however, they use the same means of analysis as Bhagwati. They therefore do not doubt that globalization serves the general interest as an essential weapon against poverty. The disagreement, which is not a matter of doctrine, centers on the ways of using this weapon. More generally, ideological confrontations among economists tend to disappear insofar as all agree on a unique and measurable criterion: growth. Growth makes it possible to classify policies and theories not in relation to their supposed virtue, such as justice or happiness, but as a function of their observed effects. This development brings economics closer to the hard sciences. It makes it less a matter of opinion, as economics becomes a *science of results.*

Apart from economists, the enemies of globalization are numerous, but their arguments are not economic. Workers' unions or associations of businessmen, for example, defend the interests of their members (which is their right), while certain ecologists recommend a return to the life of nature, a dream of wealthy countries. This rejection of globalization also proves fertile ground for lobbies, which obtain access to significant resources through clients, whose interests they defend, in agriculture or a particular industry. At the same time, they manage to present themselves as defenders of the general interest by playing on nationalist, nostalgic, or ecological passions.

Lobbies favorable to globalization have a harder time, since the potential beneficiaries are dispersed or unaware of the advantages they might gain. For example, the consumer who acquires clothing or electronics at a lower price and whose purchasing power increases does not necessarily make a direct connection between globalization and his improved standard of living. We would not expect to find him participating in some collective action in support of globalization. The same consumer who, in Europe or the United States, pays seven times more for sugar than he would if imports were not hindered is not going to join a free-trade lobby; he is not aware of the added cost of protectionism, which is modest for every individual because it is spread out over millions of consumers. These consumers have no way to compare the price of a protected product with what the global price would be, since the latter has not been offered on the market. To mobilize consumers who would benefit from free trade, it would be necessary, for example, to make all the televisions, telephones, and computers made in China or Korea disappear overnight.

Though defenders of free trade complain of the harm done to it by lobbies and governments, and though the media influenced by these lobbies report the misdeeds of globalization much more fervently than its benefits, globalization still progresses. What explains this mystery? Gene Grossman, a Princeton economist and free-trade expert, proposes two explanations. First, he supposes that governments are capable of resisting special interests and that they know that free trade encourages growth. This "statist" theory applies to foreign policy, an area in which governments often make decisions in the general interest, independently of public opinion. A second theory is based on electoral calculation: Governments behave as if they had assessed the respective weights of lobbies and concluded that antiglobalist groups were in the minority. One might also suppose that globalization develops spontaneously, through the initiative of entrepreneurs, as long as states do not prevent it—even getting around state prohibitions.

The World Is Our Country

Aren't these controversies concerning free trade archaic? The economic world, according to Grossman, has changed faster than its commentators. We continue to talk of trading products among nations: France buys soybeans from Brazil or sells automobiles to Poland. In reality, however, nations are no longer the main actors in trade, and it is no longer products that are traded, but tasks. Businesses have become transnational; they depend little on states and determine their strategies without regard to patriotism. They are no longer content just to import or export finished products; they also distribute tasks all over the world, seeking the comparative advantages of various locations. These advantages are not only a matter of labor costs. A country, a city, a neighborhood in Sweden, Sri Lanka, or Silicon Valley can offer a comparative advantage that is unique in the world because of local craft traditions (textiles in northern Italy), language (call centers in Morocco or India), creativity (Paris, New York), the reliability of the justice system (Germany), a scientific tradition (pharmaceuticals in Basel)—or wage rates.

On this global map of comparative advantages, businesses conceive, distribute, and gather tasks that lead to a complete product or service. Trade between Germany and France is a significant example. The more these two economies look alike, the more they exchange. France and Germany are each other's major trade partners. This apparent paradox can be explained by the contemporary nature of what trade has become: less an exchange of products than a distribution of functions between companies. Today's American, French, and German cars are in fact manufactured out of different parts originating in twenty or more countries. We still consider a Chrysler an American car and a Mercedes German, but only because they have been conceived in America or Germany, not because they were built there.

Then, too, we buy many "Made in China" products that are assembled in China from parts made elsewhere and then reexported. The nationality of a product or service no longer has much meaning; it is impossible now to name the originating nation of a computer or of an automobile, unless we say that that nation is the world. Good policy therefore consists not in building walls but in studying one's interests: Thanks to the distribution of functions, we have access to better and cheaper goods and services, while all nations bring to the global economy the best they can offer.

PART 2

The American Laboratory

*I*s the science of economics American? Most economists we meet are either American or have come through the United States at one point or another in their educations or careers. This is true not only of economics; American influence is strong in all disciplines. The quality of American universities is the reason. These universities are the main American advantage in the global market of knowledge, innovation, and growth. According to Paul Romer, the economic future of nations will depend on their capacity for innovation, which in turn is determined by the quality of higher education.

The primacy of education leads some American economists—Caroline Hoxby in particular—to recommend educational reforms based on the business model. Is this a typically American approach to education? Whatever is American tends to become global, not because the world is becoming Americanized but because the United States plays the role of experimental laboratory for the rest of the world—the new is generally tested there.

This ability to anticipate sometimes leads American economists to confuse what is American with what is universal. Gary Becker sees a latent entrepreneur in every individual, but is his theory of rational action valid for all civilizations? Criticisms of this rationalist theory by behavioral economists such as the Brazilian José Scheinkman, the Israeli Daniel Kahneman, and the Frenchman Jean Tirole blame Becker for not adequately taking into account our compulsive choices. In the name of pure reason, the rationalists preach a minimal state, while their critics prefer the welfare state that protects us from ourselves. But no one supposes that what is good for the United States could be bad for the rest of the world.

84

CHAPTER FIVE

The Production
of Ideas

SINCE THE EARLY 1980s, growth in the United States has tended to accelerate. Traditional economists, on this point in agreement with Marxists, had bet on a series of cycles and crises instead. What about the 2008 crisis? We assume that the fluctuations in the stock market and even sizable bumps in the road are not "final" crises but purges of the system that clear out bad businesses and bad debts. In the United States and the rest of the developed world, growth may be slow or rapid, but on a global level it has been uninterrupted. Is this still true in 2009? One cannot deny that one or two years of economic stagnation carry a dramatic human cost, one which requires collective action, private and public. The current downturn, however, has not annihilated the long-term growth trend. Innovation and entrepreneurship are still there. Only a perverse economic policy could permanently stall American growth.

What is the engine of this unprecedented growth? Ideas, says Stanford University's Paul Romer—a notion not to be confused with another economic parameter, human capital. Human capital produces ideas, but ideas then become autonomous objects that have a life of their own, independent of those who conceive

85

them; nothing is simpler than copying an idea once it has been conceived.

Sources of Contemporary Growth

Paul Romer belongs to the generation that became economists in the era of computer programs and the Internet, a technical revolution he believes comparable to the coming of electricity. Before Romer, everyone thought that development resulted from the conjunction of capital and labor, the effective combination of which produced growth. In this so-called classical model, the meeting of capital and labor, of money and people, takes place in the market. This market is run by a third force, which in modern times has been the state. Theoretical disputes circled around oppositions between capital and labor, between the market and the state—until Romer published a theory in 1990 under the title "Endogenous Technological Change." This theory introduced a third factor, innovation, and a third partner, nonprofit institutions, into the economic game. Romer thus founded what the press called the "new economics" or the "economics of knowledge." Romer privileges mathematical language so much that he condemns the media to metaphors—since journalists cannot use mathematics in their columns, they try hard to convey Romer's findings by using metaphors; he is an ardent defender of models, which he finds clearer than words. His method is a constant back-and-forth between mathematical models and reality, each enriching the other.

What is an economic idea? It can be a manufacturing secret, a brand name, a formula, a design, a process, a management technique, an algorithm—or the legal or illegal copying of any of these. Innovation, he makes clear, is not always spectacular; it does not always have to do with a new process or a revolutionary invention. Sometimes ideas that bring economic improvement are the result of mastering trivial details. In his lectures,

Romer cites modest experiments that seem characteristic of the creativity of American firms. He loves to explain, for example, how Starbucks managed to create a single type of lid for three different sizes of coffee cups. This standardization of the lid, Romer observes, was an ingenious idea that generated considerable efficiencies. But the simplicity is only apparent. Like the making of the cups themselves, the making of the lids is an engineering marvel.

What distinguishes an idea from all the other factors of production is its ease of storage—it fits into a computer program. Other factors of production, such as energy, human capital, and material resources, can be exhausted, but the more an idea is used, the more it produces. This gives an advantage to large markets, such as the United States, over small ones. Ideas are a function of human capital: The more extensive and educated the human capital is, the more abundant the ideas that spring forth from it. In the past, innovation may have appeared to be unrelated to growth. Now, says Romer, it has become the foundation of growth.

Are ideas public or private goods? Apart from the difficulty of commercializing something so easily imitated, ideas do not necessarily arise from the private market or from the state. In free societies, especially the United States, ideas germinate and prosper in a third sector, nonprofit yet nonpublic, that isn't situated in the world of business or of the state but in universities and foundations. The replicability of ideas, as well as their origin, thus places them in a separate category, neither wholly public nor wholly private.

The Global Market of Ideas

For unlimited growth to continue, states would have to adopt policies favorable to the emergence of ideas. It is therefore essential to sustain the third sector, which is noncommercial and nonpublic. Romer can find no better model than the United States, which has proved prodigiously effective, whether measured by the number of patents registered, the number of Nobel Prizes awarded, or the quality of researchers from all parts of the world who end up there. While neither public nor private, the third sector, which produces innovations, functions in the United States on the market model: Colleges, universities, and think tanks compete at all levels in fund-raising and in the recruitment of professors and students. It is beyond doubt, according to Romer, that American dominance in innovation is owing to this competition; universities, students, and professors are all responding to economic incentives. To produce more ideas, it would suffice to increase these incentives, by public subsidies and other means. In the United States, grants are awarded to research projects and not to institutions. The endowed researcher chooses the institution where he will base himself.

This American lead should not be considered a given. China? In twenty years, perhaps. What about Europe? There, Romer finds nothing new. German and French universities, which once dominated research, seem stagnant, uniform, and centralized; no major idea could come out of this bureaucratic universe. In France, at the top levels of the state and among the business elite, some are becoming aware of this problem. The creation of centers of excellence in the university setting (RTRA, or Thematic Networks of Advanced Research), jointly financed by the state and the private sector since 2006, represents an effort to retain the best scholars and to halt the ongoing brain drain to the United States. That is the ambition, in economics, of the Jean-Jacques Laffont-Toulouse Foundation, directed by Jean Tirole, and of the Paris School of Economics, directed by François Bourguignon.

But even in the United States, the attractiveness of jobs in finance has in recent years lured students away from research and from engineering; in the hard sciences, an increasing number of graduates are recruited from outside the United States, and there is no guarantee that the best will stay there. The rising power of China, India, and Brazil could bring about a reverse brain drain, in which globalization would not be a one-way street. This is not yet the case, however. So far, the surge of new nations on the world economic scene has not challenged U.S. dominance. Whatever index one chooses to evaluate innovation—the number of patents, say, or published articles in scientific journals—America's leading position remains stable, ahead of Europe and Japan; the rest of the world still lags far behind. In 1985, the United States accounted for about 34 percent of the patents established in industrialized nations, Europe for 37 percent, and Japan for 24 percent. In 2007, the numbers were 38 percent, 31 percent, and 26 percent. In 1985, Russia, China, and South Korea hardly registered in this competition; in 2007, South Korea surged to 2 percent of the total, which is not negligible but is hardly earth-shattering. The numbers for China (still) and India remain too small to register. The truly significant change during the same time frame is the total number of registered patents, which in the United States has shot up from 8,000 to 20,000 "patent families," proof of the acceleration and cumulative nature of technical progress. The company that registered the highest number of patents in the world in 2008 was IBM, the ultimate U.S. innovator. The available statistics on this topic are unambiguous—and totally disconnected from the political lamentations on the regression of science in America. Yes, American leadership in innovation may partly be due to the immigration of the best scientists from the rest of the world to the United States, but this only demonstrates that America is able to attract such talent and, in most cases, to keep it.

Is it important to know the source of ideas, if they are so easy to copy? Is it really important to attribute ideas to a particular nation or to an individual owner? And should the ownership of ideas be protected? To protect ideas too much, says Romer, slows down their diffusion; but to protect them too little might prevent their birth. Some useful ideas must be replicated as fast as possible, as in the case of lifesaving medicines and vaccines. How can we guarantee intellectual property, so as to preserve the motivation of the researcher, while recognizing that eventually every idea will be copied and that it is sometimes necessary that this happen rapidly?

The intermediate solution is what Romer calls "weak property rights." In this debate, he approves neither of the demands of capitalist enterprises nor of all the policies of governments that assist them. If growth is the priority, Romer finds it more useful to encourage the production of new ideas than to protect existing ideas too much. Intellectual piracy by China? This does not shock him. In an early phase of development, a lack of respect for intellectual property is inevitable. The imitation of processes, which must be distinguished from the counterfeiting of brands, encourages Chinese growth, and Chinese growth is good for the Chinese *and* for the rest of the world. Is this competition not dishonest? Without doubt, but it forces Western businesses to innovate more rapidly than the Chinese, which is all to the good.

Somewhat unexpectedly, Romer's position on property is shared by most economists, whose job is to encourage growth, not to protect existing businesses (which is the job of lawyers). For economists, it has not been proved that intellectual property is essential to innovation, because patents encourage monopolies and rent-seeking. In a brief against intellectual property, two of Romer's disciples, Michele Boldrin and David Levine, have proposed to show how, throughout Western history, patents have harmed innovation more than they have helped it. This paradox began with James Watt, the inventor of the steam engine. In 1769, Watt secured the protection of the Parliament of London, which granted him a patent. Protected by this patent, Watt took care not to improve his engine for thirty years: He was slow in commercializing it, he prevented his competitors from infringing on his monopoly, and he himself refused to borrow useful innovations, since these were patented by rivals. Boldrin and Levine conclude that Watt's monopoly slowed the Industrial Revolution by decades; steam engines developed only after his demise. Another example of intellectual property turning against its proprietor is the case of the French enterprise La Fuchsine, which held a patented monopoly on dyes in 1864. It stopped innovating, and ultimately it declined while its competitors left France for Basel, where patents were ignored. Basel became the European capital of dyes, to France's loss.

In the pharmaceutical industry, some argue, patents are absolutely essential to innovation because of the importance of research budgets. But it's worth noting that in Italy, the pharmaceutical industry created more medications before 1978, when patents were introduced, than after. Today, the introduction of generic drugs that do not always respect intellectual property has not prevented American and European laboratories from amassing the highest profits in the world. Do patents really motivate investment in research? Boldrin and Levin argue that the hope for patented profits directs laboratories toward the most lucrative products, not necessarily to the most useful ones. The authors do not conclude that we should abolish intellectual property, but they do not consider it essential for growth. From the moment they innovate, businesses gain a commercial advantage that does not require a patent; the patent only allows them, as it did Watt, to transform this advantage into a monopoly, an innovation into a rent.

The Watt of today, in Romer's view, is Bill Gates. Is Microsoft harmful to overall development? Romer is convinced that it is: Microsoft abuses its monopoly, smothers competitors, and prevents the emergence of new ideas that could be better than its own. And we find, indeed, that the most creative period in computer technology was in Silicon Valley before computer programs were patented at all. It is equally remarkable that modern computer technology developed in Silicon Valley instead of in the Boston area, the historical capital of computer manufacturing. Climate alone cannot explain this shift to California. Here is another possible reason: Intellectual property rights were less protected in California than in Massachusetts. In California, workers in these fields are permitted to move from one employer to another immediately; that would be illegal in Massachusetts. Silicon Valley's advantage has everything to do with the mobility of engineers and the cross-fertilization of their ideas.

A preference for "weak" property rights led Romer, in the late 1990s, to support the U.S. Justice Department's effort to break up Microsoft's monopoly. That effort invoked the ten-year-old precedent of AT&T's private telephone monopoly. It was after AT&T's dismantling by the Justice Department that mobile telephones, fiber optics, and the Internet took off. If Microsoft lost its monopoly, says Romer, imagine what could be created by the competitors that it stifles! The legal action failed in the United States, but the European Commission took up the case and, in 2007, found Microsoft guilty of abusing its dominant position.

The Perennial Gale of Destructive Creation

In a developed economy, Romer concludes, laws that encourage innovation are decisive; the rest is of minor importance. In economics, nostalgia is thus a bad counselor. Europeans, more nostalgic than Americans, pay for it with stagnation. In Europe, the dominant businesses are almost all old, even very old. The United States, by contrast, is a cemetery of failed or failing businesses: Pan Am among the airlines, Wang in computers, Chrysler under new ownership, Lehman Brothers brought down by the mortgage crisis. Unlike Europe, America is dominated by firms that are part of the new economy (Google, Microsoft, Amazon), that did not exist twenty years ago, and that have no equivalent outside the United States. And IBM? The old giant has survived by leaving behind the old economy (its computer-manufacturing business was sold to the Chinese firm Lenovo) and embracing the new: the conception of systems and tailor-made services.

All governments, to Romer's regret, tend to protect existing businesses; but every time a state intervenes to save a Chrysler or a Fannie Mae in the United States, or a Bull or a Thomson in France, it freezes innovation. What if the U.S. government had protected the Pony Express against the competition of the telegraph—and then the telegraph against the telephone? Whom would it have benefited? Above all, the stockholders and the managers of the older businesses. And what about the employees? It would be better to focus on people, the real champions of a nation, than on businesses, and to invest in the education of people instead of saving firms and their stockholders.

Education, Romer explains, is the only real factor in the struggle against unemployment and for better-paid jobs. Do you want higher pay? Then improve the education of workers. The fewer uneducated workers, the more businesses will have to innovate so as to use their better-educated—and soon better-paid—workers. Historically, only a rising level of education has contributed to higher wages.

What Is Good for the United States

Whether it's the role of innovation that is being considered, or the independence of universities, one must ask whether Romer's analyses are valid beyond the United States. If his theory is universal, it would explain Europe's lag in the area of optimum growth; if it is only a snapshot of the United States, it implies that Americans and Europeans have followed distinct trajectories. If these two hypotheses have found varying acceptance in different European countries, it remains the case that Romer can explain the United States' comparative advantage. The power of its third, nonprofit sector represents a critical mass of researchers and potential innovation unmatched elsewhere. Whether these students and researchers are American citizens matters little for the United States right now; most stay there and register patents there, since it is in the U.S. that intellectual property is best protected. The best environment for the commercialization of innovation is found in the United States.

Before China, India, or Europe can catch up with the United States—if indeed the notion of a race among nations makes sense—these lagging nations would have to build an infrastructure in the areas of education, research, and development equivalent to what the Americans have. How do you replicate Silicon Valley—its network of universities, investors, entrepreneurs, cosmopolitan culture, and geeks? As Romer explains, ideas do not come from nowhere; they come from an environment that encourages their emergence and application. Lacking such an environment, there is no chance that tomorrow a new Microsoft will pop up in Beijing, Mumbai, or Paris to bury the old one. Microsoft did not arise by magic, but as the concrete expression of an existing cultural ferment. If it happened tomorrow that Microsoft was dethroned, it would probably be at the hands of another American business.

Do European or Japanese governments take sufficient account of the nature of the new economy? What is called economic policy in Europe and Japan remains confined to older mechanisms such as monetary and fiscal policy. In the absence of an infrastructure capable of producing competitive innovation, other countries are condemned to follow the lead of the United States, to imitate rather than innovate, or, at best, to perfect previous innovations.

From Campus to Business: An American Connection

So far, Romer has described the production of ideas from an insider's perspective. Being an outsider and not an American, I take a somewhat different view. Yes, competition creates incentives to reach higher quality in education and research. Such a level of competition does not exist in Europe, and even less in Asia. But American universities and laboratories have another comparative advantage: huge financial resources. Some leading Ivy League universities have budgets the size of the whole education system in a typical European or Asian country. Funding does make a difference, though I admit that without competition the same resources would likely be less well utilized.

Another, even more striking difference between the American idea machine and the rest of the world is the smoother relationship in the U.S. between the academic world and the business community. American faculty members and their students tend to see it as perfectly normal to cooperate with capitalist entrepreneurs. Private companies have contracts with universities, professors are employed as consultants by businesses—indeed, one could argue that American universities and corporate America entertain a kind of business relationship.

When examining this relationship, one often finds that universities prove best at fundamental research but unfit to develop and market their own ideas. The American entrepreneur, on the other hand, is obsessed by the market. The market, he believes, is where the money is, and it is the ultimate way to separate bad ideas from good, ideas that sell from those that do not. A recent illustration of this distribution of functions can be found in the revolutionary field of nanotechnology. Europe might well be ahead of the U.S. in this field; but it is in America that entrepreneurs eagerly await what comes out of the laboratories and work to bring it to market, much more aggressively than European companies could act. Google is another illustration. It is significant that the Google headquarters, in Mountain View, California, pretends to be not a company but a "campus." Located near Stanford University, its design and relaxed working atmosphere seem to replicate an authentic university campus—but it is not a school. Google's employees may wear shorts and work whenever they feel like it, but ultimately, they have to generate profits. By blurring the distinction between academia and business, between art and life, Google reveals a uniquely American relation between them. Europeans would find this shockingly promiscuous.

It is, of course, permissible to prefer unquantifiable values, such as social solidarity or a pristine culture; many Americans prefer these as much as Europeans do. But one cannot assume that these nonmaterial values have no need of a material foundation. It would be still more incoherent to look for growth along paths that do not lead to it. This is the main teaching of the science of economics—an objective and cold teaching, but one that conditions our destiny.

CHAPTER SIX

The Business of Education

STANFORD UNIVERSITY's Caroline Hoxby, an authority on the economics of education, sees education as a business like any other. Stripping it of all romance and all political considerations, she asks whether this business is profitable. Since the resources invested in education are considerable, she argues, the question is not inappropriate. But how can we measure productivity in this area?

To calculate the initial investment is relatively simple. As with any kind of activity, it's a matter of money. But at the other end, when a student leaves an educational institution, how should we evaluate the "product" of this business? At the national level, the product is human capital, and its quantity and quality will determine the pace of economic development. In theory, one would want to know the cost of each individual's education, then compare this initial investment with the productivity of the same person over a whole lifetime. Since this is impossible, economists make do by measuring the average educational results demonstrated by students leaving the "business." In the United States, a national test based essentially on the mastery of the English language and of mathematics allows comparisons over time. The

97

trend for students leaving high school is unfortunately downward. Another worrisome statistic is the high number of dropouts.

In France, no comparable measure is available. The success rate on the *baccalaureat* exam (the culmination of the *lycée*, or secondary school education), which might be an indicator, does not work because it is not homogeneous over time. One cannot know whether the student's educational level has risen or that of the examination has fallen. In the United States, educational decline is a source of national concern. It also casts a shadow over America's economic future. The more an economy is based on the quality of human capital, the more its future also depends on this quality.

Is There a Decline?

National tests are imperfect as a measure, but they are significant. They enable us to predict with adequate certainty the personal itinerary as well as the economic productivity of students. Bad students can become exceptional entrepreneurs, but on average this will not be the case. The market recognizes this probable relation between scholastic achievement and economic effectiveness, as starting salaries are largely based on diplomas obtained. The premium on education continues to grow in the United States along with the economy's dependence on gray matter; if it were not in practice justified by results, salaries would go down.

Human capital is decisive because the growth rate is tied to its development. But who is responsible for it: the individual—as a function of his or her intellectual capacities—or the educational system? In Hoxby's view, the educational system is unquestionably responsible. When the national results for graduating students are falling, this is not a sign of the erosion of intelligence in the population but of a drop in productivity in the educational system. The level falls when schools decline; this is true on average, though it may not be true for a given individual. Thus there are bad schools, run badly, and there are bad teachers; a reformer is more likely to have a direct impact on them than on children, who are what they are. It is up to educational economists to propose reforms of the business of education to improve its productivity. This is no easy task. In a world where everything is changing, schools are paradoxically immutable—not, Hoxby explains, because imagination and solutions are lacking but because the forces of resistance are considerable.

The first obstacle, it turns out, is nostalgia. In the United States, as in Europe, we idealize the past—the good teachers of yesteryear and the local public school. This idealization, according to Hoxby, is groundless. In earlier periods, the investment in education was slight, there were few students, and the influence of education on preindustrial or industrial economies was negligible. It was also easier to recruit high-quality teachers with low salaries, since the social value of a teacher's status, high at the time, was a sufficient incentive; the economy was less competitive, and college graduates—especially women—were less in demand by more profitable businesses. The labor market has totally changed. A diploma can now lead to a career in business as well as in teaching, and the former generally pays more and better rewards effectiveness and initiative. In American schools (up to the university level), again as in Europe, compensation is mediocre, with promotions based on seniority, not on merit. There is no longer any guarantee that the best will go into teaching, and still less that they will stay there; this problem differs little from one side of the Atlantic to the other. What is needed, then, is to improve the productivity of the business of education via economic incentives, without too much concern for tradition. The highest priority in this effort should be the high schools, Hoxby maintains, since, in the United States, they constitute the weakest link.

As for elementary schools, Hoxby sees these more as glorified child-care facilities than as places for teaching. Instilling a little discipline and elementary vocabulary and arithmetic does not require deep economic reflection or an overall reform. Children do not drop out of elementary schools, whereas in high schools absenteeism has become a real problem. High schools are the truly critical factor—it is at the end of the high school years that a decline is observed. And in another proof of their ineffectiveness, whereas the overall number of students entering university from high school is growing, the rate of success in higher education is declining. The achievement level of high school graduates is too low to enable many to succeed at the next level.

School Vouchers

How can high schools be made more productive? In theory, nothing could be easier. In the marketplace of ideas, Caroline Hoxby finds only one idea to defend, one originally conceived by Milton Friedman in the 1970s: school vouchers. Because of Friedman's controversial reputation, some consider vouchers to be on the libertarian fringe, a capitalistic invasion of public service. But they are nothing of the kind. The voucher system is compatible with public service; it does not privatize public education but works within it. It represents a kind of third way, maintains Hoxby, with the potential to make public service in education more productive, not to eliminate it.

The voucher principle is straightforward. The federal government, the states, or the local bodies responsible for public education assign to each family or (ideally) each child a voucher valid for any school, public or private, that they have under contract. One can then expect that the interested parties, given a free choice, will select the superior educational establishments. Friedman believed that the "consumers" of education know best what is good for them; thus they are allowed to escape the particular school districts that, in the United States, are imposed on parents. For the educational establishments, the vouchers would represent all or part of their budgetary resources. If a certain school is chosen, it prospers; if not, it declines and may fail. Participating in this process, schools will have the incentive to compete with one another to attract students. They likely would do this by recruiting the best teachers and adopting the best pedagogical methods, which would then be remunerated according to their quality. The voucher system can thus only function properly if there is total freedom in the management of each school. In theory, the system would create a virtuous cycle, with schools behaving like businesses, seeking the optimum.

Teachers' unions unanimously oppose the voucher system. They argue that the system would encourage discrimination by motivating parents to group their children based on ethnicity (which already happens, in any case, because of population patterns that create ethnically homogeneous neighborhoods). Union leaders imply that neither parents nor children would be capable of recognizing the top schools but would be duped by fallacious arguments. (In reality, a school's published test results provide a good indicator of its quality.) Thus, though the voucher system has been available in the political marketplace for some thirty years, the teachers' unions have managed successfully to oppose it just about everywhere. A good example is a referendum in California in 1993, in which voters rejected the voucher system. Parents said no to a reform that, on its face, was in their interest. What argument allowed the unions to carry public opinion? Essentially, it was nostalgia: The television ads financed by the unions played on fond memories of the public schools. People are all the more sensitive to such an appeal because in a nation of immigrants, schools traditionally have been the melting pot in which citizens are made.

A Convincing Experience

Despite this resistance from the unions and the general population, the voucher system has partially taken hold in a few places, particularly in Florida and Milwaukee. It is possible to verify the validity of Friedman's theory based on these experiments.

Florida's case, Hoxby acknowledges, is only partly convincing. Its main virtue is political: Florida was equally divided between Republicans and Democrats, and the voucher system was accepted by both parties in an attempt to bolster the declining performance of high schools. Thus the system belongs neither to the Right nor to the Left. It is hardly used, currently representing only a minute fraction of the schools' budgets. But the mere threat of a wider implementation may have motivated those who run the schools to focus on improving their productivity—so perhaps the voucher system has another kind of "pedagogical" value.

The Milwaukee experiment is more convincing; from the point of view of economists, it is almost perfect. The voucher system was established there in 1998, then canceled in 2002 following a change in the majority at the municipal level, and then restored in 2004. It has been possible for Hoxby to measure the effects of all these changes. Milwaukee, moreover, has a significant Hispanic minority, mostly Mexican immigrants, whose scholastic performance had been mediocre. Before the voucher system was introduced, these students were assigned, by a mandatory geographic districting, to "ghettoized" neighborhood public schools. Offering vouchers to poor Milwaukee families had the effect of spreading voucher students over all of the city's schools. Hispanic parents made their choices of schools based on the published test results of the various establishments.

Following this large-scale experiment, Hoxby measured the verifiable results. The outcome was a 5–10 percent improvement for Milwaukee's students overall, with more significant progress for Hispanic children than for other groups. Freedom of choice for parents led, as Friedman's theory predicted, to productivity gains for the system as a whole, with a more pronounced benefit for the disadvantaged. These improvements are not spectacular, but they will change the lives of the beneficiaries and will have positive secondary effects for the economy as a whole. Hoxby also thinks that the implementation of the voucher system created a dynamic of change throughout the entire school system—an improvement in the general equilibrium—whether the schools were involved in the voucher experiment or not. Here again one sees the pedagogical virtue cited in the Florida experiment.

Despite the demonstrable virtues of the voucher system, it continues to encounter the same interest-group resistance everywhere it is tried. In Chile, where Friedman's theories have much influence, the voucher system prevails, but the results have been mediocre because governments (which have been leftist since the departure of General Pinochet in 1990) have refused to fund the vouchers sufficiently to give access to private schools, which are more expensive than the public ones. Even within the public school system, parents do not have transparent choices, since school officials refuse to publish their results. This particular application of the voucher system, even though the system has been accepted in principle, harms the poorest students, who remain in poor public schools while the privileged go to private schools. The interest-group pressure of public school teachers reinforces social discrimination, which the voucher system could theoretically reduce.

Charter Schools

Despite its uncontested benefits, the Milwaukee example has not ignited a movement. The voucher system remains marginal in the United States, more refused than refuted. But it retains the potential to provide the outline of a strategy for reform. There is another reform movement, still modest, in which Hoxby has also invested her hopes: charter schools. These make up barely 1 percent of the secondary education market, but they are expanding more rapidly than vouchers, doubtless because the idea better matches distinctive American habits and attitudes. A charter school is a secondary school created by a private enterprise, either a for-profit company (the most prominent being the Edison Company, directed by a former president of Yale University, Benno Schmidt) or, more often, a nonprofit foundation. These organizations enter into detailed contracts with local authorities that delineate the content of instruction, pedagogical methods, and methods of management. Within the framework of these contracts, schools enjoy the freedom to recruit and compensate teachers as they see fit; as a general rule, the charter schools cost the public less than the traditional public schools, doubtless because of better management. For the children, the school is tuition-free, like French private schools, but American charter schools enjoy greater freedom, and, unlike the most common examples in France, they are not religious.

One original feature of charter schools that situates them within the American tradition is that many belong to "chains." In their methods of management and teaching, the chains share certain standards, allowing each school to benefit from the experience of all the others; managers and teachers can pursue careers within the chain. The chain comes with a brand name that lets parents get their bearings and learn in advance about the characteristics of the offered "product." For a mobile population inhabiting a vast territory and accustomed to commercial standards, the marketplace of education thus can offer the same kind of guarantees as any other branded product.

Will this logic of brands have more influence over education than vouchers have had so far? Hoxby hopes so, without expecting a major transformation. Teachers' unions oppose charter schools, too. In Southern California, the Inner City Education Foundation (ICEF), a twenty-year-old charter-school network, enrolls more Los Angeles minority children, black and Hispanic, than do the traditional public schools; it sends 100 percent of them to college, compared with 25 percent from the regular public schools. How do the unions react? The California teachers' association asked the governor to pass a law that would make opening new charter schools next to impossible.

Moreover, the very success of charter schools, where they exist, tends paradoxically to limit their expansion. The public entities that finance charter schools have trouble accepting profit-making within education; as soon as a charter school works too well, to the detriment of the public schools with which it competes, or as soon as it proves less expensive, the state or the city tends to reduce its public subsidy. The Edison Company, mentioned earlier, has never been able to make a profit or to remunerate its stockholders. It remains the case, nonetheless, that the rise in educational productivity demonstrated in these experiments, with the voucher system as well as with charter schools, gradually acclimatizes public opinion and public officials to the idea of productivity in education. Educational expenditures are such that elected officials will eventually start questioning the supposed relationship between public money spent and good results. It's worth noting that Barack Obama, when he was running for the White House, made positive comments about charter schools. As president, can he convince the unions to go along?

The Best Universities in the World

It is surprising that public opinion in the United States remains so suspicious of competition in secondary education, since such competition is the rule in higher education. Unlike in continental Europe, no one in the United States objects to the complete freedom that universities enjoy in admissions, teaching, and financing. Hoxby has attempted to understand why this principle of competition does not spread from universities to secondary education. No doubt the reason has to do with the role of integrating citizens that secondary schools perform; because universities select elites, they seem to escape this democratic criterion. It is also true that American universities, both public and private, have made great efforts to avoid the appearance of discriminating, while remaining elitist. This is called "diversity."

Since the 1960s, admissions criteria in the universities have evolved so that teachers as well as students reflect the diversity of American society. This pursuit of diversity, like the scholarships and loans offered to poor and minority students, cannot be explained, according to Hoxby, by the judicial constraints of affirmative action. Nor can the explanation be found in altruism. As for quotas, these have been rejected as discriminatory. Economic productivity suffices to explain diversity. Through her studies of students' educational careers, she has shown that applicants favor the most diverse universities; it is in the students' interest, in the course of their studies, to confront society as it is, the same kind of society in which, as graduates, they will probably become business managers. By taking diversity into account, students and universities behave in an economically rational fashion.

Economic logic also explains why attending an American university is becoming increasingly expensive. At one time, universities were local and recruited students and faculty in neighboring areas. More recently, however, they have competed vigorously on a national level, which has led them to invest in costlier academic disciplines and to recruit the best possible teachers, offering them bigger salaries. And now these universities must even compete on the global educational market, since students from all over the world wish to study on American campuses and professors from all over the world want to teach on them. As a result, prices rise, disciplines specialize further, and teachers profit even more. Students also profit insofar as their investment in expensive studies will later translate into higher salaries in the employment market. Free access to higher education as practiced in France and in Germany is therefore not a factor to which the market is sensitive: Many students prefer to attend an expensive private university, financing their tuition by loans, than go to a less expensive public university, if the former is more prestigious (as it usually is) and guarantees greater subsequent remuneration. This reasoning is valid for foreigners who are searching in the global marketplace using the same criteria; it is easy to verify that free access to French or German universities does not give them a comparative market advantage. Further, free access impoverishes these universities by making them dependent on states alone for their financing. The gap between the continents is widening: $6,000 per student per year in Europe, compared with $40,000 in the United States.

Non-American universities that are not involved in this global competition risk losing their best students and teachers—a downward spiral that results in the erosion of national capital. Aware of this threat to France, Jean Tirole notes that the departure of a researcher for the United States leads to a loss of human capital beyond that person alone: A whole generation of students will not benefit from his teaching, and the innovations that he and his followers produce will be lost for the country left behind. The American lead might get too big for other nations to catch up, assuming that the United States retains most of the students educated in its universities. This is the current tendency, not yet counterbalanced by the return to their home countries of U.S. students from China, India, and other foreign countries. The intellectual trade balance still favors the United States. In the future, this brain drain toward the U.S. may even reach secondary education; it is becoming common among Asian, African, and Middle Eastern elites to send their children to study in America or in American schools abroad prior to university to facilitate their later access to higher education. It is conceivable that this global education market already provides an outline of tomorrow's economic map.

CHAPTER SEVEN

Rationality Everywhere

"Ideas have little influence on political choices," Gary Becker proclaims. "The true engine of societies is material interests." Such modesty from the most libertarian—and one of the most influential—of contemporary economists is surprising. But the theory of "rational action" that Becker has originated at the University of Chicago clarifies his vision of the world. According to this theory, we never act except to maximize our material advantages, just as an entrepreneur seeks to maximize his profits.

This collective "we" does not allow us to describe the behavior of a single individual. Still, on average, for a given group, we can say that economic optimization determines choices. These choices may be conscious or unconscious: Becker refuses to ponder individual psychology or to analyze cultures. He remains content to observe that we behave *as if* we were rational; whether we are does not affect the final result. In a family, for example (the economics of the family was the point of departure—a controversial one in its day—for Becker's work), choices get made that are similar to those a business would make in pursuit of an optimal economic outcome. Comparing a theoretical

109

model of a firm operating within a marketplace with familial behavior, such as the number and the education of children, the age of marriage and divorce, and so on, Becker notes the similarity of strategies and of results, and he concludes that our actions, on the whole, are rational. The market economy thus reflects human nature, and the partisans of government intervention, by going too much against human nature, risk producing consequences other than those they hope for.

The Determinism of Interests

This interest-based determinism contradicts a famous prophecy of John Maynard Keynes, who, in the concluding notes of his *General Theory of Employment, Interest and Money* (1935), wrote: "Practical men, who believe themselves to be quite exempt from any intellectual influences, are usually the slaves of some defunct economist.... [I]t is ideas, not vested interests, which are dangerous for good or evil."

Intellectuals, and especially economists, would like to believe Keynes on this point, but his theory is indemonstrable, while Becker's, like it or not, bases itself on statistical studies. It is, in fact, easier to demonstrate that political choices are determined by power relations among pressure groups than to show that they are influenced by an evaluation of economic ideas. Becker illustrates this supremacy of interests over ideas by using the history of the free market. Since the eighteenth century, economists have been practically unanimous concerning its usefulness, but it took three centuries for the superiority of the free market to win acceptance, and policies dictated by particular interests have continually contradicted it.

If certain ideas prevail over the long term, Becker adds, it is because they coincide with new interests—for example, interests that arise following changes in power relations. An idea arises to cover these new interests, but this is merely a way to dress up the interests that really drive new policies. Nevertheless, like his mentor, Friedrich Hayek, Becker considers ideas indispensable during crises. When a political or economic system collapses, it is good to have on hand an alternative system, what Hayek, as we've noted, called an "alternative utopia."

Notwithstanding these precautions, and perhaps somewhat ironically, Becker has for fifty years tirelessly promoted his own theory of rational action. This theory isn't limited to analyzing and recommending what are ordinarily considered economic policies. Becker has brought *homo economicus* into domains formerly reserved for sociology or psychology, the family included. Sociologists, especially those unfriendly to the free market, do not welcome this economic imperialism. Such scholars denounce the theory of rational action as ideology. But unfortunately for sociologists, economics is a science that deals in measurable results, which is not always the case in sociology.

A new generation of economists, following Becker's example, is applying the theory of rational action to ordinary or deviant behaviors, with a certain predilection for the latter. Are not criminals, prostitutes, and drug users seeking a maximum profit, or don't they at least behave as if they were? In this vein, in the name of rationality, Becker (along with Milton Friedman) was one of the first economists to recommend legalizing all drugs—a perfect example of an idea that has had no influence.

The Legalization of Drugs

If we legalized drugs, Becker explains, ordinary private businesses would produce and distribute them. The firms would compete without having to resort to violence; mafias and cartels would have no purpose. All this would represent considerable progress for civil and international peace. By the logic of the market, better-quality drugs and good brands would reduce the number of accidents due to defective hygiene. The price of drugs would fall, so that drug users would have less incentive to commit reprehensible acts—thefts, murders, and prostitution—to procure their supplies.

But wouldn't lower prices lead to increased consumption? Becker acknowledges the possibility. But taxes could help contain demand. As we know from the case of tobacco, price influences consumption. A price increase reduces the temptation for a young person to smoke a first cigarette, making him less likely to become dependent on nicotine. The smoker, in this view, is a rational consumer like any other, responding to market signals; the economic reflex prevails over biological dependence. Then wouldn't we raise prices by taxes to the point of eliminating all consumption? No, because too great an increase in taxes on tobacco would encourage smuggling. The creation of a black market in tobacco becomes attractive as a business from the moment the margin between the taxed legal market and the black market generates profits that are higher than the risk run by the trafficker. The trafficker, a rational entrepreneur, calculates the cost of fines and the risk of imprisonment. If the profit he can make by smuggling tobacco becomes considerable, he will run the risks.

The same reasoning would hold for hard drugs if they were legalized. A well-calibrated tax would make it possible to regulate demand at a tolerable level while not encouraging illegality and violence. Becker proposes one last argument in favor of modest taxes on tobacco and, if applicable, on drugs: These taxes weigh hardest on the most disadvantaged, who are the biggest consumers of these products. An excessive taxation of tobacco, which affects the poorest consumers, is disproportionate and unjust.

In order to moderate consumption, a legalization of drugs would require the severe punishment of illegal acts committed under their influence. Drugs do not remove personal responsibility. Evidence shows, for instance, that the enforcement of more severe sanctions reduces driving under the influence of alcohol—

and does so in all countries. Even drunk drivers, in other words, behave in a relatively rational manner. Similarly, a drug user in a free market would become less irrational than he is under a regime of prohibition.

Does Becker's logic run against conventional ideas? Yes, but cultural myths or social prejudices don't trouble him. His examples are not intellectual concepts. Moreover, every stage in his argument finds support in studies of behavior; he does not offer mere opinion but relates quantified facts. The facts are true—only the conclusions he draws from them are original, even disturbing. Others can draw other conclusions and make different recommendations. Yet policies that contradict human nature, Becker reminds us, lead to results that differ from those they promise.

Immigration for Sale

In the area of immigration, Becker again offers an economic solution to a social problem. Looking at the immigrant as an entrepreneur, Becker observes that the immigrant invests money to reach the country of destination, and all the more if his project is clandestine. He pays smugglers, corrupts officials, and runs personal risks, estimating that in the end his profit will justify his investment. Becker concludes that the best way to control migratory fluctuations would not be to regulate immigration but to make it conditional on payment. The distinction between legal and illegal immigrants would disappear, replaced by that between those who pay and those who defraud. The price of entry would vary according to the gains expected by the candidate and by the receiving country. The country derives an economic advantage from immigration, but it also undergoes social costs; these costs would be assessed and would determine the price of a truly chosen act of immigration. Once again, Becker's approach appears provocative, but it is already somewhat followed in the United States: An important investor automatically receives a green card. In 2007, President George W. Bush proposed (unsuccessfully) that illegal immigrants be granted legal status by paying a tax—implicitly acknowledging the validity of Becker's theory.

Crime Pays

Becker's proposals have not yet influenced drug policy and have influenced immigration policy only a little. The same isn't true for criminal legislation. As Becker himself might say, it happens that new interest-based coalitions have found it advantageous to support his rationalist projects.

Beginning in the 1960s, Becker quantified the economic behavior of criminals. When laws became more lenient, judges more tolerant, and police less effective, he found, crime came to be seen as a more lucrative activity: The risk was diminishing. When there are so many criminals, Becker says, crime must pay. Does his argument also work for the death penalty? It seems to have little deterrent effect, but in Becker's view, that is because it is not enforced, or enforced infrequently, even when applicable. The criminal does not define himself by existing laws but on the basis of reality, as he perceives it: Is crime effectively punished? Crimes that go unpunished, punishments that are not enforced, and automatic releases from prison are the true signals—much more than laws—that encourage criminal activity.

It is therefore legitimate, Becker concludes, to oppose the death penalty on moral grounds—but not by refuting its effect as a deterrent. Beginning in the 1980s, this so-called utilitarian interpretation of crime gained public acceptance in the United States. It translated into tougher crime legislation and police practices. At the same time, criminal behavior declined. Was this because it was less profitable? This is Becker's argument in favor of what is known as "zero tolerance"—there is a direct relationship, he maintains, between the reduction of crime in the United States and zero-tolerance policies. In Becker's logic, the increase in the number of prisoners, a controversial characteristic of American society, sends a deterrent signal to potential criminals.

Dissuasion by repression, Becker notes, works also on crimes of passion and apparently uncontrolled acts of violence, such as barroom brawls. Comparative statistical studies of different nations have proved that even under the sway of passion or of alcohol, an assessment of the associated risk tempers violence. The delinquent, whether in the grip of liquor or of emotion, is rational—or acts as if he were.

In the case of the reduction of criminality in large American cities, rival explanations to Becker's exist. One can cite, for example, the transition, in criminal circles, from crack cocaine, a stimulant drug, to heroin, which relaxes. So it may be that the use of heroin instead of crack helped drive crime down. Some believe that the downward tendency of the price of cocaine results in less violence because it becomes less difficult to procure it. These alternatives, Becker notes, do not contradict the theory of rational action but enrich it. Is the abandonment of crack due to the high risk that this drug imposes on the consumer? If so, then the consumer is rationally directed toward another substance. Far from renouncing his hypothesis, Becker proposes more complex models that incorporate a greater number of factors.

One of his disciples, the Brazilian economist and Princeton professor José Scheinkman, has completed Becker's theory of criminal behavior by investigating the surprising dispersion of crime across American soil. Waves of crime come and go with none of the clear connections to culture or income that one might expect. Scheinkman thus quantified a phenomenon familiar to sociologists: imitation. Crime spreads by imitation in social environments where it is considered acceptable. This observation would be banal if Scheinkman had not organized crime statistics into a mathematical model that makes surges in crime predictable.

It is now possible, thanks to the model, to predict the population density, in a given sector of society, at which crime will likely appear. This model shows how quantitative economics, without replacing sociology, can sometimes elevate it from empirical observation to relative mathematical predictability.

The Origins of Virtue

Rationality explains not only crime but virtue as well: Many so-called bourgeois virtues evolve as a function of economic signals. Becker has shown how taxation policies encourage or discourage marriage and divorce. The wealthy divorce less, since they have more to lose than the poor. He has also shown the degree to which laws affect whether a father cares for his children, pays child support, and stays with his wife. State interventions are thus never neutral when it comes to values. Are state interventions and values therefore at odds? Becker cites Tocqueville, who observed, in *Democracy in America*: "Since the state interferes little, citizens are all the more responsible and capable of taking initiatives."

For Becker, arguments in favor of little government regulation of the economy serve not only the principle of efficiency but also what we like to call morals—that is, bourgeois morality, the rationality of which, until recently, seemed evident and useful to the social and economic order. If he has to, each individual becomes thriftier and develops good habits and personal responsibility. He loses these habits if the government tends to things that should be the individual's responsibility.

Sociologists and moralists counter this rational explanation of virtue with the notion of altruism. Is altruism not economically irrational, proving that we obey incentives that are not material? Becker has always rejected this apparently irrefutable argument by showing that, outside the family, altruism is all but insignificant. In the United States, he says, much is made of charitable donations. But what do these really amount to, and to whom are they given? Altruism represents only 2.5 percent of household income, and half of this sum, he adds, goes to churches from which one expects something in return: masses, weddings, or funerals. On the other hand, it is undeniable that altruism is constantly at work within the family. Becker believes that this does not weaken but reinforces his theory of rational action, since familial altruism indeed arises from calculation. The most common and important strategy is the sharing of resources. This may be explained by conjugal love, Becker says, but even without love, it is clear that this sharing is economically advantageous and lets a couple optimize its resources.

Using the same method, Becker has addressed another objection concerning generosity that has been raised by Jean Tirole and Roland Benabou. Is it really rational, the two French economists argue, to give to humanitarian organizations from which nothing is expected in return? But Tirole and Benabou have also shown by laboratory experiments that one is more generous when the gift is visible. Generosity proves readier to show itself than to remain hidden, and the anonymous giver is an exception. Under total anonymity, giving falls to almost zero, and material interest prevails. Becker concludes that an expectation of reward, the gratitude of others, and even self-love usually motivate generosity. Thus the snare of rationality takes in what appeared to be altruism.

The Rise of the Irrational

In 2008, I asked Becker what recent developments were hardest to deal with for his theory of rational behavior. "Islamic martyrs," he answered without hesitation. He is familiar with Islam, his wife being of Iranian origin, but he has not succeeded in integrating the suicide bombers into his model. Is this a limit of Becker's theory, or a limit of economics in general? The science of economics runs up against the reality of collective myths.

Becker also confesses to being at a loss when considering environmentalism. "We do not know with certainty if there is global warming," he observes, "but it is certain that it is impossible to discuss the question rationally." Becker does not doubt that if climatic risks are eventually demonstrated, technical solutions will be found. But he notes that the debate is quasi-religious and that to doubt is to expose oneself to the outrage of fanatical "greens."

The science of economics is threatened by myths; it also has a tendency, at times, to slip into triviality. Without wishing it, Becker has become the godfather of what is called "Freakonomics," after the title of a bestseller by one of his students at Chicago, Steven Levitt. Freakonomics examines deviant phenomena and behavior: why athletes cheat, how a prostitute calculates her prices, at what price a football fan will buy a ticket on the black market. These studies attempt to demonstrate that individuals, as calculating beings, are independent of the norms of the society in which they live and of the culture that supposedly conditions them. Everyone in all civilizations is rational, and all behavior can be explained by this rationality.

To illustrate how this research into economic maximization illuminates the most unexpected and least explicable behaviors, Levitt published a study titled "Why Do Drug Dealers Still Live with Their Mothers?" Based on data gathered from the subjects, he calculated that the average income of a drug dealer in Chicago, in a competitive market, was equivalent to that of an unskilled employee, such as a server at McDonald's. The dealer thus cannot afford to live anywhere but with his mother. If he remains a dealer despite the risks, it is because he dreams of moving up the ladder of crime. Levitt nonetheless observes that over time, when the price of drugs falls, commissions also tend downward and the dealer ends up reentering the legal economy. Dealers are rational entrepreneurs.

CHAPTER EIGHT

The Limits of Pure Reason

What is scientific is falsifiable, Karl Popper famously explained—that is, it is susceptible of being proved wrong. Ideologies or religions are irrefutable, by contrast, because by their nature they cannot incorporate criticism. One might conclude, then, that the theory of rational action as Gary Becker conceives it is eminently scientific because it is always being refuted. Here we will consider two such refutations. The first concerns speculation, which appears to be the least rational of economic activities. The second, known as behavioral economics or neuroeconomics, goes so far as to contest the very capacity of individuals to demonstrate rationality. On this view, we're all neurologically illogical, unable to distinguish our interests from our drives. The reader looking for absolutes will find no definitive response here to these challenges, however. This is typical of scientific progress.

The Logic of Passions

Princeton's José Scheinkman has sought to explain the logic that leads speculators in the grip of a passion for gambling or for money to participate in speculative ventures that appear irrational. Speculative bubbles, Scheinkman notes, are as old as economic history—from the Dutch passion for tulip bulbs in the seventeenth century up to the Internet bubble of 2000 and the mortgage-credit crisis of 2007–08. How is speculation born? Whether it involves tulip bulbs or the unthinking acquisition of every new Internet firm that makes a public offering, the mechanisms are identical and one can capture them in a model.

At the outset of all these phenomena is something real, some discovery or innovation: Imported bulbs in Holland were a novelty that everyone wanted to have, the Internet was a technical innovation, and derivatives were a financial invention. But innovation by itself is not enough. What is necessary is the intervention of a third person who rouses passion. Scheinkman names this person the "advisor." The advisor may be a recognized expert, a financial consultant, a journalist, a commentator, or an art critic. Such an advisor's first concern is to manage his or her own reputation, which is the foundation of his business—and he is in business as much as anyone. If somehow he overlooks some innovation or tax shelter, he loses his reputation and his clients. And so the advisor lies in wait. As soon as he spots—or thinks he spots—an innovation, he will exaggerate its significance to serve his own interests. His excesses only contribute to his reputation for expertise and bring him new clients.

The conjunction of innovation and its enthusiastic promotion by advisors begins the process in which people find themselves swept up in a wave of interest in tulips, in contemporary art, in certain stocks, or whatever. The expansion of a speculative bubble can be identified by the number of transactions. On the stock market, a stock normally gets traded 100 times a year; if one is traded 100 times a week, a bubble has been created. All the bubbles that Scheinkman has observed follow the same arithmetic trajectory, configurable in models.

Besides its trajectory, a bubble is characterized by the disappearance of any relation between the value of what is acquired and the value of the business or benefits that one can expect from it. Has the buyer become irrational? Not altogether, for the speculator does not buy in order to receive dividends; he buys in the hope that the speculation will continue and that he will be able to sell at a higher price. The speculator is not irrational, but a not uncommon psychological trait affects him: an excess of self-confidence. Speculative buyers believe that they know more than others and that they can beat the market. As in a lottery, a few succeed, which reinforces their excessive confidence. Thus it makes sense for them to ride the speculation as long as it lasts. Scheinkman imagines an investment-fund manager's dilemma. He knows that a bubble is speculative. Does logic dictate that he stay on the sidelines? If he does, he might seem reasonable, but not necessarily, since his clients might blame him for forgoing a chance for big profits. This clear-sighted manager risks losing clients who would abandon him to invest with bolder competitors; as reasonable and risk-aware as he may be, therefore, he feels pressure to join the speculators. Where speculation is concerned, what is rational is not necessarily logical.

Scheinkman's model (which, in its mathematical version, is built on empirical data) applies to areas as diverse as the contemporary art market and investments in China—whether direct investments within China or purchases on the Shanghai stock market. Is China itself a big bubble? Prices have no relation to the value of businesses (which no one really knows). Advisors warmly recommend investing in China: If you don't, your clients or stockholders will leave you! The number of transactions on the Chinese market, along with the characteristics already mentioned, confirms that we are dealing with a bubble. Should a person ride it? In other words, is it possible to know when the bubble will burst? No. Scheinkman's model makes it possible to point out the formation of the bubble and its expansion, not to predict its ending point, though this end is certain. How does a bubble burst? The timing is unpredictable, but the market eventually collapses when supply surpasses demand. Values plummet until they reflect the real value (or lack of value) of the businesses or things that fueled the speculation. And then we await the next frenzy and the exact repetition of Scheinkman's model.

All the characteristics of a bubble as Scheinkman describes one apply to the subprime-mortgage crisis. At the beginning, there was an innovation: financial derivatives, which allowed mortgage risk to be spread to a large number of financial investors. Advisors then intervened, promoting the new financial instruments to investors and buyers. The reasons to join this market looked stronger than the reasons to stay out of it. Boosted by easy credit, real-estate prices ratcheted upward, just as they did for tulips and Internet companies. Buoyed by euphoria and profits, all participants bet that they could beat the market, at least for one more day.

Is there a political lesson, or some safety measure, to learn here? No: Speculation is at once rational and irrational, reflecting recalcitrant human nature. Should speculation be regulated in order to avoid bubbles? But bubbles tend to appear on the fringes, where markets are unregulated. Thus regulation always comes too late, as a political reaction to the bubble. Moreover, an excess of regulation could kill in its infancy a genuinely useful innovation. Despite the 2000 Internet bubble, the Internet is still with us—after the market cleared away the excesses. The same holds true of financial derivatives; the sophisticated repackaging of debts by the mortgage industry—"securitization"—will survive the subprime bubble. Without it, many creative companies could not be born and many deserving Americans would have no hope of ever owning a house. If subprime-mortgage credit were forbidden, the primary victims would be the poor, the main beneficiaries of subprime loans. Most will avoid foreclosure and remain homeowners.

"Selves" in Contradiction

Neuroeconomics takes us still deeper into the contradiction between human nature and economic reason. David Laibson asks his guinea pig if he would prefer to receive $100 immediately or $110 in a month. The average subject prefers the immediate $100, an economically absurd choice but a revealing indicator or our bias towards instant gratification. Then Laibson asks the same subject whether he would prefer to receive $100 in one month or $110 in two months. Generally, people prefer $110 in two months. These choices aren't coherent, but they indicate irrational behavior, contradicting the Beckerian belief in economically sound decision-making by individuals.

In a comparable experiment, the subject is asked if he would prefer immediately to eat some chocolate or some fruit. He prefers the chocolate. In a week, would he prefer the fruit or the chocolate? The fruit. Whether it's chocolate or dollars, the subject thus chooses immediate gratification over his long-term interests; it would be healthier, in the end, to eat the fruit, and better to receive $110 in a month with its very advantageous interest rate. The subject adopts a short-term position that he knows is harmful in the long term. Depending on whether the question concerns the short or the long term, different parts of the brain leap into action. One can see this on a laboratory scanner taking pictures of the test subject's brain. In such tests, Laibson, a pioneer at Harvard in neuroeconomics—or behavioral economics, as it's also known—got the result that he had foreseen. All experiments of this kind conducted so far, whether on individuals or on groups, corroborate the founding hypothesis of behavioral economics: that *homo economicus* is not as rational as classical economics claims.

Two Israeli-American researchers, Amos Tversky and Daniel Kahneman, are credited with founding in 1979 this new economic approach, which brings together the findings of economic science, psychology, and, more recently, neurology. This new economics has been recognized with a Nobel Prize, awarded to Kahneman in 2002. Behind the new approach lies a philosophical dissatisfaction with classical economics and especially with the theory of "rational action" formalized by Gary Becker. The classical models based on statistical aggregates cannot account for the way in which individuals actually make economic choices. As Becker often says, everything happens "as if," in an average population, these choices were rational. Laibson replies that "as if" is unsatisfying. Behavioral economists prefer to press the question: How do we *really* make choices? Their observation of actual choices has led them to doubt the rationality of individuals.

In Laibson's view, we are divided at each moment between contradictory demands and drives, and still more divided over time. At each moment, an individual can be split between opposing desires: to do good or bad, to be concerned with self or with others, to invest or to spend. In sum, the instantaneous self is multiple. And if one situates the self in time, then all the "selves" that are in a person diverge still more. Smoking gives me pleasure right now, but finally harms my future self. Will I stop smoking? Yes … tomorrow. This behavior is dominant in all forms of addiction. But tomorrow, I will put off changing my ways until the day after tomorrow, because the present counts much more for me than the future. People are impatient in the present and patient about the future.

Classical economics does not take this contradictory behavior into account; it assumes that actors are rational, or at least act as if they were rational, at every moment. Behavioral economists propose an alternative model that accounts for the bias toward the present and for the relative concern for the future. Following experiments that he conducted in American businesses, Laibson was able to quantify the gap between rational behavior, as imagined by classical economists, and real behavior. In reality, we are led to make irrational choices that are against our interests; we go more against our interests when things are offered to us in certain ways. In a well-known experiment conducted by Kahneman, a subject is asked if he will accept a bet on a coin toss, knowing that he will gain $150 if he wins but lose $100 if he loses. By simple logic, the player has an interest in accepting. But almost all players refuse. Our risk-averseness, a strong psychological trait, prevails over rational calculation: The player plays against himself, just as I play against myself.

Laibson conducted similar experiments among groups of employees of American businesses that offered very advantageous retirement plans; he notes that these employees selected the plans only as a function of the way the choice was formulated. When a retirement plan was automatic, allowing individuals to opt out, 95 percent of employees joined. But if an express choice was required to join the same plan, only 50 percent chose to join, and 50 percent did not commit themselves. Under a third possibility, in which employees had to choose either to join a retirement plan or not to join (one was free to choose, but one had to choose), 75 percent joined and 25 percent refused. To ensure the validity of these experiments, Laibson carried them out within one and the same business, in real time, dividing employees into comparable groups.

If one applied the theory of "rational action" to this business, you would expect 100 percent of the employees to join an advantageous plan: This would be the logical optimum. But in real life, the rate of choice varies between 50 percent and 95 percent as a function of its formulation. This gap between the optimum and reality reflects our temporal inconsistency. The further away the future, the more the present self sees itself in conflict with the future self. And we have to consider that in a complex world, employees often give up exercising their personal judgment and rely upon the recommendations of leaders—not very democratic, perhaps, but quite rational.

The preference for immediate gratification that Laibson describes, without being modeled or quantified, is familiar to all salespeople. To offer a sale with no payment the first month or the first year is a proven technique for selling everything from cars to insurance policies. In the United States, the mortgage crisis was the direct consequence of this method. Unqualified clients were taken in by offers of credit without immediate payment or with no interest for the first year. An adherent of "rational action" theory would conclude that these clients, knowing what they were doing or behaving as if they knew, had taken a calculated risk. But behavioral economists like Laibson denounce abuses on the part of the underwriters, who knew how irrational their clients were and thus how they could be manipulated.

The State Rehabilitated

These two theories, according to which action is either rational or driven by passions, respectively, have distinct political consequences. If the first is true, it is important not to regulate, for example, the insurance market. But if one adheres to Laibson's view, then it is appropriate to forbid irresistible offers that are too enticing to be true. Does it follow that Laibson advocates state regulation of the economy? If we are irrational, shouldn't the state protect us from our drives, taking over the management of our future for our own best interest? Obligatory retirement systems responded to our irrationality long before the emergence of behavioral economics.

But the new theory isn't based on intuition; it quantifies our irrationality and links it to a certain neural determinism. Thus we move from intuition to science. To conclude that behavioral economics must lead to statism would be unfair to the theory, since it denounces the irrationality of all economic actors, including the state. State actors, Laibson points out, also manifest a preference for immediate (electoral) gratification and discount the long term. And since the state is more powerful and thus more dangerous than individuals, it is best to limit its power, as it too is irrational. Whereas theoreticians of "rational action" make the case for totally free markets and for the quasi-disappearance of the state, behavioral economists tend to favor the welfare state, but without excess.

The same invitation to prudence can be found in the work of George Akerlof, an American economist at the University of California at Berkeley who found his place in the scientific literature in 1970 with a simple story of used cars. The market economy would be perfect, he wrote, if all economic actors disposed of the same information, but this is not the case. When a used-car salesman offers a customer a deal, the salesman has information that the customer lacks; their information is asymmetrical. The same holds for another example of Akerlof's: In the real-estate market, agents possess information that potential buyers do not. To prove the asymmetry of this information, Akerlof showed that real-estate agents in the United States acquired their own housing at a lower average price than that set by the market; they cannot use an information asymmetry against themselves. Akerlof concludes that a third party must watch over the market. But this third party is not necessarily the state; a brand or label can also reestablish fairness of information. In these and other cases, Akerlof, like Laibson, warns against excessive zeal. No actor is perfect, and every system has its vice.

Tirole's Criteria

How can a line be drawn between the state's legitimate protection of consumers and totalitarian paternalism? Jean Tirole believes that the criterion should be social demand. He cites two circumstances in which this demand has been expressed and it is legitimate, in his view, for the state to protect individuals from their own passions. Tirole argues that the addictive quality of tobacco and the desire of the majority of smokers—either active or passive—to rid itself of that addiction, a desire frustrated by the power of the desire for immediate gratification, justifies state intervention. Similarly, the demand for consumer credit has led to such a large number of payment defaults and expressed regrets that it is legitimate for the state to impose a waiting or "cooling-off" period—an expression that makes it clear that it is an instinctive passion that must be countered.

Tirole thus parts company with Becker, who believes that the incentive of a market price suffices to manage behaviors optimally. For Becker, tobacco must be sold at its fair price, while Tirole suggests taxing it to force consumers to be more clear-headed. Becker ignores passion, whereas Tirole would reintroduce it into the market. Tirole also distinguishes himself from Laibson, whom he finds too interventionist. In the mortgage crisis in the United States, according to Tirole, the majority's desire for access to home ownership justifies maintaining the free market; the defaulting of a minority of borrowers does not amount to a social demand that would justify a state sanction. Like José Scheinkman, he rejects excessive regulation that would deprive the poor of any chance to participate in the real-estate market.

A middle way may be found in the obligation to inform. Since behavioral economics reveals a tendency for consumers to inform themselves insufficiently of the future consequences of an immediate choice, information can force them to become aware of the implications of their choices. Still, it is essential, Tirole adds, that this obligation to inform not become too bureaucratic. Tirole's criteria aren't measurable under all circumstances, but they sketch a middle way between the absolutism of the market and state paternalism. Economics is like that: Whether in theory or in practice, there is no perfect solution, only solutions less bad than others.

PART 3

The Convergence of Nations

A *third of humanity remains mired in poverty, but two-thirds have escaped it. This progress is without precedent in history. Over the last thirty years, 500 million people, many of them in China and in India, have joined the path of development. In the end, all nations should converge toward a higher standard of living and participate in a way of life comparable with that of the most prosperous. On the scale of human history, this convergence is rapid: At a growth rate of 6 percent per year, which is common in countries that are taking off economically, the standard of living doubles every twelve years. This historical trend has been partially interrupted in 2008, but there are no structural reasons why it should not start again after the current cyclical downturn, since these nations have now built a capacity for growth—they understand the proven path to development. A crisis in capitalism is thus not a crisis of capitalism, nor is it the end of the free market and globalization. It is now widely understood in these poor nations that their destiny is globalization, a new civilization that a temporary, even severe, credit crunch will not derail.*

These attainments and this universal achievement are in large part the work of economists. It is now possible to mark the path that leads from poverty to the wealth of nations. It has been proved time and again that natural resources are not absolutely essential for prosperity, that international aid is not the key to development, that planning and state control of the economy are counterproductive, and that freedom of entrepreneurship and trade is the right recipe for growth in any culture.

The experiences of the Asian Tigers since the 1960s, followed by the examples of India, China, and Brazil, demonstrate that the convergence of nations is predictable in all latitudes once the right economic policy is in place. This is what the Catalonian economist Xavier Sala-i-Martin, originator of the theory of convergence, explains, and what is proved by the following case studies in Asia and Latin America. Then there is Africa—the last to get started, but equally a place where growth is the key to a desirable future.

CHAPTER NINE

The End of Mass Poverty

HAD HE BEEN BORN twenty years earlier, Xavier Sala-i-Martin would likely have stayed in Barcelona and studied the crises of capitalism. But in the space of a generation, it had become clear that while the market economy might suffer downturns, it was not in its final crisis—and indeed had displaced socialism, national self-sufficiency, and planning. At one time, market economics seemed confined to the West and a few Asian Tigers. Then it took over the planet; the resulting economic growth is global. Sala-i-Martin took note of all this. The duty of an economist, he writes, is to embrace his times and be of service to his contemporaries. This duty brought him to Columbia University in New York and led him to become a recognized expert in the development of poor countries.

The Two Meanings of Growth

Development economists distinguish between two kinds of growth: extensive and intensive. Growth is extensive when the population is expanding and productivity increases at the same

133

rate—for example, by the cultivation of new territory—but at a constant technological level. Growth becomes intensive when productivity per inhabitant increases substantially. This takeoff can be called "Smithian" (after Adam Smith) when it is the consequence of economic freedom. Thanks to the division of labor and specialization, in this scenario, each market exchange improves the economic condition of both parties. Eventually, this exchange-based growth exhausts itself if it is not followed by "Promethean growth" (Eric Jones's expression) or growth based on innovation. Since the end of the eighteenth century, first in England and then in Europe and in the United States, growth reached a rapid pace and appeared limitless because it was Promethean.

And what of crises? Some years are better than others, some countries are less dynamic, but all progress over time. "No nation involved in the market economy stagnates, none regresses for long," says Sala-i-Martin. The world crises of 1930 and 1973, which slowed down the United States and Europe, have been overcome. The recession that started in 2007 is, no doubt, "a serious crisis in capitalism but not a crisis of capitalism." I agree with his prediction that once more the doomsday prophets and revolutionary dreamers will be disappointed by the capacity of the market to heal itself.

Going from Catalonia to the United States was no problem for Sala-i-Martin. Recruiters from American universities travel the world to find the best students and make them irresistible offers. Why stay in a poor Spanish university, Sala-i-Martin asks, when you can find fame and fortune in the United States? Almost all Nobel Prizes in economics and other scientific disciplines go to Americans or to foreigners residing in the United States. In the United States, Sala-i-Martin notes, universities force everyone to achieve at a high level; intellectual accomplishment and research respond to the same motivations as all other human activities. If European universities are in decline, he believes, it is because they reject selectivity and competition.

The Theory of Convergence

Sala-i-Martin's renown sprang from the 2005 publication of his study of the reduction in world poverty. Based on a statistical examination of national income in 136 nations (the Democratic Republic of the Congo was excluded for lack of data), he showed that since 1970, poverty (measured absolutely and not relatively) had been on a path to elimination. Sala-i-Martin calls this the "general convergence of nations." By the World Bank's criterion for poverty—$1 per day per person (or the equivalent in local purchasing power)—the percentage of poor persons has fallen by two-thirds over the last thirty years. More than 425 million individuals have escaped poverty. The origin of this economic good news lies in commercial globalization and the spread of the market economy. Both have transformed civilizations that had never known anything but destitution. Sala-i-Martin thus concludes that nations are converging towards the dominant model: that of the rich countries of the Organization for Economic Cooperation and Development.

Will the poor eventually catch up with the rich? Possibly, since imitation is less expensive than innovation. Lower costs explain how poor countries progress faster than rich ones and close the gap with them. But then, as copying becomes less profitable, the growth of poor countries slows and aligns with that of rich countries. In the long run, it follows that all economies will progress in a rhythm with those that are masters of innovation. The less developed will stay behind the more developed, unless they in turn become pioneers of innovation.

Sala-i-Martin's conclusions contradict conventional ideas on the subject. It is not the case, he maintains, that poor countries grow poorer and rich ones grow richer. The rich continue to increase their wealth, but the poor are getting less poor and converging with the rich. Though this theory of convergence is based on verifiable data, not all economists accept it. Some—notably, Harvard's Lant Pritchett—hold on to the theory of divergence.

How can people arrive at opposite conclusions starting from the same observable reality? By modifying the criteria. Instead of using national income, as Sala-i-Martin does, Pritchett, who is already hostile to globalization for its leveling effect on culture, studies declared family incomes and finds divergence there. Opinion surveys often reveal incomes inferior to those shown in financial statistics. But doesn't self-interest lead in all regimes to the underestimation of declared income?

Another bone of contention separates partisans of convergence and of divergence: The question of whether public spending should be included in national income. Sala-i-Martin includes this spending, reasoning that spending on schools and public health helps alleviate poverty. His opponents reply that such expenses include military and other public spending that in no way benefit the poor. This method is wrong, observes Sala-i-Martin, for all comparisons across time and space are valid only so long as criteria are held constant and comparable; since 1960, there are no such criteria except the gross domestic product (GDP) of nations. For periods before this date, all is guesswork. No one knows whether the Chinese standard of living in 1600 was higher than that of Europeans. But since contemporary data are incontestable, we can be certain of the truth of convergence.

The Theory Contested

Instead of comparing the national incomes of states, would it not make more sense to compare individuals' incomes without respect to their nationality? Lant Pritchett sets himself apart in this respect from the international institutions concerned with development: For him, the best development policy would be one that enriched individuals, whatever their nationality. And there is no more rapid method for a human being to get rich fast than to migrate from a poor country to a rich country. Pritchett therefore suggests that rich countries such as the United States, European nations, and Japan admit large numbers of immigrants for a limited time in "guest-worker" programs.

Sala-i-Martin replies that in theory, Pritchett is not wrong. But is it progress to take a worker from his home community, exploit him, and then send him back? In practice, Pritchett's project has no chance of working, as much because of opposition in the host countries as because of skepticism in the countries of origin. The more practical Sala-i-Martin wishes to demonstrate the effectiveness of good economic policies as opposed to bad. Since policies are national, only comparisons among nations produce useful results for fighting poverty.

Would the actual curtailment of poverty disappoint some who might not find it to their advantage? Sala-i-Martin denounces Marxist economists. Far from having disappeared from American universities, these incurables, ever in search of a crisis of capitalism, imagine the world's poor in the role of revolutionaries. He also takes aim at a more influential category: the international aid professionals, organizations like the World Bank and large NGOs like Oxfam. Since poverty is their raison d'être and helps them raise money, he contends, they welcome every bit of bad news.

Quarrels among economists do not escape the influence of ideologies, but some economists are more rigorous than others. Without hiding his free-market commitments, Sala-i-Martin roots himself in economic reality, not in political desires. He finds it unfortunate that not all economists support those models that have passed empirical tests; he reminds us that bad policies have killed more people in the twentieth century than epidemics or wars. "More die because of economic mistakes than from AIDS," Sala-i-Martin points out.

African Divergence

Convergence is a general phenomenon, but it is not uniform. It is thanks to China and, more recently, India that the total number of poor is diminishing massively. But there is no question that it is a revolutionary development. In 1970, poverty was essentially an Asian problem, with 27 percent of the world's poor living in eastern and southern Asia. Today, poverty has become an African problem. Africa stands outside the convergence trend, but convergence outside Africa shows that it is possible to escape poverty—if one adopts an economic policy that works. Theoretical inquiry into development has been superseded, since the right way has already been marked out and adopted by many different nations. The question of development no longer centers on development in general but on African development in particular, Sala-i-Martin maintains.

It is important to acknowledge that the economic convergence between nations does not always hold true *within* nations. In China, Russia, and the United States (but not in Brazil or Thailand), the gap between rich and poor is increasing to various degrees. But these local divergences within a larger context of generalized growth do not stand in the way of global convergence. In other words, individuals everywhere are getting richer, and they are doing so fairly rapidly. In countries where inequality is deepening despite general growth, Sala-i-Martin points to flawed or corrupt domestic policies: unequal access to education, say, or the plundering of resources by bureaucrats (as in Russia or in China). It would be a pity, he thinks, if local imperfections cast doubt on a global model that remains essentially progressive.

It is hard for Sala-i-Martin to accept resistance to his conclusions. We have heard him castigating those swayed by ideological prejudices and material interests. But the reasons behind his unpopularity—which all economists suffer, whether or not they advocate a free market—reflect the nature of the discipline. By reducing human existence to numbers and all individuality to statistical categories, the economist condemns himself to a certain unpopularity. How can cold statistics stand up to media sympathies or measure the value of the compassion evoked by the picture of a starving child? The asymmetry between the economist's objectivity and human emotion plays into the hands of misinformed parties moved by compassion or indignation. But to each his own emotional and intellectual register: The economist deals with large groups in the hope that a good economic system, by raising the general level of prosperity, will eventually create a better future for everyone.

From Growth to Happiness

There are few personal outcomes, Sala-i-Martin writes, that economic prosperity does not determine. We do not know how to measure happiness exactly, and yet it is still the case that disposable income has an influence on the factors that make up happiness.

Is this verifiable? At Erasmus University in Rotterdam, Ruut Veenhoven created a database that classifies the "gross national happiness" of ninety-five nations. Unlike the gross domestic product, this notion is not objective but based on opinion surveys. (In his book *Gross National Happiness,* economist Arthur Brooks has applied this notion to the American people.) The results are never surprising: The countries in which people claim that they are happiest are the richest countries, with competitive economies and well-governed democratic institutions. International organizations not known for their affection for the free market—the United Nations in particular—have invented other, less economic criteria to measure a nation's progress. The most accepted is the United Nations Development Programme's index of human development, which takes into account education and life expectancy. Again, the resulting ranking does not differ from that obtained by using GDP. Gross domestic product affects life expectancy and education. If the economy does not produce happiness, it contributes to it.

Ultimately, Sala-i-Martin believes, development resolves most of society's problems. Take two classic examples: the environment and democracy. We know that in the first stage of development, nature is mistreated; however, beyond $5,000 per capita (the current level of Thailand and Malaysia), productivity comes into play, and intensive growth becomes less greedy for natural resources. Similarly, rich countries tend to become and to remain democratic, while poor countries are rarely democratic and often do not remain democratic for long when they become so. Is there a correlation between democracy and income? All agree that a market economy stimulates growth, the rise of civil society, and the establishment of institutions. From these, democracy flows almost naturally. Sala-i-Martin notes this but does not explain it; it's a fact, and that is enough for him. He also observes that globalization and growth progress together. Where globalization, free trade, or capital markets are absent, as in sub-Saharan Africa, growth is absent, too. This is another settled fact, and so to question the relation between globalization and development, Sala-i-Martin reasons, is no longer worth one's time.

This correlation between the growth of material income and other sources of well-being also addresses the objection of the Anglo-Indian economist Amartya Sen, who introduced into the assessment of development certain nonquantifiable criteria called "instrumental freedoms": political freedom, economic capacities, social opportunities, guarantees of transparency, and protective security. But growth produces these intangible values, whereas the absence of growth does not. The supposed contradiction between classic quantifiable development and Sen's qualitative development could have been the stuff of an interesting debate, but it does not really exist.

Complexities

The path of development appears straight. It seems sufficient to replicate the conditions that have characterized Western economies—innovation, an entrepreneurial spirit, private property, good education, the rule of law, and solid institutions. The experience of the last thirty years has proved that these conditions can appear in the most diverse civilizations, whether Christian, Confucian, Buddhist, or Muslim (as in Turkey and Malaysia). In making this well-attested statement, one nevertheless sets aside a thousand local circumstances that cannot be generalized. Developing nations have indeed adopted the Western model but have adapted it to their own cultural and political practices, sometimes with surprising results. No Western economist would have foreseen, for example, that China would develop with capitalism and competition but without private property. And no non-Chinese expert, Sala-i-Martin admits, would have advised taking that path. Circumstances particular to China, including the role that bureaucracy has traditionally played there, probably explain this Chinese synthesis. But the experiment is so singular that it cannot be replicated (except in Vietnam, for the same reasons). The Chinese system thus lies at the margins of free-market theory, rather than contradicting it. It achieves development only by following the norms of a market economy, first and foremost the principle of competition. Nevertheless, the relative success of China is perplexing to advocates of the market.

In adapting the universal model of development to local circumstances, we know quite well what we need to do, but not so well how actually to do it. Foreign experts are the least well equipped to carry out such adaptations. Sala-i-Martin finds proof in the case of the World Bank—for forty years, it has tried strategy after strategy without producing any significant development. From one era to another, its bureaucracy (18,000 officials) has imposed on poor countries investment in infrastructure, investment in human capital, balanced budgets, good government, the fight against corruption, and now the creation of good institutions. In Africa, where the World Bank concentrates its efforts, nothing ever works. Is this because the advice comes from the outside? Or is it because the World Bank wants to believe that aid is the key to development? Is it not troubling that northern countries see aid (or forgiving debt) as the basis of development, while none of these northern countries first developed thanks to such aid? Might it not be aid that *weakens* Africa?

Africa as a Victim of Charity

Sala-i-Martin asks: Is Africa responsible for its own hardships, or are Africans the victims of others? One cannot deny some local responsibility: Wars, tribalism, and the plundering of natural resources are the work of African leaders. Take Nigeria, a good illustration of a resource-rich country plundered by its leaders. From 1965 to 2000, the per-capita income of Nigeria hasn't grown, though the country has taken in $350 billion in oil revenues over that period. These revenues have been grabbed by just 2 percent of the population—and these people have no interest in establishing a more equitable economic model. For the last thirty years, African states, with the sole exception of Botswana, have regularly declared war on their neighbors and on their own peoples.

Yet Africa is also a victim, even if it is not only a victim. Sala-i-Martin holds European protectionism responsible. He considers agricultural subsidies in Europe, Japan, and the United States "obscene," not only because they block trade, but even more because they discourage entrepreneurship among Africans. But the most disastrous of all the errors committed by Africans or by Westerners is the refusal to perceive Africans as potential entrepreneurs. As Sala-i-Martin observes, Westerners want to produce everything themselves and so leave no room for African businesses. By giving aid, we feel we are purging our historical sins, but we are condemning Africans to the status of welfare recipients. He adds that aid is necessarily inefficient because its logic is the opposite of that of the market. In the market, the producer tries to satisfy a consumer, while with aid, one tries to satisfy the donor. Is the unacknowledged goal of aid to make the United Nations, the World Bank, and the sponsors happy?

In Africa, the best intentions lead to the worst results. Consider "fair trade," which in Europe and in the U.S. has such a fine reputation. In the name of cooperation, certain humanitarian organizations or Western businesses acquire African products at prices higher than the market dictates. And what is the result? African producers see the chance for a windfall and rush to produce what the North is looking for. Overproduction follows, supplies pile up, and prices collapse. In the end, the producer winds up ruined. The only legitimate aid, Sala-i-Martin thinks, is help in solving medical problems like tuberculosis, malaria, and AIDS, which the Africans cannot do by themselves.

It is unfortunate, Sala-i-Martin adds, that economists—good ones, anyway—are not heeded in Africa. He expresses annoyance that so many listen to his colleague at Columbia, Jeffrey Sachs, who is always campaigning, with the help of the rock singer Bono, to raise funds for Africa. Sachs's argument, as popularized in his book *The End of Poverty,* holds that if aid has not contributed to development, it must be because there has not been enough of it; if the United States would quadruple and Europe double their aid, then Africa would at last take off. As proof, Sachs and his supporters finance model villages in Africa, which Sala-i-Martin denounces as Potemkin villages, albeit sunny ones. Sachs receives star treatment from African heads of state and large Western aid institutions. Is he more interested in popularity than in truth? Sala-i-Martin would rather not consider that possibility. But this naïveté is no doubt feigned: Columbia recruited Sachs as much for his charisma as for the quality of his research. In competing to attract students, donors, and other professors, universities seek not only pure researchers but also scholars who attract media attention.

Sala-i-Martin's hopes rest, in the end, with the Chinese. Since Chinese businesses first landed in Africa, Westerners have feared that they would plunder the continent's raw materials. In the short term, prices would rise, but this increase rarely benefits a people. Yet Chinese intervention has another face that could unleash a more genuine process of development. The Chinese come in as entrepreneurs, recruit local workers, and manufacture on site, at a lower cost than in China. Could this be the outline of an African industrialization?

It is common, in poor countries, for the entrepreneurial spirit to arise within minority groups not bound to local traditions and constraints. Will the Chinese in Africa become the equivalent of what Protestants once were in Europe, or Greeks in Turkey, or Lebanese in Brazil? Meanwhile, Sala-i-Martin sees a great virtue in the Chinese presence. Unlike aid workers, they look at Africa objectively and without guilt, observe the market and the workers, and reason in business terms. This is what the Africans need; Africa will converge with developed countries if it adopts the rules of growth by industrialization.

Excessively General Theories

Sala-i-Martin has reason on his side, but does reason have any effect on development? Avinash Dixit, an American of Indian origin and a development economist at Princeton, is renowned for his ironic analyses of the literature on the subject of convergence published over the last fifty years. He divides this literature into three phases: During the 1960s, the theme was the need to accumulate capital under the tutelage of state planners; during the 1980s, it was the promotion of good economic policies based on privatization and balanced budgets; and during the first decade of the new century, the emphasis has been on good institutions as the sine qua non of development.

Behind these successive theories that have determined the course of Western aid, Dixit sees the influence of the ideologies of the day: the socialism of the 1960s, the free-market theories of the eighties, and what one might call the democratic theory of the current decade. But these theories are always latecomers in relation to reality—so many attempts to explain the previous failure rather than to offer prescriptions for the future. They are general enough to describe global situations but not operational enough to dictate concrete actions. Dixit does not conclude that these uncertain theories are pointless. But he reveals them to be explanatory rather than prescriptive. He also sees great preventive value in them: They alert us to what must not be done. A theoretician of development can explain to practitioners that if one wants to arrive at a certain destination, there are certain places not to start.

François Bourguignon, another development economist, is both a theorist and a practitioner, having spent many years at the World Bank. He takes an equally cautious view of convergence theory. The universal harms what is essential, he thinks, and the essential lies in the details. The general progress noted by Sala-i-Martin can be explained, above all, by the economic engines of India and China—meaning that convergence theory is too abstract to capture the stagnation that afflicts the poorest. Questioning the categorization of Africa as a uniform whole, Bourguignon prefers to examine economies country by country or region by region. In Africa, there are thirteen countries—Bourguignon calls them the "G13"—that have been participating in a growth cycle at the respectable rate of 5 percent per year. But the G13 comprises nations like Mauritius, which is as much Asian as African; Botswana, which is well endowed with minerals; Ghana, where the progress has been quite real; and Benin, where the progress is less certain. Bourguignon also questions all extreme judgments on international aid—Sachs's enthusiasm as much as Sala-i-Martin's nay-saying. Once again, Bourguignon asserts, the truth is in the details. It is impossible to know, he says, what might have happened in Africa without aid. Poverty might have been even worse.

Beyond these controversies is a consensus that Sala-i-Martin, Dixit, and Bourguignon share. All agree that to escape poverty, a nation must undergo industrialization and urbanization; no rural economy can absorb a surplus of labor or integrate a large cohort of youths into remunerative activities. And industrialization in Africa turns out to be particularly difficult. Is this because of the prejudices that Sala-i-Martin denounces? Or because of the continuing effects of colonization? Or because African states are ill-governed? Or because they are corrupt? Bourguignon believes that all these reasons apply. But another factor is that Africa is a latecomer, while China and India have already taken over the low-cost markets. Also, the competitive rules imposed by the World Trade Organization now prohibit the use of once-classic subterfuges, such as export subsidies and the closing of domestic markets. Yet it is these methods that launched industrialization in Asia and Brazil. Should Africa receive an exception? If it did, non-Africans would in turn demand preferential treatment, which would risk disorder throughout the global marketplace.

In the end, is it not hypocrisy that is preventing Africa's convergence? All three economists grant that nothing in the various cultures of Africa opposes development. But the question of African industrialization is not a priority in international debates, though nothing can take the place of industrialization as an engine of growth. Should we, like Sala-i-Martin, count on the Chinese to industrialize Africa? The project might seem strictly theoretical. But remember that fifty years ago, no one foresaw that the Asian Tigers, led by Korea, would become industrial societies.

CHAPTER TEN

Asian Tigers

TAKE A PARTICULARLY POOR and badly situated country, surrounded by enemies, once colonized, ravaged by civil and foreign wars, inhabited by illiterate peasants, dominated by a reactionary aristocracy, and deprived of natural resources. Cut this country in two along an arbitrary line, say the forty-second parallel, so as to hinder trade, split provinces, and divide families. Having thus brought together the conditions most unfavorable to progress, apply to the northern and southern sections of this battered nation two diametrically opposed economic policies. Let a half-century pass, and then compare.

Per-capita income in North Korea has been estimated to be anywhere from $1,000 to $7,000; in South Korea, it is $20,000. After taxation, the gap between incomes available for consumption is still more spectacular: perhaps $300 a year in the North (the data are unreliable) and $15,000 in the South. The success of the South and the failure of the North are now uncontested, but this was not always the case. After the partition of Korea between the Soviets and the Americans in 1945, and then the civil war from 1950 to 1953, North Korea had the advantage: It had access to coal, and Japanese colonizers had already established industries there during the 1930s. The South, on the other hand, was entirely agricultural.

Note as well that during the 1960s, the Communist regime in the North applied the strategy that development economists then recommended: heavy, state-planned industrialization, protected by tight borders. Inspired by the Soviet precedent, this model of "import substitution" appeared rational and was not ineffective in the short term. After Stalin's Soviet Union, China had adopted it, as well as other countries seeking to develop, such as Argentina, India, and, of course, the part of Europe then under Soviet domination. Seen hastily and from the outside, this model could impress a visitor. Factories rose from the earth, and people were working. A closer look, however, would have revealed that much of what was produced was of low quality and had no outlet, and so was destined for the trash heap; salaries did not encourage consumption because there was nothing to consume. All this, now so well known, was for a long time not understood. Sometimes this ignorance was deliberate—the rejection of capitalism, Marxist propaganda, and dreams of a third way (neither capitalist nor Communist) long obscured the science of economics.

During the 1970s, economic education in Europe gave equal consideration to the rival economics of socialist planning and free-market capitalism, to the strategies of import substitution and what was known as export promotion. The best European schools considered it mandatory that these strategies be put on an equal plane, as if both led equally well to development. This foolish equation, which ignored the facts, would leave traces in the minds of a generation of bureaucrats and politicians formed—or deformed—in this period.

The case of the two Koreas, an exemplary laboratory, should have made it possible to understand as early as 1970 that there were good and bad strategies that would lead either to development or to underdevelopment. Geography, climate, natural resources, culture, religion: All these factors, linked theoretically to development since the origin of the science of economics, were shown to have no decisive impact. Korea settles the question, proving that an economic policy can be right or wrong. What is necessary is that the right policy be chosen and applied. So how did South Korea manage to do it?

Economists in Power

"We have benefited," Il Sakong says, "from a favorable confluence of circumstances that is not necessarily reproducible." Educated at Berkeley, Il Sakong, who is both an analyst of and an essential actor in South Korea's development story, acknowledges that "Korea was lucky." That luck wasn't politically correct. In 1962, General Park Chung-Hee took power; he was a dictator, but an enlightened one. North Korea was threatening, and the South survived only thanks to American aid. How could independence be preserved except through development? Park, though not an economist, noticed that Japan, Taiwan, and Hong Kong were growing economically at a rate of over 10 percent a year. The same observation attracted the attention of dictators in other regions who were no more economically literate than Park but whose thinking was just as practical: Franco in Spain and Pinochet in Chile.

Was a dictator necessary in Korea for the imposition of a good economic strategy? More generally, is strong power indispensable to development in poor nations? Il Sakong, who would serve dictators and democrats in turn, concludes that despotism isn't necessary. Didn't democratic India embrace the free-market model in 1991? Experience has shown that the key is not so much the nature of the regime as its strategic choice and its capacity to stand by that choice—leadership, that is. With Park, South Korea benefited from such leadership. Having no energy resources, and with American aid bound to dry up, the only solution was to export. Park gathered a team of economic advisors, the Korean Development Institute (KDI). Counting among its members economists trained in the United States and in Germany, the KDI laid plans for Korean development. These were not command-based plans of the Soviet type but catalogs of goals. At the time, Il Sakong recalls, Indian plans were commonly considered the best in the world, but none of their goals were attained. In Korea, the reverse was true.

It may not seem unusual that economists should conceive and direct a nation's economic system, but the Korean case is exceptional. The KDI had no comparable equivalent except in Japan (the Ministry of International Trade and Industry) and in Taiwan. In the United States, there is the President's Council of Economic Advisors, but it plays a minor role, as the Commissariat au Plan in France did once.

Il Sakong says that the classical Korean administrative tradition explains the nation's willingness to place confidence in experts. Inspired by the Chinese imperial model, Korean sovereigns recruited their administrative officials through competitive examinations; the best educated joined the public service. In the Korea of the 1960s, the custom persisted. It is less true today, because private enterprises now offer more attractive careers than the government does. But academics, often including economists, typically fill out Korean administrations.

Confucius and Business

So we find South Korea during the 1960s equipped with a leader interested in development and a team of internationally trained experts who drew inspiration from Japan's successful model of promoting exports. All that was left to do was export. But were there entrepreneurs in Korea? A misguided question, says Il Sakong. Until recently, economic literature regularly raised the question of the spirit of enterprise: Does it or does it not exist in all civilizations? If it does not, is it up to the state to make up for the lack of entrepreneurs? We can blame the German sociologist

Max Weber's book *The Protestant Ethic and the Spirit of Capitalism* (1904) for this framing of the question. By locating the origins of capitalism in the existence of a social group informed by the Protestant ethic, Weber implied that the entrepreneurial spirit was culturally determined. In the 1920s, he explained that Asia could not achieve economic development or adopt the capitalist model because of its Confucian culture. This culture, he wrote, promoted conformism, repetition, communitarianism—all values contradictory to the individualism that is indispensable to the spirit of enterprise.

During the 1960s, a whole body of literature accumulated in the United States in which the numerous disciples of Weber continued to explain the inevitable poverty of Asia and the impossibility of development in China and Korea in terms of Confucianism. Ten years later, the same idealist school of thought began to produce works extolling the economic *virtues* of Confucianism in Japan, Korea, and Taiwan! Others, equally idealist in their approach (for example, Serge-Christophe Kolm in France), judged that the rise of these "Asian Tigers" was due to the influence of Buddhism and its values.

If it was because of Confucianism that South Korea hadn't developed, and then because of it that South Korea had developed, what sort of influence can Confucianism have had on behavior? Development economists have attributed attitudes of submission (rejection of individualism, conformism, repetition) to Confucianism. But these values are reversible: Confucian conformism is held to harm the entrepreneurial spirit but to be useful in standardized industry, thus explaining the Korean taste for assembly work.

In reality, these character traits exist in most traditional rural societies, whether or not they are Confucian. Wherever masses of conscientious workers toil sixty hours a week over their looms or manufacturing equipment, are they Confucians? It is more likely the desire to escape poverty that drives them. The authoritarian norms that once reigned and of which traces remain in contemporary

Korea owe more, it seems to me, to poverty—that is, to a certain peasant submissiveness and to the authoritarianism of bosses and political leaders—than to Confucius. To appeal repeatedly to Confucius is to venture into a pseudo-cultural terrain that, at best, provides a snapshot of society but does not explain its trajectory.

And here is another error of perspective: Confucianism is not the only religious tradition in Korea. It competes there with Buddhism and with Christianity, both of which are altogether individualistic. Is it possible that competition among beliefs leads to competition among businesses? This hypothesis of the necessity of pluralism would also apply to Europe, where the rivalry between Catholics and Protestants certainly contributed to the rise of Western capitalism. On the other hand, wherever a single worldview prevails, as in certain Arab-Muslim or Orthodox Christian countries, the middle class has had trouble making its way.

The entrepreneurial spirit thus turns up in Korea as it does in all civilizations, without exception. It is the rules of the game that will orient this spirit either toward activities that redound to the common good or toward others that are zero-sum in nature.

From Feudalism to Capitalism

Until its occupation by Japan and then by the United States, South Korea remained under the control of a landed aristocracy whose rents financed a life of leisure and sometimes refinement. In this unjust and unproductive society, there was little incentive to innovate or to produce, either for the property owner or for the tenant. This equilibrium in poverty was destroyed by the Japanese between 1905 and 1945, and then by the Americans.

The subject is taboo in Korea, but it is undeniable that the country's modernization began under Japanese occupation. It was the Japanese who introduced industrial efficiency. But autonomous development truly began under the impetus of the United States. Driven as much by a desire for social equity as for economic efficiency, the American administration (shaped at that time by the interventionist principles of the New Deal) imposed on Korea (as on Japan and Taiwan), from 1945 on, a program of radical land reform that broke up the great estates and redistributed the land. The Americans had also calculated the value of properties in such a way as to inculcate the Koreans with accounting notions appropriate to a market economy.

These agrarian reforms in East Asia were never anticapitalist measures but rather pedagogical undertakings intended to establish capitalism. Unlike the targets of Marxist-inspired reforms (in North Korea and in China, landed property was abolished), dispossessed South Korean landowners received compensation; peasants had to obtain their plots with the help of favorable rates on bank loans. The Americans expected that this new nation of small landowners would give rise to a just and entrepreneurial society. In places where the Americans did not impose agrarian reform, such as in the Philippines, the economy has remained feudal. In Japan and Taiwan, agrarian reform allowed peasants to escape poverty and former landowners to turn toward nonagricultural entrepreneurial activities. In Korea, inflation and war complicated this scenario, preventing an easy transition from landed aristocracy to new enterprises. And so it was left to Koreans from very humble backgrounds (the founder of Hyundai was a farm worker) to become their country's entrepreneurs, something that the old land system would never have allowed.

Cultural Value-Added

In the 1950s, caught between war and inflation, Korean entrepreneurs maximized profits by taking advantage of speculation and scarcity; they imported the most necessary consumer goods, stockpiled them, waited for prices to rise, and then resold them.

From their own point of view, these entrepreneurs were acting rationally, but the result for the collectivity was negative. There was no lack of entrepreneurs in Korea. What was lacking, rather, was a good economic policy to channel their energy into more useful and profitable activities. But which policy? Let the market decide, Il Sakong answers. Over the last fifty years, Korean entrepreneurs have shifted their efforts to accommodate international demand. Public works, textiles, naval construction, electronics, automobiles—such has been their upward path toward ever more sophisticated enterprises.

In the beginning, Korean labor was abundant and cheap. It was profitable for firms to employ it on construction sites (in Vietnam or Saudi Arabia, for instance). Then labor became scarce, and the level of education increased. Businesses transformed themselves through research and innovation in order to sell goods and services at a greater value-added. At the same time, other countries embraced the Korean model, including China, Malaysia, and Turkey. This competition pushed Korea to innovate even more.

The evolution of the label "Made in Korea" reflects this trajectory. Originally, it designated a cheap product of mediocre quality. Now it suggests cutting-edge design and technology (think of Hyundai or Samsung). South Korea's most recent success is in exporting its culture, especially in film and music. A "Korean wave" has swept across Asia and is reaching the United States. Of all possible exports, cultural "products" involve the highest value-added and are the most resistant to imitation. More generally, the image of a nation reflects its economic success and in turn contributes to that success. Early in its rise, Korea had no image except an archaic one ("Land of the Morning Calm") or its reputation as a producer of inexpensive goods. As Korea has become better known and its products more sophisticated, its image has evolved. "Made in Korea" today conveys something meaningful; the "brand" enables the exporter to increase its profit margin thanks to a kind of cultural value-added. The great internationally known brands contribute to this evolution: Samsung stands for the new Korea.

As a general rule, if one classifies nations as a function of how the world sees them culturally and how many of their brands are recognized, the image of nations would match their economic performance. No doubt such perceptions consist of stereotypes (France represents luxury, say, or Germany, technical prowess). But such stereotypes sell goods and also have some basis in reality.

Crony Capitalism

This Korean epic could not have been written without cooperation—some would say collusion—between the state and certain entrepreneurs, in particular the bosses of the conglomerates (the *chaebol*) that dominate the Korean economy. These organizations (Hyundai, Samsung, and Daewoo, among others) could never have become national, and then international, giants without state support.

This characteristic of Korean development is explicable in terms of the nation's history. As South Korea emerged from colonization and civil war, it was keen on independence—and on revenge. Economic logic, as it operates today in developing countries, would have favored a call for foreign investment, the path that China is now following. But because Koreans worried about the Japanese returning, this time as investors, their leaders chose another way, that of indebtedness. President Park solicited governments and institutions sympathetic to his anti-Communist arguments (this was during the 1960s), especially the United States and Germany. Inflation ran high at the time, and debts were assumed without compunction, in the belief that repayment would be in devalued currency. The government, finding itself in a position to finance the entrepreneurs of its choice, picked future winners by granting them loans at negative interest rates.

In principle, explains Il Sakong, who played a role in setting this policy, this selection was based on efficiency. The boss who succeeded in some sector received government financing to reinforce his positions in the global market or to allow him to venture into promising new businesses.

Thus the chaebol formed, and during the 1980s, they came to control 30 percent of everything produced in Korea and 80 percent of everything exported from the country. In such a selection process, it proved impossible to preclude collusion, corruption, and simple mistakes; not all chaebol made the best use of the funds lent them. During a difficult financial crisis in 1998, it became evident that some of these conglomerates financed long-term investments with short-term money or had ventured into inflationary real-estate speculation. Some chaebol disappeared, and other bosses wound up convicted and incarcerated (including the founder of Daewoo). Others survived this "Asian crisis" of 1998 by increasing their specialization and innovation. Is an overall judgment on the behavior of the various chaebol possible? If we consider the question from a strictly utilitarian and economic standpoint, putting aside all moral questions, we will note that the Korean economy progressed at an average rate of 12 percent between 1960 and 1980, a speed that China has yet to attain. Without the chaebol, South Korea would probably never have reached that level.

But the experiment is over, and Il Sakong believes that it is not replicable, since the rules of the game have changed in the world at large, as they have in Korea. When the chaebol set out to conquer external markets during the 1960s, competition was weak and demand gigantic. The idea of protecting against an invasion of Korean products never entered American or European minds. The world market, with its demand for low-cost products, wasn't as regulated as it has been since the creation of the World Trade Organization. Most earlier Korean practices, such as dumping and state loans and subsidies to the chaebol, would today be prohibited out of respect for the rules of competition.

Chinese exporters now face obstacles that they manage to surmount but that the Koreans never experienced. International commerce was simpler before it entered the age of globalization.

Thus it was easier for a government to pick out economic winners during the 1960s. In a rapidly changing world, by contrast, there is no way to predict the industry of the future. Since Il Sakong chairs the Presidential Council of National Competitiveness, created in 2007, his strategy is to remove all obstacles to entrepreneurship. Deregulating the market, opening the borders to foreign investors, introducing competition everywhere, increasing the flexibility of the labor market—all this should increase Korea's chance of catching up to the "First World" economy. In the West, skepticism erodes support for the free market, but in Asia, the welfare state and regulations are perceived as a luxury. Il Sakong and his peers in China and Japan are certain that the free market is the only road to becoming as prosperous as the West. The 2008 financial crisis has not changed their conviction: It has reinforced it.

Democratic Uncertainty

Without much violence, step by step, the military rulers of South Korea ceded their political power to elected parties. Since 1988, South Korea has become a regime alternating between administrations of the Left and of the Right. It is without a doubt more democratic than its neighbor, Japan, and indeed more democratic than all the other countries in the region. Its public debates are vigorous; whatever the written press, largely controlled by the chaebol, tries to hide shows up on the Internet. And the influence of democracy is not limited to political institutions. The society is being transformed as worker attitudes become less submissive and discipline becomes less strict within businesses, families, educational institutions, relationships, and churches. As they shed a Confucian morality once considered the most rigid in Asia,

Koreans appear to have become as individualistic as Americans. Doubtless they were always so, but authoritarian institutions repressed them. The South Korean economy is changing, too. Its growth potential has slowed considerably, to a rate on the order of 4–6 percent, only half the rate experienced under dictatorial rule but twice that of the more developed economies of Europe and the United States.

Should we hold democracy responsible for this slowdown in the growth rate, or is it simply the result of South Korea's reaching another stage of development? Il Sakong blames not democracy but a lack of strategy on the part of the leftist governments that held power from 1992 to 2007. This is not a very socialist Left, since the example of North Korea has been sufficient to discredit Marxism. But it is a redistributive Left, less respectful of the power of business leaders, less infatuated with the United States, and more attentive to union demands than the political opposition. Under this Left, growth is no longer the absolute priority it once was. Wages rise, and union protests interrupt the rate of production without government intervention. Business profits shrink while investment slows or goes to countries with lower wages, such as the Philippines, Thailand, and China.

Should we follow Il Sakong in holding the Left alone responsible for the compromising of the Korean model and its consequent loss of dynamism? No doubt his judgment is partisan, since the slowing of growth can also be explained by the multiplication of competitors taking the place of Korean firms. This foreign threat is healthy: It brings Korea into the cycle of innovation. It is Korea's very success that compels it toward destructive creation; it is necessary to leave the old behind in order to look for the new, as we see in the case of Samsung, and to get into future businesses where Korea can excel—biotechnology, for example. In number of patents, South Korea lags far behind Japan but remains ahead of China. In this rising cycle, education will play a decisive role; but the threshold of quality has not yet been attained. What remains of Korea's Confucianism has retreated to its schools and universities, where authoritarian teaching still has little use for the participation or creativity of students. The United States remains decisively ahead in this area, and that is where the best Korean students are going. However, unlike the Chinese or the Africans, they usually return home.

When the 2008–09 global downturn hit South Korea, President Lee Myung-bak, instead of running for protectionist cover, chose to increase the competitive edge of Korean higher education in order to boost innovation, following the American model. He also pushed for labor-market deregulation. From the Asian Tigers' perspective, a crisis offers an opportunity to become more flexible and creative, not less.

Cultural Diversity in a Global Economy

Cultural explanations of development have gone out of fashion. By becoming too theoretical, however, economists sometimes overlook local circumstances. If social norms do not explain development, they still tend to give it a certain orientation. The same strategy can lead to different results in different places because civilization and history give a certain bent to general principles. It is customary in the economic literature to lump the Asian Tigers into one category. After all, four of them took off at the same time, at the same speed, and by the same method of emphasizing entrepreneurial spirit and exports. But South Korea, Hong Kong, Singapore, and Taiwan, having benefited from a common strategy, are alike only in their newly achieved standard of living. Though they are all Asian, they are quite dissimilar. Cultural diversity in Asia remains more noticeable than in Europe. A Korean is less like a Taiwanese than a Frenchman is like a German; the gap between Hong Kong and Singapore is as vast as that between Rome and Stockholm.

Take Taiwan, which has been, in effect, an independent state since 1949, the year it seceded from the Communist regime in

Beijing. According to economic theory, Taiwan followed the same path as Korea: It developed a private economy distinct from the state, with an emphasis on exports. And much like Korea, Taiwan was a Japanese colony until 1945; American economic aid was significant until 1965.

But Korea is dominated by large industrial dynasties, which were initially selected by the state. Taiwan, by contrast, is bursting with small and midsize businesses. Korea has specialized in high-value-added industrial products that require large investments, such as naval yards and automobile manufacturing. Taiwan prefers exploring the niches of the textile industry, biotechnology, and computers. Koreans are industrial. Taiwanese tend to gravitate toward trade, management, and financial services. A visit to a Korean business leaves the impression of a visible hierarchy and a quasi-military management style. In Taiwan, one notices a lot of muddling through and a somewhat disorderly hyperactivity. The Taiwanese are more mobile than the Koreans; they found their first investors in the United States and in mainland China. As Wu Rong-yi, president of the Taipei stock exchange, has said, "Taiwan is more a network than a nation." Koreans, anchored in their national territory, are patriots. A person from Taiwan finds it somewhat difficult to define himself in terms of nationality. When global competition threatens Korean businesses, the managers turn to banks and to the state for help, while the unions demonstrate to save their businesses and their jobs. In comparable circumstances, the entrepreneur in Taiwan changes jobs or even countries.

Koreans regard their former Japanese masters with undying rancor: The will to surpass Japan is a motor of economic activity. Anti-Americanism also flourishes there. The Taiwanese, on the other hand, love the United States, going there to study and often to live. Still more surprising, Japan is the Taiwanese's favorite country. The Koreans will not acknowledge that it was Japan that initiated modernization in Korea. The same Japanese colonizers modernized Taiwan's infrastructure, agriculture, and industry, and thus the Taiwanese feel deep gratitude toward them; they see their colonization in a positive light. There is no other example of a colonized people showing such gratitude to their former colonizers.

These behavioral differences, with identical incomes, have little to do with the two countries' comparable economic strategies but are rather the clear consequence of national histories and cultural differences. South Korea is the heir of a nationalist kingdom and the most rigid Confucianism in Asia. Many Taiwanese are the descendants of migrants who left mainland China in the eighteenth century to escape the emperor. On this island without a state, they became fishermen, pirates, and tradesmen. Beginning in the nineteenth century, Taiwan profited from exporting agricultural products to Japan. When the nationalist army of Chiang Kai-shek, defeated by Mao Zedong, withdrew from the mainland to Taiwan and formed a government, the Taiwanese already there denied all legitimacy to the new state and took refuge in the economic sphere. The Taiwanese state became democratic in 1997, but its authority remains weak, divided between a pro-independence party and the "mainlanders" who remain faithful to a "greater China." Such a state is not much of a burden on entrepreneurs. For them, Taiwan is not so much a mother country as a territory on a world map; a Taiwanese is, above all, a *homo economicus* with a Chinese background. For a Korean, the economy is a means to national greatness rather than an end. Thus the Asian Tigers remain diverse, since neither economic development nor globalization wipes away cultures; in fact, they give cultures new ways to flourish.

The Peacekeeper

Asian development can also be explained by an unquantifiable factor that economists mention too rarely: the American military guarantee. If the United States Army and Navy, present on

Korean territory as well as in Japan and on neighboring seas, were not protecting their security, the South Koreans and their neighbors would have been more preoccupied with defense than with seeking wealth. This observation holds for the region as a whole, including China. The flow of commerce among North America, Europe, and Asia, upon which both regional and global prosperity are founded, endures only because of this American military and maritime protection.

From its headquarters in Yokosuka, Japan, the U.S. Seventh Fleet cruises the Pacific from San Diego to Madagascar. The Navy, combining soft power with hard, sails from port to port, showing its military strength and simultaneously delivering humanitarian support. That so little piracy and conflict has broken out in this region for fifty years is proof of the Seventh Fleet's success. If it were to disappear, Korea and Japan could easily find themselves in a conflict over some minor disputed islands; Vietnam, China, and the Philippines might go to war for the possession of the disputed and oil-rich Spratly Islands; and so on. Piracy would doubtless hinder Chinese exports, and oil tankers would have a harder time reaching Japan. As Vice Admiral John Bird declared in 2008, "The role of the navy is not to fight but to deter confrontation just by being there." In the nineteenth century, similarly but on a smaller scale, the British navy made possible the first globalization. If for some reason the United States ceased to play the role of global policeman, the economic model under which we prosper could disappear.

CHAPTER ELEVEN

India:
A Market Revolution

ALL EYES ARE ON CHINA these days—but the media and investors may be looking in the wrong direction. True enough, China is growing faster than India, but it's looking more and more like a tortoise-and-hare race, with India steadily catching up. India's economic growth—an 8-percent trend—is based, unlike China's, on private entrepreneurship, on small business as much as large companies, on the domestic market as much as the global market, and on a balance among industry, services, and agriculture.

Above all, the Indian growth strategy is rooted in democratic institutions. The opening of the economy and the drive toward privatization was initiated in 1991 by a left-wing government after years of national debate. After that government lost elections in 2000 and found itself replaced by a conservative majority, the economic strategy has been maintained. The Left returned to power in 2005 with Communist allies—and proceeded further down the same road. The free market in India represents a consensus choice, not something that an enlightened despot imposed from the top.

163

Indian journalists constantly debate the free-market revolution and its benefits and problems. People are for it or against it—few Indians are neutral or ignorant about economic matters. Westerners have not recognized the extent of free expression among the Indian people and in the Indian media. Because of the diversity of Indian religions, we often hear that each Indian has his own god; each Indian is also entitled, as it happens, to express his own opinion. "Every Indian is a dissenter," says sociologist Ashis Nandy, "and the cost of dissenting amounts to zero." India's democracy makes the nation's economic strategy more predictable; China's inscrutable tyranny makes its long-term strategy unpredictable.

An Ancient Democracy

India is first and foremost a democracy. Democracy is the one thing that the fair, blue-eyed Muslim tribes of Rajasthan in the north and the dark-skinned Muslim, Hindu, and Christian Keralites in the south have in common. India comprises a bewildering array of beliefs, cultures, languages, and ethnicities. Eighteenth-century European philosophers, upon discovering the multiplicity of religions in India, were amazed at the Indian capacity to worship many gods without religious conflict breaking out. Voltaire and several others used the word *tolérantisme* to describe Indian religions. In the nineteenth century, the British coined the term "Hinduism," a unifying Western concept that fails to convey the diversity of sects in India.

Indeed, Indian civilization defies all definition. In China, a far more homogeneous nation than India, the force of tyranny holds the country together. In India, it is the fact that the residents are all citizens. Do they have the British and colonization to thank for this? Not really. After publishing *Democracy in America* in the 1840s, Alexis de Tocqueville turned his attention to British reports on the functioning of local democracy in India. Indian villages, it appeared, elected committees of five elders, the *panchayat,* which ran the affairs of their communities in the same way that local councils did in the West. Was democracy universal, therefore, even if it assumed different forms? Alas, as Tocqueville began preparing to travel to India, he contracted tuberculosis. Had he made the journey, the world might have had another work of genius, *Democracy in India,* to complement *Democracy in America.* And the entire debate on the compatibility of oriental values and Western democracy might never have taken place. The British eventually left India, but the democratic institutions that they established endured, built on fertile ground.

Democracy has given India stability, making it the only non-European postcolonial nation that civil war or revolution has not torn apart. Yet democracy does not automatically generate economic growth. Postcolonial history shows that political freedom and economic development tend to evolve at different rates. From 1947 until 1991, India was democratic but its economy stagnated; an authoritarian but market-oriented China has experienced continuous growth since 1978. This is to suggest not that authoritarianism is a precondition for economic takeoff but that the free-market economy holds the key to economic growth, irrespective of the nature of the political regime. It took Indian leaders forty years to understand this essential point—forty years of stagnation before the unleashing of market forces in 1991 and the integration of the nation into the global economy.

From the time of its independence in 1947 until the late 1980s, India's growth rate was about 3 percent per annum, barely enough to keep pace with the annual 2 percent increase in population. Real income did not go up, a state of affairs that seemed so natural that both Indian and foreign economists talked in all earnestness of a "Hindu" growth rate, pegged at a measly 1 percent. It had to do with the Indian ethos, they said, not with faulty economic policy.

This smug rationale for stagnation collapsed in 1991. Until then, the Indian economy had survived thanks to the support of the Soviet Union. India was then the leader of the nonaligned nations, which meant that they were anti-American and pro-Soviet; the Soviet economic support reinforced this strategic choice. India could sell its poorly manufactured goods to the Russians. Russia, in exchange, would provide the oil lacking on the Indian subcontinent. These exchanges weren't based on real prices: It was a barter economy. All that changed in 1991 when the new Russian state, in dire need of currency, required the Indians to start buying oil with U.S. dollars, which they did not have. To find dollars, India had to open its borders to foreign investors and export valuable goods to the rest of the world. It was an economic revolution, in the same category as the so-called shock therapy that took place in Russia and in Eastern Europe in the 1990s, and in China during the early 1980s.

When thrown into international competition, Indian entrepreneurs had to adapt—or perish. And they did adapt, at all levels of Indian society, from the small service sector to the major industrial groups. Engineering this market revolution has been a remarkable duo of economists: Manmohan Singh, finance minister in 1991 for the left-wing Congress government, and his associate, Montek Singh Ahluwalia. Both have worked in the U.S., at the World Bank and the IMF in Washington. Since 2005, Singh has been prime minister, while Ahluwalia has been in charge of the planning commission, a kind of a ministry for economic affairs. Neither was taken by surprise in 1991. They knew that the closed, statist economy was doomed to fail. Still, they could not predict the moment when the final failure would occur—no one could. They also knew that the free market would work in India, since the country had an ancient tradition of entrepreneurship, a tradition that the ruling socialist ideology had repressed. They proved to be correct. Since the 1991 market revolution, India has boasted an annual 7–9 percent growth trend. The "Hindu rate" has vanished.

Stagnation by Consensus

Today, you might wonder how India could ever have been a socialist economy. While Jawaharlal Nehru and, later, his daughter Indira Gandhi were ruling the country, the feeling of self-satisfaction was strong, as they considered their socialist policies in step with the dominant ideologies of the time. Development economists and major international institutions agreed on the merits of social democracy, planning, and autarchy. This was the "Prebisch" doctrine, named after the Argentinean economist then seen as an authority on the subject. The doctrine combined British socialism, Keynesian theory, the Soviet model, and the nationalism of the recently decolonized Third World.

Beyond theory, socialism also appealed to the Indian leaders' mind-set. These leaders, Nehru foremost among them, belonged to the Brahman upper caste, dedicated to religious and scholarly leadership. These upper-caste members tend to look down on lower merchant castes. They believe themselves entrusted with the responsibility to lead and enlighten the nation. Socialism was to grant a modern and scientific legitimacy to the ancient superiority of the Brahmans. Beyond India, one could argue that the history of socialism in various nations has been determined by the existence or absence of an "enlightened" ruling caste in those places. The Catholic hierarchy, the aristocracy, the upper caste— socialism has tempted each group. In Protestant democratic nations, socialism took root with far more difficulty, or never took root at all.

Postcolonial India faithfully followed the socialist economic formula. Within its closed borders, industry was strictly national, which suited a handful of private industrialists, like the Tata and the Birla dynasties, which enjoyed a near monopoly on the domestic market. For forty years, Tata was virtually the sole automaker in India. The Ambassador, which Tata churned out during the socialist era, was styled on an old British Austin car.

This heavy car, driven by a chauffeur, was an icon of self-sufficiency and the bureaucrats' vehicle of choice. It is significant that in 2008, Tata introduced a light and cheap popular car, the Nano. The Nano aims to become the icon of the new middle class generated by the free-market economy, just as the Ambassador represented the former socialist economy.

Nehru, who admired the Soviet Union for supporting decolonization and for its apparent industrial power, borrowed from Lenin the idea that the state must control the "commanding heights" of the economy. The key sectors—industry, energy, and transport—were nationalized and managed Soviet-style. Production was expensive and technically backward, but it was national, and the state-employed Indian economists, as in Labour-controlled Great Britain, were reputedly excellent planners. The elegance and complexity of their plans won them laurels from pundits, but the plans were far removed from on-the-ground reality: No Indian plan ever achieved its stated goals. The West revered Nehru and his self-righteous daughter, Indira Gandhi; in their own country, opinion was more nuanced.

Even during this socialist phase, a strong free-market current ran through India, represented by a vast body of small traders and businessmen. Many took pride in calling themselves "Nehru haters." During the eighties, they supported the BJP, a pro-market nationalist party advocating the revival of conservative Hindu values. This alliance of capitalism and religion has similarities to American neoconservatism.

Socialist India managed to avert the worst because its leaders did not nationalize property, a step that the nation's largely peasant population would probably have rejected. If India did not starve, it was thanks to its peasants. Then came the remarkable Green Revolution of the sixties, when the American agronomist Norman Borlaug (awarded the Nobel Peace Prize in 1970) and his Indian disciple M. S. Swaminathan introduced new wheat seeds, doubling production in a period of ten years. Once a continent plagued by famine, India became an exporter of food grain, enjoying a large surplus. Yet until the 1990s, one could still hear some Marxist Indians and foreign economists lamenting the inequality caused by the Green Revolution. It is true that the new high-yielding seed varieties helped the more enterprising become richer faster than others.

This outmoded critique apart, the main result of the Green Revolution was that in 2000, an Indian population twice as large as it was in 1947 consumed twice the number of calories per capita. Malthus had been proved wrong: Food production increased faster than the population, and as food supply went up, population growth slowed. The Green Revolution also silenced the economists who advocated birth control as a condition for development, as China had. In fact, development proved a more efficient contraceptive than the forced sterilization that Indira Gandhi imposed in 1975. Everywhere in the world, as development takes place, parents spontaneously start having fewer children; they act more rationally than their governments. When the future is looking up, spending more on the education of fewer children seems a better investment. When government enforces birth control despite development—this is still the case in Communist China—the aim seems less to promote growth than to keep the people in check. Family planning in China is an easy way for bureaucrats to supplement their income, since you can violate the law as long as you're willing to grease the palm of an official. Indian bureaucrats are often corrupt, but in more mundane ways.

The License Raj

"The license raj was the novel institution of slumbering India," Gurcharan Das recalls. Educated at Harvard and a former CEO of Procter & Gamble in India, Das is also the author of the worldwide bestseller *India Unbound*, published in 2001, which was the first book to announce the surge in India's economy.

India was the land of the license raj, or permit, until the early nineties, recalls Das. Even more pernicious than self-sufficiency and nationalization, this institution was most responsible for the country's stagnation. No firm, no matter how small, could get started without an administrative license. The more ambitious the firm, the harder it was to obtain it. Often, one had to go all the way to the minister to obtain a permit, but corruption flourished at all levels of the political-administrative hierarchy. One had to offer a bribe or a vote bank to open a shop or a factory, for instance. Naturally, the political leaders defended the system with seemingly rational arguments. The equitable distribution of work to all Indians and among all regions was a primary concern. Without the license, the enterprise of some and the passiveness of others would lead to social and regional imbalances, they said. But the real result was the elevation of prevarication to the rank of state policy and the suppression of the spirit of enterprise. The Indian diaspora, which has a considerable presence in Canada, the United States, and Great Britain, consisted mainly of economic refugees, exiles of the license raj ready to try their luck elsewhere.

The license raj crumbled in 1991, the year India's development took off. Why did it last so long? Indian leaders were intellectually isolated, according to Ahluwalia, who, as chairman of the planning commission, is the most influential economist in India. Nehru and Indira Gandhi, he says, saw countries like Korea, Taiwan, Singapore, and Hong Kong emerging, but they were dismissive of these Asian Tigers, seeing them as tiny clients of the United States. How could one compare India with such dwarfs? Meanwhile, the Soviet Union was viewed with respect until the day it fell apart.

India's main rival has always been China, but until the eighties, China's development was slower than that of India. The Chinese takeoff, Ahluwalia says, shook India out of its complacency. It was only when China opened to the world and freed up the spirit of enterprise that Indians became conscious of their own country's stagnation.

Rajiv Gandhi, prime minister from 1984 to 1989, was the first Indian leader to understand this point. Unlike his predecessors, this Gandhi was cosmopolitan. He wasn't really a politician; his coming to power was an accident necessitated by his mother's assassination. He had spent a large part of his life abroad, and when he returned, he was horrified to see that nothing worked. Even making a telephone call was difficult. Rajiv recruited Ahluwalia and Manmohan Singh, free-market economists. Air transport was liberalized: Indian Airlines lost its monopoly and private companies thrived, proof that even in India, the free market was efficient. The bureaucracy was not enthusiastic, and neither was the Left, which lost its main point of reference when the Soviet Union disintegrated. As the new Russians demanded dollars, which India didn't have, it had no choice but to open up to foreign investors and allow its own entrepreneurs to export, thereby bringing in foreign exchange. Thus the license raj came to an end and development took off. However, the free-market revolution was not purely a product of circumstance. Having anticipated the crisis, Singh and Ahluwalia had an alternative economic model ready.

The Free-Market Economists in Control

Free-market economists have been steering India's economy ever since 1991. Singh was the finance minister from 1991 to 1996 and prime minister from 2004 onward. Irrespective of the party in power, Ahluwalia has headed the planning commission. Singh's elevation to the post of prime minister was completely unexpected. Looking at him, one wonders how this slight, almost frail man with a reedy voice can lead so complex a nation and such a loose social-democratic coalition, dependent as it is on both free-marketers and Communists for its survival. His authority is, above all, intellectual; he was the man who saved the economy from bankruptcy in 1991.

While Singh shares the British sense of decorum, Ahluwalia has opted for a more informal American style; he's always ready to argue his case and prove the rationality of liberalization. He seems more readily available to foreign visitors than to the numerous supplicants waiting patiently in his antechamber. The economy is changing, but traditions die hard. One still needs the help of people in high places to deal with the bureaucracy or settle personal problems. In the waiting rooms of the powerful, time has no meaning. Petitioners return day after day, hoping for an audience. While they wait, minions prepare milky tea and sweepers lethargically swab the corridors. The economy may be growing, but the state continues to move at its own languid pace.

Ahluwalia and Singh are both Sikhs. Is this a coincidence? Sikh culture encourages the generation of wealth, unlike the Brahmanical tradition from which most of the socialist leaders emerged. Except for this elite, Indians are generally favorable to the spirit of enterprise. Capitalism has become legitimate, a process in which diaspora Indians (otherwise known as non-resident Indians, or NRIs) have played a major role. Seen as heroes, the NRIs were those who had the courage to leave their own country and seek their fortune abroad, returning only when they had succeeded by dint of hard work. Most Indians dream of setting up their own businesses, and liberalization has made their dream come true. Within the space of a few years, India has become a hub of small-scale enterprises.

This spontaneous and decentralized surge of capitalism, for the most part far removed from the state, distinguishes the Indian path from the Chinese and Korean models, in which the state names the winners. The West may be struck by spectacular takeovers by Indian tycoons—for example, Mittal's buying the steel giant Arcelor—but according to Ahluwalia, it is the myriad small projects that contribute most significantly to the modernization of the economy. Small and midsize enterprises set out to conquer the domestic market and the rest of the world, exporting goods and services and acquiring foreign firms to acquaint themselves with far-off markets and the latest technology. The NRIs are helpful partners in this drive toward globalization. The traditional familial, religious, and cultural networks have morphed into business connections, and the movement of the Indian diaspora between North America, Europe, and India has become an engine of growth. These overseas Indians invest in India. Some return for good and create new businesses in the motherland, as in the information industry in Mumbai, Bangalore, and Hyderabad. Indians working as engineers in Silicon Valley have exploited new opportunities back home while simultaneously keeping a customer base in the U.S. or Canada.

A newfound respect for intellectual property rights is a clear sign that the Indian economy is going global. In the past, Coca-Cola was banned in India; in its place, a local company produced the much-touted Campa Cola, which tasted like Coke and came in similarly shaped bottles. Today, however, India protects foreign trademarks. Indian entrepreneurs who have built their own brands, especially in the fields of pharmaceuticals, software, and biotechnology, have realized the importance of intellectual property, in both the domestic and international markets. This shift has still not happened in China (though when breaches happen, the wheels of justice move just as slowly in both countries).

Access to the American market is vital for the new Indian entrepreneurs. This is one reason for the strategic rapprochement between India and the United States, which marked a break with India's earlier pro-Soviet neutrality. India's desire to access nuclear technology, its fear of Islamic terrorism (India has more than 100 million Muslims), and, above all, the specter of a powerful China were other motivations.

Though rivalry with China has spurred Indian growth, which now almost matches that of China, Indian development is less conspicuous. Chinese development is visible to the foreign observer. India's development is imperceptible, its cities still sleepy, and its infrastructure as dilapidated as ever. On the face of it, China seems far more dynamic. Yet this is a superficial perception. In China, the central and provincial governments are all-powerful, and civil society is virtually nonexistent. The Chinese have opted to concentrate investment in a few core sectors of urban growth and in spectacular infrastructure projects; what remains hidden is China's rural poverty. In India, the central and state governments are relatively weak and do not have the clout to invest in large-scale public projects. Indian development is thus mostly the work of small firms spread across the country, a reflection of India's society and democracy.

"I won't hide the fact," says Ahluwalia. "Sometimes I envy the Chinese leaders." The Indian state's limited reach slows down work on major infrastructure projects that are essential for industrial progress. To travel remains an adventure. To fly to or within India on domestic airlines has become easier, but finding a landing spot at a congested airport is another matter. Many Indian firms use obsolete technology because of their geographical isolation and lack of communication. The service sector is more developed than in China, but this is no indicator of economic health. Typically, these are local services that cannot absorb the excess rural population.

Rural Exodus, the Rule of Thumb

Like all development economists, Ahluwalia is convinced that the rural exodus is a necessary stage of development. Urbanization and industrialization will take India forward. He does not share the economic romanticism widespread among Indian intellectuals, who paint an idyllic picture in which rural India, as if by a miracle, will begin to thrive, leaving the cities to concentrate on high-tech services and letting the nation bypass the manufacturing stage and leapfrog over industrialization. The millions of hamlets in which peasants live are too dispersed for adequate public services to be provided to them all. If they are to have running water, schools, and health-care facilities, they will have to be grouped together.

In India and beyond, the trend toward urbanization responds to an economic rationale and the human desire for a better life. Only in cities can access to energy, good jobs, good schools, decent health care, and social interaction be fully provided. It is significant that in 2007, for the first time in human history, the number of people living in cities worldwide outnumbered the rural population. This is part of the globalization process, and we should consider it progress.

In India, doesn't the success of the IT sector indicate an original strategy, different from what happened in Europe, Japan, and China? The achievements of Wipro, Infosys, and Tata—firms that enjoy worldwide respect—are of greater symbolic than economic value, admits Narayan Murthy, founder and CEO of Infosys. This diminutive software engineer has trained in France and Great Britain and is also one of India's richest men, though his modest demeanor and the quiet Brahmanical charity he practices would never let you think it.

The IT sector accounts for no more than 3 percent of Indian production and exports—less than the textile sector, he says. "Yet Indians like to believe that they are genetically gifted for computers, even if the success of Infosys has nothing to do with genetics," he adds. The IT success story resulted from a happy combination of hard work and circumstances, namely knowledge of English and the time lag. Americans can send their work at night and have it on their desks the next morning, thanks to an army of well-trained, if underemployed, Indian mathematicians.

Does an Infosys cubicle in Bangalore look exactly like a Microsoft cubicle in Seattle? Well, not exactly. The software will be the same, but in Bangalore a small statue of Ganesh will usually preside. The elephant-headed god has the gift of removing "obstacles"—a power that works for computer engineers grappling with problems as well as for writers suffering from a block. In the same vein, most Infosys workers will undergo purification rites in a campus temple before work. There is no contradiction in the Indian mind-set between modern science and eternal traditions, between reason and mystique. For a Westerner, conversation with Indian scholars can be somewhat difficult to follow, as they jump from the seemingly rational to irrational in the blink of an eye. Indian civilization is built on the addition of traditions, not on substitution. When a new god emerges, imported or home-bred, it joins the pantheon of existing gods. None is ever removed.

Ensconced in his New Delhi office, Ahluwalia says that the brilliance of Bangalore, Hyderabad, and Mumbai IT firms has put India on the world map, but they will never be able to absorb the millions of landless peasants. Indian manufacturers will therefore have to compete with Chinese firms and prove themselves second to none in producing and assembling electronic goods, textiles, and cars for the world market.

Does Democracy Slow Down Growth?

No discussion of the Indian economy can overlook the relationship between democracy and development. Ahluwalia perceives democracy to be a retarding factor, so completely does he focus on increasing India's growth rate. Indian democracy, he says, is less about representation than about argumentation and dissidence; everything is the subject of incessant controversy. Indeed, there are few nations in the free world where associations in defense of one cause or another are so active and numerous. Infrastructure projects habitually wind up in the dock, thanks to campaigns championing the environment, the landscape, or tribal culture. The Chinese government decides and acts unmindful of the feelings of its people; Indians prefer to argue. The Three Gorges Dam has displaced millions of Chinese peasants and submerged historical sites, yet there was not the slightest protest. Meanwhile, the proposed construction of dams on the Narmada River in northern India has become a major social controversy, mobilizing public opinion, the judiciary, the media, Bollywood, and leftist intellectuals. The dams will go up eventually—but many years later, and on a much less ambitious scale.

Democracy also slows the rural exodus that would be necessary to accelerate industrialization in India. Local politicians obtain state subsidies, which allow the peasants to remain in their villages, but mired in poverty. One understands why foreign investors, who play a decisive role in the development of India and China, prefer putting their money in China by a ratio of four to one. But they could be proved wrong. Democracies may work slowly, and infrastructure and industrialization may get held up. But the political consensus built over time will make Indian development sustainable. The conservative parties are more wary of foreign investment and the Left more attached to the public sector, but the difference is marginal and does not affect the overall consensus.

The Communists, who have been in power in West Bengal for thirty years, are now the most ardent prospectors for foreign capital and builders of free-trade zones around Calcutta. The Indian Left has also acknowledged that tough labor laws and the impossibility of laying off workers act as a deterrent to industrialization and competition with China. The paradox is that under-industrialized India overprotects the relatively small proportion of workers in the organized sector, while China, Communist in principle, offers no protection for its vast industrial manpower. At present, Indo-Chinese economic relations are almost nonexistent, but eventually, both countries will be competing in similar areas of production, at which point labor laws and wages will likely converge.

Comparing India and China is somewhat audacious, given the completely different nature of the two civilizations. But to take the comparison to its logical conclusion, India—slowed down though it is by democracy—appears to be more predictable in the long run than does despotic China. India's free-market consensus has been tried and tested over time, whereas China's economic strategy only mirrors the preferences of the dominant faction within the Communist Party. No one dares oppose the Party in China, it is said, but who can tell what lies ahead? Further, as things stand, India's growth, based on the domestic market, is less dependent on global demand than China's. When American consumers reduce their spending, China's growth is threatened more than India's is. In addition, Indian firms have developed cheap and reliable brands that, while not sold in the U.S., do well in the developing countries of Asia and Latin America.

The Excluded 30 Percent

Ahluwalia no longer claims that the market has an answer for everything. In 1984, when he left his job at the International Monetary Fund to formulate Indian policy, his confidence in the virtues of the free market was total. He was certain that growth would "trickle down" to the lowest rungs of society. Twenty years of experience have somewhat tempered his enthusiasm. He calculates that the benefits of growth have not reached the 30 percent of the Indian population that remains outside the market. It seems that India's robust economy has run into a cultural wall, built on rural traditions and the resilience of the caste system.

For instance, a lack of hygiene and the practice of defecating in the open remain basic problems in rural India. Mahatma Gandhi had asked Indians to bury their own excreta and set the example himself, but few followed. This has had disastrous consequences for public health, the worst being the pollution of waterways and groundwater. In 2007, the Indian government decided to finance the construction of latrines in the countryside.

Keen on promoting the scheme, the prime minister readily traveled long distances to inaugurate them, giving prizes to the villages that earned the ODF ("open-defecation-free") label. But the government hadn't reckoned with the caste spirit. In the large cities, belonging to a caste no longer governs behavior, but this is not the case in the countryside. The caste that builds the latrines is not going to maintain them; and if no caste is ready to keep them clean, the latrines will be abandoned, which occurs frequently.

Caste remains a major obstacle to development. Every Indian belongs to a caste, and each caste has a specific set of rules that regulate the daily life of its members as well as their relations with other castes. Even in the highest strata of society, people marry only within their own caste. The complexity of the caste system limits economic mobility, but the Indians are loath to give it up. One way of escaping from its clutches is to move from the village to the city. Yet even in the cities, Indians tend to seek out members of their own caste and group together. A caste may be restrictive, but it also provides a safety net to the poorest of its members. And far from becoming irrelevant, the notion of caste is strengthened by the constant reinforcement of an affirmative-action policy introduced to benefit lower castes during the 1930s. Indeed, the lower castes have a vested interest in perpetuating the system, since there are quotas for them in grade schools, universities, and the civil service. In exchange for their votes, caste leaders demand that they be declared a lower caste. Many a high-caste IT entrepreneur from Bangalore was once refused admission to the university because most of the seats were reserved for the lower castes. Yet civilizations evolve. The media are highlighting ODF villages and stressing the essential Hindu principles of purity and impurity—so much so that at times, marriages take place only between people of ODF villages.

Amartya Sen, the Nobel Prize–winning Anglo-Bengali economist, deplores another alarming custom: the Indian family's preference for male children. In rural areas, where female feticide is common, mothers look after their sons better than their daughters. Undernourished girls in turn give birth to malnourished children. Sen believes that human development is a better indicator of growth than quantitative parameters. He points out that one reason that India seems to lag behind China is that available statistics do not take human development into consideration. In China, political oppression retards human development, just as in India, backward traditions impede it. However, Sen believes that governments are ill equipped to change the mind-sets of people and reduce female feticide. This is a task best left to NGOs, which thrive in India but that China prohibits. Without doubt, compassion and grassroots efforts will improve the lot of the excluded 30 percent.

Gandhi and the Free Market

As M. S. Swaminathan's exemplary efforts illustrate, the market, too, can be an efficient instrument for alleviating poverty. After co-fathering the Green Revolution during the 1970s, Swaminathan set up a foundation in the southern city of Chennai that bears his name and helps poor Indian women gain access to technology. Swaminathan is one of the most respected personalities in contemporary India; he is certainly among the most upright. Modest and spartan in his habits, this great scientist is very active even in his late seventies. It was his ability to adapt Borlaug's seeds and introduce new agricultural techniques that saved millions of people from famine and malnutrition. The foundation still pursues its scientific work, selecting seeds capable of surviving brackish water and drought and genetically modified organisms (GMOs) adapted to local conditions. Swaminathan does not share the apprehension of ecologists from affluent countries who demonize GMOs because they can do without them. In India, agriculture is a question of life and death.

Apart from being a great scientist and innovator, Swaminathan is moved by a vision of India that Mahatma Gandhi first articulated. His stated goal is to use scientific progress in the service of the poorest of the poor: women whose standards of living and civic awareness must be raised. In India's caste-ridden hierarchy, he believes, women are the most vulnerable. They also stand to gain the most from progress and are the best agents of growth in society. Swaminathan makes no distinction between scientific, economic, and political progress: Everything is interlinked. In the Union Territory of Pondicherry (south of Chennai), he organizes village women into pressure groups, educates them, and initiates them into new agricultural techniques.

India, says Swaminathan, is not lacking in food, but there are some too poor to afford it. They need income, not charity. So he is urging landless single women to engage in income-generating activities—introducing household mushroom cultivation in Tamil Nadu and Pondicherry, for example, so that women can live off their own produce. To produce mushrooms and earn a living, all one needs is a hut. His foundation has also provided Internet access in villages to help peasants know the market price of their produce and avoid being cheated by middlemen. Such activities are being carried out by thousands of NGOs in other Indian regions as well; they show to what extent the Gandhian spirit can accommodate progress. Gandhi's economic philosophy was not averse to the free market. Indeed, its intention was to direct the poorest of the poor to the market.

When Indians fought for independence under Gandhi's leadership, they wanted development, not stagnation and poverty in the name of the diversity of civilizations. There are many misconceptions about the India of Gandhi's dreams. He was not against progress, as we tend to believe in the West. His main fear was the injustice and loss of human dignity that an uncontrolled industrial revolution could cause. To the ailing, after all, he recommended Western medicine, which he knew to be more effective than traditional Indian medicine. When he traveled, he did not hesitate to ride the train instead of the bullock cart. The yardstick for measuring progress, he said, should be the extent to which the lives of the poorest Indian women improved. For

Gandhi, development was good and just only if it raised the standard of living of the poorest. Then came Nehru, who wanted a modern, powerful India and thought that in socialism he had found a way to reconcile development with justice. His aim from the outset was development, but the road he chose was not the right one. Will the road to globalization and the free market bring Indians where Gandhi sought to take them?

The free market is now taken for granted in India. Few question its efficiency or its capacity to spread wealth. In India, as in all economies that are in a period of takeoff, capitalism has also given rise to an ostentatious class of nouveaux riches, whose attitudes and lifestyles find themselves mirrored by Bollywood, the Mumbai film industry. The contrast in India between vulgarly displayed wealth and stark poverty comes as a shock to many Westerners. Poorer Indians themselves are used to injustice and caste segregation; if they had a choice, they would willingly embrace the opulence of Bollywood.

The questions people ask are: How long will it take for a more even distribution of wealth to occur? How long will it take for the poorest Indian women to benefit from economic progress? How long will it be before affluence trickles down to the lowest level? The fact that these questions are asked all the time is Indian democracy's greatest virtue. The best response, to my mind, is a combination of what Ahluwalia suggests at the top and what Swaminathan is doing at the grassroots level. This alliance between an export-oriented strategy and grassroots development will protect India from a backlash against globalization. The 2008 economic slowdown has not sparked any attempt to return to the old socialist system.

The Risks of Globalization

The free market will not solve all social contradictions, nor will it eliminate all religious tensions, as the 2008 Mumbai terrorist attack made clear. Globalization introduced India to a new kind of Islam, a global Islam that is more often connected to websites than to local traditions. Relationships between Muslims and Hindus in India have always been complex, but in general, until recently, they could live together, in villages as well as in cities. Local customs have always influenced Indian Islam, which emphasizes, as does Sufism, nonviolence and a pluralistic tolerance among religions.

This traditional coexistence had already begun to fray in the 1930s, as religions became politicized. Muslim leaders created Muslim political parties, which paved the way for the bloody partition of Pakistan and India. Hindu leaders today exploit old resentments against the Muslim colonization of previous centuries; this has led to confrontations between religious communities and to the creation of an all-Hindu party, the BJP. And with globalization, Indian Muslim workers, returning from the Persian Gulf countries where they had found temporary employment, have brought back to their homeland a "purer" Islam, along with Arabic customs. Coexistence between radicalized minorities—Muslims and non-Muslims—thus has become more difficult than it has ever been in Indian history.

With the acceleration of economic growth, uprooted youngsters who migrate from the villages to the big cities tend to create a new Islam, a new Hinduism, or a new Sikhism—inspired by overseas Muslims, Hindus, and Sikhs—and are usually more radical than the conservative Indians who have remained in their own country. Increasingly, one can hear young Muslims in Delhi or Mumbai talking as global, not Indian, Muslims; they use jihadist code words, a lingo common to disgruntled urbanized Muslims around the world. Until very recently, when violent clashes broke out between Indian religious communities, the causes were local or traceable to "foreign interventions"—meaning the Pakistani enemy or the Kashmiri independence-seeking guerrilla. Now, bombings in Delhi and Mumbai can often be attributed to domestic fundamentalist Muslims. They remain a tiny minority, but they represent a major challenge for the Indian government. To predict that they will disrupt the Indian social fabric would be far-fetched. But India has become one more country involved in the global fight against terrorism.

This new war, though, will not reverse India's market revolution and democratic development; one hopes that it might reinforce both. Poverty and tyranny may not be the only or chief causes of terrorism. But the eradication of poverty and the establishment of political freedom could limit the attraction of fundamentalist violence.

CHAPTER TWELVE

In Brazil, the Future Is Now

Everyone calls him Fernando Henrique; no one would think of calling him Mr. President. Brazil is a unique civilization, where the greatest inequalities hide beneath a warm familiarity. Fernando Henrique Cardoso, a mirror image of his country's economy, has lived two successive lives. First he analyzed Brazil as a sociologist. Then, from 1995 to 2002, he served as its president. At the University of São Paulo in the 1960s, and later as an exile in France and in the United States during the military dictatorship, Cardoso was not a Marxist, he explains, but a Marxian, like his whole generation of intellectuals. In the universities, a number have remained Marxian, that is to say, inspired by an understanding of the world in which the poverty of the periphery, including Brazil, is explicable by the wealth of the imperialist center, the United States and Europe.

This "dependency" theory, the Latin American version of Lenin's theory of imperialism, is traceable to an influential Argentinean thinker, Raúl Prebisch, who was head of the Economic Commission for Latin America and the Caribbean (ECLAC), a United Nations office still located in Santiago, Chile. Until the early 1980s, this laboratory conceived the economic policies of the Latin American continent. Cardoso, like Prebisch, deduced from dependency theory that the true decolonization of the continent required its industrialization. This is undeniable. But neither man could imagine this industrialization except as a state-guided process, sheltered from all internal and external competition. In Brazil, this strategy was called developmentalism. The industries that arose from it were inefficient, but they enriched the bureaucrats who ran them, the military officers who owned them, the middle-class clients of the industrial state, and the unions that had a share in the project. One of the unexpected consequences of developmentalism was the deepening of social inequalities; great fortunes were amassed under the wing of the state. For small entrepreneurs and poorer Brazilians, this "greenhouse" industrialization was of no benefit. Many said in those days that Brazil was a country of the future—and would remain so.

During the 1970s, certain Brazilian economists, the most prominent being Delfim Netto, made a surprising contribution to this tropical statism: They justified hyperinflation as a factor in economic progress. During the 1980s, Brazilian money was worth nothing. Prices changed every day, and in 1993 the rate of inflation reached 6,000 percent a year. But the Brazilian administration, which inherited a great sophistication from its Portuguese forebears, had set up a system of generalized indexation, which pegged remuneration to the prices. With this indexation, hyperinflation supposedly became inconsequential. The state could print money without shame to pay for investment in infrastructure and industry, pulling from a bottomless financial well without victims—in theory. This Brazilian model achieved such authority that for a few years, it was taught in European universities, primarily for ideological reasons. Did the Brazilian experience not demonstrate that monetarists like Milton Friedman, partisans of sound money, were wrong? In reality, hyperinflation enriched the rich, who lived on American dollars, and ruined the poor, whose income always lagged behind prices. Cardoso's thinking was shaped by this social horror, which is how a Marxian sociologist became the first free-market president of Brazil.

The Social Horror of Inflation

The influence of inflation on the course of history is well known. The French Directory and the Weimar Republic, among other regimes, went down along with their bad money. In Brazil, inflation contributed to the fall of the military dictatorship in 1986. The newly elected leaders—José Sarney, Itamar Franco, and then Cardoso—understood that the people expected monetary stability before political liberty and even before growth. This would be Cardoso's great work: a new money that was real, authentic, and stable. Everything else in Brazil's new economy flows from this achievement. For the currency to remain stable, the state had to balance its budget. To eliminate the deficit, it stopped recruiting bureaucrats and subsidizing public works. What followed—privatizations, opening the market to competition—was not a choice based on free-market ideology, Cardoso explains, but the rational consequence of monetary stabilization. One should note that Cardoso's success would not have been possible without Brazil's effective state and competent administration, in which the government's orders get carried out. The attempt to stabilize Argentina's currency during the 1990s was technically comparable, but it failed in 2002 because the mafia-like state continued to spend beyond its means.

After the reestablishment of democracy, Cardoso says, elected officials were surprised to find how much their popularity was tied to the stability of prices. Many people understood faster than political elites—and better than some economists—that inflation was a tax on the poor. The Brazilian political experience provided a point-by-point confirmation of classical economic analysis.

As president, Cardoso implemented a monetarist program. For money to remain stable in the long run, it was necessary for it to escape political power and for the state to balance its budget. Thus Brazil needed economic institutions insulated from political changes and populist temptations. Cardoso created an independent central bank and established total budgetary transparency. Using the Internet, every Brazilian citizen can know instantaneously the state of all public expenses, the level of debt, and any threats to monetary stability. This transparency binds the political class and the bureaucracy. And no transgression escapes Brazil's very free press, the third pillar (along with the central bank and transparency) of the new Brazilian order.

The Just Society

Cardoso does not define himself as a free-market thinker. This is understandable. In Latin America, there is a strain of economic fundamentalism—an extreme free-market ideology that reduces everything to the market, that refuses to see society as it is, and that prefers enlightened despotism to democracy—that would embarrass such masters as Hayek and Friedman, the heroes of their Brazilian disciples. In Brazil, public opinion perceives free-market economics as the ideology of the big bosses who once got along quite well with the military dictatorship.

Cardoso thus calls himself a social democrat: His appreciation for the market does not exclude direct action against poverty. The first Brazilian chief of state to take a concrete interest in the poor, he established a model of public assistance that is remarkable in conception and application. Recognizing the fact that the worst poverty in Brazil is rooted in ignorance, he granted financial aid to families, conditional upon their sending their children to school; these allocations go to the mother. (The market-friendly government of Vicente Fox created a comparable aid program in

Mexico, and there is also one in Chile.) The quality of public schools still needs improvement, but thanks to these "family scholarships," illiteracy is falling. Cardoso made the strategic—and cruel—choice to help the next generation instead of today's poor. In effect, Brazil gave priority to the future. It did this first with Cardoso, a president from the Right, and then with Inácio da Silva, commonly known as Lula, a president from the Left.

In economics, institutions are better predictors of a nation's future than the occasional interventions of passing governments. But one cannot bet on these institutions until they have proved resistant to recessions and changes of administration. Since 1995, Brazilian political and economic institutions have shown such resilience. Lula, who came from a background of antimarket syndicalism and who enjoyed the support of liberation theologians and Trotskyite academics, has maintained the integrity of Brazil's economic institutional legacy. Cardoso himself finds this surprising. "Did some intuitive sense of goodness prevail over ideology in Lula's mind?" he asks. Another factor is that Brazil is traditionally a land of accommodation, not confrontation.

Lula's adversaries do accuse him of hiring too many bureaucrats and of increasing, for electoral reasons, the range of families benefiting from welfare well beyond the truly needy—that is, of having created a base of welfare clients. The accusations aren't without foundation. But compared with the benefits of institutional continuity, these missteps are negligible. The independence of the central bank, monetary stability, the opening of the market, privatization, fiscal transparency, and conditional assistance to families: All this has been maintained. Lula even deserves credit for containing the public deficit better than Cardoso did. This achievement is comparable with India's politically ecumenical economic strategy. Brazil, like India, has made a successful economic transition and now boasts the institutions necessary to sustain development and improve social equity.

The Rise of the Middle Class

The solidity of financial institutions, the predictability of the currency, and the transparency of transactions have allowed for a modernization of credit in Brazil. It is now possible for a new entrepreneur to obtain loans at rates compatible with his economic capacity, and a family can look forward to acquiring housing or a car. Thanks to credit, a new middle class is forging a decent life through its labor, no longer dependent on partisan clientelism or on the blessings of the state.

The new economic rationality leads entrepreneurs to modify their behavior. Whereas in the old Brazil, one sought out speculative niches or privileged situations, now managers take a long view of things; they invest in market research. The old habits have not disappeared, but they are in decline. The rigor of Brazilian businesses has not yet reached the level of "First World" firms. But as economist Maílson da Nóbrega observes, "Brazil has unquestionably left the Third World."

The main remaining obstacles to sustained development are no longer those of a Third World country—administrative corruption, say, or state capriciousness. Brazilian entrepreneurs, like those of the "First World," are always protesting against an excessively high minimum wage, which makes it hard to compete with China; against labor laws that make it difficult to dismiss workers; against anticapitalist unions; and against the inadequacy of public infrastructure, which slows down exports and makes the case for privatization. These complaints, sometimes legitimate and sometimes excessive, characterize a world that has discovered rationality and left structural poverty behind. Brazil needs administrative reforms, true, but it has accomplished its economic revolution. The virulent Marxists and the partisans of dependency theory still have their jobs in the media and the academy, but they no longer have the capacity to alter the course of history. Buried by Cardoso, such Marxists belong to Brazil's past. The new middle class more modestly represents its future.

The new Brazil is developing not only economically; it is also becoming more egalitarian. In 2007, Brazil was the only country in the world, other than Thailand, whose Gini coefficient improved. This universally accepted index measures the distance between the richest 10 percent and the poorest 10 percent of the population. In every country besides Brazil and Thailand, the gap is growing. In all developed and developing countries, that is, the rich are getting richer faster than the poor, even where the poor are becoming less poor. In the United States, for instance, everyone is getting richer, on average, but the rich are doing so faster than others because of the premium on education, which is worth ever more on the world market. In China and India, the condition of the humble is improving, yet not as fast as that of the most fortunate. In Brazil, however, the poor are progressing faster than the rich; for the first time in the history of the country, the gap is closing. Da Nóbrega ascribes this to the transition from state-driven development to a free-market economy. The pursuit of wealth by clientelism and the establishment of monopolies have been replaced by the majority's access to the market. It is the market that generates social mobility, while statism reinforces rent-seeking. "The free-market economic model improves equity better than fiscal redistribution or social welfare does," says da Nóbrega.

Direct aid to families also contributes to this equity, but in an accessory manner. Assigned to some 12 million families, the Brazilian government's "family scholarships" represent only 0.5 percent of national wealth. It is the next generation that will benefit from education and really gain from this assistance. The market not only generates more equality than statism, it also propels the rising curve of the Brazilian growth rate, which progresses for no other reason than the opening up of credit, commerce, and trade. The Brazilian breakthrough, its coupling of equality and progress, is not accidental; it is a lesson in good economics, as taught by today's theorists of development.

Finally, there is a nonquantifiable factor in the new Brazilian economy that we should mention, whether or not it is a cause: the replacement of Catholicism by evangelical and Pentecostal churches. The shift in church membership is massive. In the state of São Paulo, the most prosperous in the country, evangelicals have become the majority. Evangelical churches do not promote the same values as the Catholic Church does. The Church, especially in Brazil, has been hostile to market economies and favorable to social revolution in the name of the liberation theology long embodied by the "Red Cardinal" of Recife, Dom Hélder Câmara. During the 1970s, Dom Hélder saw the shantytowns as a hotbed of revolution against savage capitalism.

Today, far from being revolutionary, the shantytowns have become centers of drug trafficking and other organized crime. This is by no means progress, but neither is it the fulfillment of the liberation theologians' hope. Under the influence of John Paul II, the Catholic Church in Brazil and its activist Jesuits have moderated their political activism, but this has come too late to counter the evangelicals, who recommend individual effort as a remedy for poverty and idealize the spirit of enterprise, even the pursuit of wealth. It is possible that this ethical-religious displacement has contributed to the emergence of new norms and behaviors that are more in tune with the transition to a market economy and globalization than Catholicism has been.

Getting Rich by Paying Taxes

In Brazil, as in all poor countries, the informal economy remains powerful. The street merchant, the artisan, the handyman, the landless peasant—all work outside the law, and for meager results. Without a title to property and a legal right to earn a living, a person turns to informal work as a survival strategy in the face of criminal states, rapacious bureaucrats, or colonial aristocrats. The Peruvian economist Hernando de Soto has showed how, in his country, the near impossibility of obtaining legal property blocked access to credit and condemned many to marginal activities. In the countryside, the peasant, occupying land without title, cultivates the coca plant because it requires no investment and the crop rotation is rapid. The number of steps necessary to open a legal business in Peru is so great and the cost, including corruption, so high that it is impossible to become an entrepreneur without a bureaucrat's personal protection. De Soto's observation is valid to varying degrees for Brazil and for most of Latin America, where the rule of law has not yet completely replaced the personalization of law and clientelism.

The informal economy sometimes inspires a certain romanticism, an idealization of barefoot capitalism and of the brave entrepreneur outwitting the bureaucracy. It was left to two Brazilian economists, José Scheinkman and Áureo de Paula, to demonstrate that this underground activity was simply a survival strategy that locked the poor into a downward spiral of increasing poverty. Their study, based on a sample of 50,000 informal companies, showed that Brazilian informal businesses were necessarily badly managed and unproductive. Their managers were mediocre because the better ones went into the formal sector; their capital was insufficient because access to credit was impossible or onerous; yet wages were comparable with those in the formal sector, wiping out profits and hopes of long-term development.

The informal sector thus slows growth. Moreover, it is contagious: Informal businesses tend to deal only with other informal businesses in order to escape taxation and regulation throughout the cycle of production. Because of the importance of the informal economy in a relatively poor country like Brazil (where it amounts to 40 percent of national production), moving this sector into the formal economy would speed growth. Following the recommendations of Scheinkman and de Paula, the government has, since 2006, offered fiscal amnesty to businesses that will agree henceforth to pay their taxes. Paying taxes makes it possible for firms to access bank credit at the market rate; according to de Soto, the average interest rate in the informal sector in Latin America is five times higher than in the formal sector. Paying taxes—the Value-Added Tax, in Brazil—benefits both the entrepreneur and the country. With the VAT, formal chains replace informal ones, in one more proof of the universal relation between the rule of law and development.

The Two Latin Americas

Globalization, Cardoso argues, has divided Latin America into two parts: one adapted to the new reality, and one that denies the other part's very existence. Among the countries that have adapted, Cardoso puts Chile first. He observes that the Chileans were the first to understand that the true natural advantage of nations was not climate or mineral wealth but their capacity to create stable institutions. From Pinochet, chief of state from 1973 until 1990, until and including Michelle Bachelet, the socialist president since 2005, Chile has hardly changed its economic rules; it has successfully joined the global economy by adapting its production. Mexico, Brazil, Uruguay, Colombia, Peru, Costa Rica, and the Dominican Republic have all taken part, at differing paces and to different degrees, in the same reconciliation with liberal democracy, the market economy, and globalization.

In Cardoso's view, Brazil is now more a part of the world than it is of Latin America. This is doubtless the fortunate result of good political and economic choices, but a number of historical predispositions were also necessary. Brazil and the other ascending Latin American countries have benefited from a certain political and legal tradition inherited from colonization. All have an old entrepreneurial middle class and a free-market tradition dating back to the nineteenth century, and all benefit from a relatively homogeneous national culture, which allows for democratic citizenship. Brazil is ethnically diverse, true. But from the landed aristocracy to the racially mixed peasantry, Brazilians share a feeling of national belonging, a common multiethnic civilization, and an orientation toward the future comparable to what U.S. citizens recognize as "the American dream." "We are Americans rather than Europeans," Cardoso writes. "We also have a 'black problem,' but it does not undermine the nation."

The other Latin America—the one that Brazil, Colombia, and Chile are leaving behind—is better characterized by the magical realism of the writer Gabriel García Márquez. Its heads of state are never more than caudillos, whose clients expect them to redistribute wealth; the redistribution of oil, minerals, land, and government jobs takes the place of economic policy and of development. This old Latin America remains fertile ground for the myth of revolution—Communist revolution and, still more, indigenous revolution. This revolutionary tension can be explained by the failure to integrate indigenous peoples—in Bolivia or Paraguay, for example—into a national society. In Europe and the United States, the error is commonly made of translating the problems of a country like Bolivia, which are rooted in a racial struggle inherited from colonization, into the Western ideological language of class struggle.

In the old Latin America, democracy is a fiction: Every political leader strives to redistribute more than the others, not to produce more. The best that can happen is that global commodity prices will rise, producing an illusion of prosperity (in Venezuela when oil gets expensive, for example, or in Argentina when soybeans do). The movement of international capital as it searches for windfall profits, along with global commodity prices, makes and unmakes these economies, based as they are on speculation, not on a local entrepreneurial middle class. When prices fall and capital flees, as happened in Argentina in 2001, society collapses all at once. The only certainty, according to da Nóbrega, is that everything in the old Latin America always turns out badly, albeit in degrees—very badly in Venezuela, not so badly in Argentina. After the euphoric period ends, economic recession and military dictatorship always return.

Despite the strange fascination that this old Latin America holds for intellectuals nostalgic for revolution, we are no longer living in the 1960s. Chávez-style populists contest the global order, but they propose no real alternative. The disappearance of the Soviet Union, as well as the experience gained since its fall, has produced a new situation: There is no known path to development other than integration in the global order through democracy and the market. Cardoso calls this a new social democracy, his Brazilian translation of the German-style social-market economy. Call it social democracy, then, if the free-market label has been discredited by its most extreme enthusiasts. In Brazil, says da Nóbrega, the future is now.

Why Doesn't Latin America Progress as Quickly as Asia?

The economic situation of Latin America has never been as favorable over the last thirty years as it is today. This progress is essentially due to market-friendly economic policies, the creation of relatively stable and predictable political and financial institutions, and improved control over inflation and indebtedness. In years when the global economy grows, there is also the boon of a significant increase in the price of raw materials exported from the continent: soybeans from Argentina and Brazil, grain from Uruguay, copper from Chile, gas from Bolivia, oil from Venezuela and Ecuador, and so on. Despite these favorable circumstances and this new economic rationality, the Brazilian economist Eduardo Giannetti notes that the growth rate of the Latin American continent as a whole, including in the best-run countries, has lagged distinctly behind that of China, India, the

Philippines, and Thailand. The argument that certain Latin American economies have already achieved a level of maturity—and that their growth should properly be compared with that of developed countries, not developing ones—might be valid for Chile, Argentina, and Uruguay. But it certainly does not hold for Brazil, nor *a fortiori* for countries as poor as Peru, Bolivia, and Colombia. Doubtless there are structural factors intrinsic to the Latin American continent that explain this gap. According to Giannetti, the classic tools of economic analysis shed more light on this question than cultural explanations do.

In Latin America, people borrow and invest less than in Asia, and they attach less importance to mass education. In Brazil and in Chile, to consider only the most dynamic economies, people save and invest only half as much as they do in China. The evidence is apparent in the lack of industrialization and the inferiority of the infrastructure. There is also less investment in basic education, though elites benefit from excellent universities. If there is less investment, it is because there is less incentive to invest—in the short term or in the long. The reason is simple: The tax rate in Latin America, particularly in Brazil, is extremely high. Taxes on businesses finance oversize state sectors, which have no equivalents in the developing Asian countries.

One can cite historical reasons for these burdensome states. The Latin American governments in question are heirs to extensive and meddlesome Spanish and Portuguese colonial bureaucracies. In Brazil, the complexity of the procedures necessary to create businesses, and still more to close them, discourages their creation. This bureaucracy explains the significance of the informal sector. The fact that in Brazil, about half of all business activities are informal—an anomaly—shows that the rule of law does not touch half of the population, underscoring the still-dysfunctional character of the Brazilian state, despite its recent improvements. Scheinkman has shown us how informality slows the development of businesses.

Historical reasons and the colonial heritage are not enough, however, to explain why half of an economy might escape the rule of law and its bureaucratic administration. The states of Latin America are not expensive simply because they are perpetuating a colonial heritage; a greater factor is that they attempt, by major social expenditures, to appease protest movements that are altogether contemporary. In the profoundly unequal societies of Latin America, social injustice is badly tolerated. It is not an accident or a matter of a particular local government that Latin America has been so fertile in socialist revolutions and remains agitated by so-called populist movements. The careers of Che Guevara and Fidel Castro, Hugo Chávez in Venezuela, Subcommandant Marcos in Mexico, Evo Morales in Bolivia, and many more like them reflect social cleavages that the majority often finds unbearable. These divisions go back to an onerous past that never seems entirely over: the exploitation of indigenous peoples by conquerors, economies based on large-scale agricultural enterprises and on the extraction of rents, minerals, and oil. In North America, European colonizers chose to develop their territory and increase its value; in Latin America, they exploited it. Is this to be explained by the colonists' origins, or by the fact that labor was abundant in South America and scarce in North America? In any case, North Americans have tended to invest, whereas South Americans have exploited.

The statist policies in place from the forties to the seventies did not radically modify this regime of exploitation. The nationalization of the copper industry in Chile by the Marxist government of Allende, for example, simply took the rents formerly paid to foreign proprietors and transferred them to the bureaucracy. This was also true of tin in Bolivia and of oil in Venezuela. Latin American socialism transferred property and its profits from a private aristocracy to a public aristocracy, but without bringing the society as a whole into the process of economic development.

The democratization of Latin America—the reforms of the 1930s and their renewal during the 1980s after the eviction of military dictatorships (which also failed to involve the people in development)—forced governments to buy social peace by distributing public jobs and subsidies; the clientelism that characterizes Latin American democracies seeks at once to buy votes and to defuse social protest movements. Thus, during his presidency, Fernando Henrique Cardoso surely built economic institutions for the future—but he also substantially increased public expenditures to ward off the specter of revolution.

This revolutionary threat, which swells social expenditures to the detriment of investment (whether public or private), has been aggravated by the recent concentration of the poor in the cities. When Che Guevara tried to mobilize Bolivian peasants, or when the Brazilian Catholic Church stirred up landless farmers, their rebellions were invisible in the faraway cities where the elites lived. But with the massive rural exodus to urban centers, the proletariat has settled in the suburbs. In São Paulo, Bogotá, and Lima, the poor have entered the cities, where they have set up shantytowns not far from the richest neighborhoods. Public subsidies represent a kind of evasive response to a fear of the poor and to the real violence that breeds in these settlements.

The threat of revolution, added to the disincentive of taxes, limits entrepreneurs' desire to make long-term investments. The short term is preferred—or foreign investment, or consumption while it is possible—because the future remains uncertain. Perhaps Latin American culture contributes to this predilection for the present and for consumption, and objective economic and social circumstances then reinforce this culture.

In theory, the remedy for social inequality is the extension of education. A significant increase in human capital in these countries would reduce discrimination and lead to an economy based more on quality and less on extraction. But the reverse is happening: Almost everywhere in Latin America, education reflects economic inequalities and crystallizes them. From Argentina to Mexico, the universities are excellent (especially those that are private and expensive), and private schools are likewise pricey and of high quality. Public schools, by contrast, are the preserve of the poor, and they are mediocre. Latin American leaders have not understood the extent to which mass education could strengthen the nonmaterial capital of their countries and defuse social protest movements—unless the traditional elites are comfortable with this discrimination, which sustains their privileges. Or perhaps these two reasons reinforce each other.

Also, it is not easy for a democratic and market-friendly government to invest in education, for this will increase public spending, whereas limiting the state's budget is necessary to encourage investment. This is a universal dilemma that Chile is attempting to negotiate.

The Chilean Solution

Chile is a laboratory of economic and social experimentation for Latin America, a pioneer that the rest of the continent observes attentively. This has been true, strangely, since the presidency of General Pinochet (1973–90), less because of Pinochet himself than because of the surprising group that surrounded him. Ignorant of economics, faced with inflation and with a broken system of production following the nationalization of enterprises under Salvador Allende, Pinochet called upon the economists of the most highly regarded university in Chile, the Catholic University of Santiago. It happened that these economists, owing to an old agreement with the University of Chicago, had all, to varying degrees, drawn inspiration from the theories of Milton Friedman.

So they entered into the history of their own country, and into the general chronicles of economic history, as the "Chicago Boys." They applied the principles of free-market economics to Chile just as they might have done on a blank page or on a blackboard. They privatized businesses, stabilized money via an independent central bank, deregulated markets, and opened borders. Only copper mining, which represented half of Chile's exports, escaped the application of the theory, doubtless because the army preferred to maintain control of the resource. Even today, long after the reestablishment of democracy in 1990, 10 percent of copper sales are assigned directly to the military in order—in principle—to purchase weapons to use against an imaginary enemy. With this exception, and after a few false starts in the execution of pure market-based theory, Chile is the Latin American country that has grown the fastest and where poverty has shrunk the most. Free trade has been particularly effective, allowing Chileans to consume low-priced goods from the global market and motivating businesses to export products with a growing value-added to the whole world, such as wine, fish, and fruit. After Pinochet's departure, most of the Chicago Boys returned to teach at Catholic University, but no subsequent democratic government, Christian Democrat or Socialist, has turned against the market economy. This continuity has proved beneficial to the country and inspired its neighbors—in particular, Peru and Brazil.

But it is no longer the establishment of economic freedom, which is now the rule in the new Latin America, that constitutes Chile's originality. What was achieved was banal, as one of the Chicago Boys, the economist Rolf Lüdders, has observed. Its only unique feature was the unexpected alliance between Pinochet and the free-market economists. The true innovation, which today earns Chile its rank as a pioneer, was in social policy.

Chilean growth raised the overall standard of living and reduced poverty, but it did not close the gap of inequality. The success of the most educated only underscored the slower rate of progress among the less educated. Demands for social justice were thus no less urgent in Chile than in the rest of the continent, but the concern was more with redistribution than with poverty. How might it be possible to redistribute without increasing public expenditures and stifling the growth of businesses? The answer was found in Milton Friedman's proposal concerning school vouchers: to support individual demand rather than offering additional public services.

In Chile's education system, every poor family, based upon a precise assessment of real needs, receives a voucher that makes it possible to choose a child's school, whether private or public. This formula—which is, in principle, fair and egalitarian—so far works badly in practice because, as noted earlier, the value of the voucher is insufficient to allow children to attend private schools and because the public schools refuse to publish their educational results. A family's power to choose therefore remains somewhat illusory. On the other hand, a similar method has proven effective in the area of housing. The state guarantees the least advantaged access to mortgage loans and the ability to acquire housing in the private sector. Thus the state does not build the housing that it assigns publicly, and government spending is kept within bounds. (The Chilean way being cautious, the country has avoided the risk of subprime mortgages.)

It is in the area of retirement plans that the Chilean method is most admired for its success in combining social justice and economic efficiency. All Chileans can choose to join either a public system of minimum retirement income or a system of private investment; everyone must choose one system or the other. The private retirement investment plans are run by insurance companies, are licensed by the state, and are in competition with the state system. The logic of the system is thus comparable with that of school vouchers. It is not a matter of the total privatization of education, housing, or retirement, since the state guarantees access to everyone and offers public assistance to the poorest citizens. But the private sector is responsible for managing public services in education, health, housing, and retirement. The Chilean method is neither socialist nor free-market; it brings together the principles of solidarity and efficiency without doing too much damage to economic dynamism. The Chilean Left denounces the imperfections of the system, which indeed are incontestable, but it does not question its essentials. The new Latin America will probably come to resemble the Chilean model. The old Latin America will remain unpredictable.

PART 4

Coming Out of Socialism

Until the 1980s, teachers, economists, and journalists felt obliged to make evenhanded comparisons between the organization and the results of Soviet socialism and those of Western capitalism. The French sociologist and conservative thinker Raymond Aron predicted that the two systems would remain distinct and unchangeable; the political scientist Maurice Duverger prophesied the convergence of the two systems, with each taking the best things from the other. These have proved to be so many pointless wagers. Since the disappearance of the Soviet system, capitalism is no longer Western, but universal. It must be criticized—but by the standards of its own ambitions, not by comparison with a model that no longer exists. What is surprising is that we were able, in the East as well as in the West, to take Soviet socialism seriously for so long. It was never a realistic alternative; it functioned for some sixty years only to the extent that military discipline imposed it, and it did not even respect its own principles completely. Behind the façade of omniscient planning, the Soviets and the Chinese Communists survived—and badly at that—only by going around the system. The black market became a spontaneous survival strategy mitigating the prohibition of open markets.

Another surprise was the unheard-of rapidity and the peaceful nature of the transition from what János Kornai calls the socialist system to what he calls the capitalist system. After the collapse of Soviet socialism, some expected or hoped that the Russians or the Poles would invent a third way, a collective economy based on cooperatives, neither Soviet nor capitalist, in the manner of the utopian socialist dreams of the nineteenth century. Even among those who did not believe in this third way and favored capitalism, many feared that it would be necessary to wait another generation before homo sovieticus would give way to homo economicus.

Such a long wait was not necessary, as it turned out, so great was the desire of the interested parties—in the words of Donald Tusk, a member of Solidarity and later the leader of Polish free-market liberals—to "live in a normal economy." If the debate between socialism and capitalism belongs to a past that is already vanishing, other questions have taken its place—in particular, questions concerning the relation between the market and democracy. Developments in Central Europe, Russia, and China seem to suggest that capitalism and democracy evolve on two distinct planes. For those convinced that capitalism leads necessarily to democracy, the Communist Russian and Chinese leaders are an embarrassment. In these two countries and in Central Asia generally, an authoritarian capitalism is emerging, and no one knows whether it will prove to be a stable form. Must we conclude that the truth is asymmetrical—that capitalism can do without democracy, but that there is no democracy without capitalism?

Readers may be surprised to find a consideration of Turkey among chapters devoted to transition. The reason for its inclusion is that Turkey's earlier stagnation was due to its statist economy, not to its Islamic culture. The Turkish transition from statism to free-market liberalism has produced rapid growth—proof that the market can function in all cultures, and statism in none.

CHAPTER THIRTEEN

The Great Transition

FROM HIS BALCONY overlooking the Danube, János Kornai contemplates what remains of real socialism in Budapest: long blocks of concrete, the Soviet architecture of the 1960s, identical in all the cities that made up the "socialist camp." Before Central Europe's transition toward liberal democracy in 1990, Hungary was not the worst off of the vassal nations. In that camp, Kornai recalls, it had "the happiest barracks." The regime imposed on the Hungarians was known as "goulash socialism," from the name of the national dish. To reduce the temptation to rebel, the government authorized unofficial employment and tiny private businesses. To illustrate how the old system worked, Kornai relates how state-owned businesses made bottles of beer that were hard to open, so that private entrepreneurs could prosper by making openers. Hungary's mixed economy produced a modicum of comfort not found in its sister countries. Yet Hungary was no less a barracks—and no less Communist.

In Kornai's view, there is not—nor can there be, in theory or in practice—any economic system aside from capitalism and socialism. Within each system, one can find national variants, but these never affect the foundations of the particular system. There is thus no third way, such as, for example, "market socialism." One cannot leave socialism without entering capitalism, in other words. No one can remain suspended between the two for long.

Socialism as a System

Kornai has devoted himself to the economic analysis of these two systems and the transition paths between the two. His life as an economist, the most famous of those who remained in the socialist world, is inseparable from the history that he has analyzed and described—better than anyone, because he did so from the inside. How did Kornai survive repression without sacrificing his freedom to think and write? The relatively technical character of his work doubtless protected him. No shortcoming of socialism ever escaped his scalpel, as we will verify, but the censor must not have understood much. Kornai chose not to accept exile, even though American universities courted him as the best economist of socialism. When it was permitted, beginning during the 1980s, he taught at Harvard, but he returned to Hungary to share, as he puts it, the suffering and the memory of his compatriots.

No American or Western European, he says, can truly understand what life was like under the Communist regime; the experience is not transmissible. Another, earlier non-transmissible experience was being forced by the pro-Nazi Hungarian government to wear the yellow star. Was Kornai ever a Communist? In reaction against Nazism, he was for a moment seduced by his country's liberators—a brief idyll. After the massacre of the democratic uprising of 1956, not a single believing Communist remained in Hungary, or, for that matter, in any Central European country. Similarly, in Poland, Lech Wałesa likes to report that he never in his life met a single Polish Communist who was sincere about his beliefs. Yet, as in all the regimes, nomenklaturists were not lacking. Kornai did not collaborate, and he did not rebel; he analyzed. And he did this with a certain taste for paradox. While the socialist camp was crumbling, in 1990, he drafted his major work on socialist economy, *The Socialist System.* A complete view of the socialist economy, he explains, was only possible after the completion of its history. The inability of the last Communist leaders to reform the economy brought validation to his theory of socialism as a system. In a closed system, no element can be modified or removed without the whole system's crumbling. Kornai had long predicted this, without, of course, being able to predict a date for the expiration of the system. He was proved right, as against those who, like Aron, believed that socialism was eternal, as well as those who believed that it was reformable.

The Necessity of Repression

In a socialist system, as is well known, private property is abolished; the state manages all resources and sets prices. Less well known are the consequences. Socialist economies never innovated, because there was no incentive to innovate. Everything in the socialist economy was copied—or stolen—from capitalism. Imitation was an essential cog in the operation of this machine; "spying was not a choice but a vital necessity," says Kornai. Similarly, the economic outcomes of socialism were poor, not because of bad management but because it could not be otherwise. As the famous joke has it, in socialism, the state pretends to pay you and you pretend to work. Prices were as artificial as salaries. On this point, Kornai confirms one of Hayek's fundamental criticisms, which makes it possible to understand why a centralized economy can never function optimally. To set prices, Hayek wrote, a centralized state would require perfect knowledge of the desires and behaviors of all individuals at a given moment and would have to be able to predict their future behavior and desires. Even if equipped with the most powerful computer in the world, no state could manage this unlimited amount of data, which are also, for the most part, unavailable to it; the state would have to be God. Hayek called this myth of an omniscient state a "fatal conceit," and he saw in it the congenital defect of utopian socialism. Socialism was a make-believe world.

And yet the socialist economy produced goods. The socialist camp had industrialized, and objectively speaking, its people lived better than in the past. But this appeared as progress only compared with the past, not with capitalism. It was thus essential to the socialist system that information not circulate and that the press be censored and travel prohibited. An isolated Russian worker could see that he lived better than his parents under the czars, while remaining ignorant of the fact that he lived less well than an American worker of his generation. This socialist worker was also ignorant of the considerable price that he paid for his country's industrialization. His buying power was almost nothing, and the rare consumer products were distributed to those who stood in line and as special favors. Penury and standing in line, so characteristic of the socialist system, were not accidents or the results of management errors, but the very principles of socialist management.

Considering the sacrifices of the population, the results of the socialist economy were disappointing. On a scale from one to 100, Kornai gives socialism a 50 and capitalism a 90, understanding that no system functions perfectly. The socialist system, according to Kornai, fulfilled the "vegetative" functions of the economy, like a large body that vegetates. To perform these functions, repression was essential—without military-style discipline, the socialist economy could not have functioned. It was not, therefore, Stalin or Mao Zedong who perverted the good Communist model, as some in the West believed. Without Stalin, Mao, or their equivalents, Kornai maintains, the system could not have functioned. Tyranny was intrinsic to it. This tyranny could take different forms—Kádár in Hungary was more tolerant than Stalin, and Castro less than Ceauçescu—but the military imperative of the system limited these differences. This is what Gorbachev himself did not understand.

The Elusive "Third Way"

During the 1980s, because it had become technically impossible to control information, and because the objective shortfall of the socialist system compared with the capitalist system had become clear to everyone, from the lowliest worker to the summit of the state, socialist leaders were swept up in a spirit of reform. Between 1950 and 1980, the average growth rate in the West was three times higher than in the East, and it was no longer possible to hide this fact. Among the reformers, Gorbachev was emblematic, but a number of theorists preceding him had recommended introducing market mechanisms into the socialist system without renouncing the state ownership of property. This market socialism, or third way, very favorably viewed in the East as well as the West during the 1970s, presupposed, as Kornai says, that economics was a shopping mall where one could select the most advantageous products: full employment along with market efficiency, equality along with innovation, public ownership along with democracy. But the economy is not a supermarket; it is a system, as the failure of perestroika would demonstrate.

Kornai maintains that Gorbachev committed two irreparable errors. The first was to liberate both information and—even more consequential—prisoners. The whole socialist camp suddenly discovered that it had been conned. Gorbachev had not grasped the extent to which censorship and military discipline sustained the system. The second error was to believe that the market and state ownership were compatible. In the absence of competition and the profit motive, directors of state-owned enterprises never behaved as if they were directors of private businesses. The director of a state concern can either innovate or not innovate. Unlike in the private sector, he has the choice. If he fails, he can turn to the state, which never terminates a failing public enterprise. State ownership effectively prevents the creative destruction that Joseph Schumpeter showed to be the motor of capitalist efficiency. In the USSR, no enterprise ever disappeared. Industry was like a museum, with each new layer superimposed on the last; new techniques were added to old ones without ever replacing them. If socialism is one system, capitalism is another, with its own internal coherence: private property, competition, and freedom of prices and of transactions.

Gorbachev in Russia, the Solidarity movement in Poland, Pope John Paul II, the Hungarian socialists, Václav Havel—all had initially hoped to replace the socialist system with market socialism. The European socialist Left shared this dream as well. How was the illusion finally dispelled? Do certain theorists—Kornai in Hungary, Leszek Balcerowicz in Poland, Yegor Gaidar in Russia—deserve credit for dismantling it? Or Jeffrey Sachs, who rushed over from Harvard University to advise the new leaders in the East? Or Michel Camdessus, the influential director of the International Monetary Fund, who helped convince the pope of the morality of the market economy? Maybe common sense carried the day. By then, there were enough private entrepreneurs who had emerged spontaneously in the socialist camp and wanted nothing more, as Polish Solidarity member Tusk said, than to "live in a normal economy."

The myth of market socialism still has not totally disappeared. It is diminished, as Kornai notes, but it has found refuge, for understandable moral reasons, in the niches of health and education. In the now-dominant capitalist system, it is hard to accept that health and education should be left to private property and to the market. Everywhere there are attempts, with uneven results, to reconcile the irreconcilable, efficiency with centralization. The predictable consequences are like those of the old socialist system: mediocre productivity, penury, standing in lines, and distribution by favors. Depending on national cultures, education and health may tend more toward state control or more toward the market, but no government and no economist can claim to have found the right way. Doubtless it does not exist. Education and health, to varying degrees, are condemned to the gray zone of market socialism: neither entirely just nor entirely efficient. Kornai concludes that economic systems are always imperfect, paralyzed by social pathologies. The role of the economist is to recommend the least murky of all systems, the one that at least makes it possible to choose the evils to be suffered.

Chinese Capitalism

Does the Chinese experience invalidate Kornai's thesis that no economic system exists apart from socialism and capitalism? If by a capitalist economy one means the dominance of private property, the setting of prices by the market, and open competition, then the Chinese Communist Party has clearly embraced capitalism, not any third way. The sector under state monopoly is disappearing. If China is not yet capitalist, it is definitely moving in that direction. Our external perspective is merely confused by rhetoric that remains Marxist but refers to a reality that is Marxist no longer.

True, the Communist Party still holds power, though now at the head of a capitalist economy, which makes it a singular case. But capitalism, unlike socialism, can accommodate diverse political regimes. In the twentieth century, capitalism has prospered under dictators (Hitler, Franco, Pinochet) as well as in democracies. No definite relation between capitalism and democracy is empirically demonstrable. Whereas tyranny is essential to the socialist system, democracy does not appear to be inherent in the capitalist system, at least in the short term. In the long term, we see capitalism tending toward democracy, though the causality connecting the two appears neither necessary nor automatic.

This dissociation explains why Russia became capitalist even as it distanced itself from democracy. With or without political pluralism, it remains the case that the new Russian economy, like the new Chinese economy, is capitalist. Neither has anything to do with a so-called market socialism.

Socialism's Seven Veils

The seduction that the socialist system exercised on good minds in the capitalist world remains a mystery. But it is important, says Kornai, to distinguish different periods. During the 1930s, when capitalism was in crisis, the Soviet economy was effective, as long as we take growth as the sole criterion. At that time, propaganda, a lack of information, and the naïveté of Western visitors played up the visible successes of socialist industry while concealing the system's actual workings. After World War II, the socialist system was again able to advertise itself as more desirable than capitalism, which had been linked with Nazism and fascism. Meanwhile, the Gulag was almost invisible, at least until Khrushchev's report and the repression of the Budapest uprising in 1956. Clueless Westerners confused the visible with the real; failing to understand the systemic character of socialism, they imputed the failures of an economy they considered essentially just to the personal aberrations of Stalin or Mao. The absolute incompatibility between a socialist economy and democratic pluralism was lost on them. Their mistake was to believe that socialism was perfectible, when in fact it was unchangeable.

Beyond this imaginary effectiveness of socialism, many Westerners found themselves seduced by a number of the system's real features: full employment, equality, and the power of workers. By definition, there was no unemployment in the socialist camp. Though labor was inefficient, it was much in demand because it was poorly paid. This strong demand conferred real influence on industrial workers, even if the suffering that they endured to exercise it was considerable. At the same time, a certain equality obtained. Socialist workers were poor, but were poor together. The nomenklatura had privileges, but these were modest compared with those of rich capitalist bosses. For someone satisfied to observe the visible face of the socialist system without uncovering its real workings, the seduction was understandable. But this seduction appealed to intellectuals above all, Kornai observes. The Western intelligentsia believed—and still believes—that the capitalist system rewards them poorly for their talents. The socialist system, by contrast, accords class privileges to intellectuals. Of course, they must serve the regime; but this detail was mostly ignored until Solzhenitsyn's revelations. After Solzhenitsyn, it became difficult not to know. It is rare, Kornai points out, for intellectuals to love the society in which they live. Whatever utopia presents itself always seems preferable to their daily misery.

Shock Therapy

How does one go from socialism to capitalism? The challenge that confronted the Communist camp in 1990 was without historical precedent. No established method existed, so economists had to invent from the whole cloth an approach that might work. It was hard to say who owned the businesses that existed in a Communist system: the state or the people. If the people were the owners, as per Marxist rhetoric, how could the businesses be returned to them? Two schools faced off. The gradualists, led by Kornai, suggested a progressive auction of the state sector to private investors. This recommendation was followed in Hungary with a result that Kornai did not anticipate: Foreign investors, who proved to be the most numerous and the richest, were able to buy public enterprises.

Outside Hungary, "shock therapy" won out over gradualism. The Czech economist Václav Klaus, who later succeeded Václav

Havel as president of the Czech Republic, initiated a voucher system. Because the socialist economy had been built upon the exploitation of citizens, Klaus concluded that all businesses rightly belonged to the people. Every citizen should therefore receive a voucher that he or she could use to buy privatized businesses, in whole or in part. Klaus was less concerned with the economic efficiency of this redistribution than with making an irreversible rupture with the Communist past. But he failed to foresee how weak the citizens' desire to become stockholders would be—and this proved the case with the Russians, too, who adopted the same method. Most citizens resold their vouchers to investment funds, often created by former Communist bureaucrats. With these funds, the managers of businesses acquired their workers' vouchers and thus appropriated the entire old production apparatus at a low price. What had been conceived as a means of democratic restitution turned into a free-for-all. Great fortunes were made, as happens in every revolution.

Looking back, what should we make of "shock therapy"? In Kornai's view, it became a source of social and economic disorder that could have—and should have—been avoided. He holds responsible those experts who rushed over from the United States, Sachs in particular. Sachs was a convincing advocate of shock therapy but was completely ignorant of local circumstances. In Prague, however, Klaus isn't so hard on his own record. Given the priority of breaking with the Communist system, shock therapy, he argues, created an irreversible situation at a time when victory for the capitalist camp was not assured. As for Russia, we will see that the author of instant privatization, Yegor Gaidar, justified his choice at the time by the necessity of getting closed factories back into operation. The new bosses may have been thieves, but they were bosses—and industry got going again, thanks to these "oligarchs."

Fifteen years later, from Budapest to Bratislava, Warsaw to Moscow, the great controversy over the modes of transition is today merely academic. Whatever path was taken, the Communist system has been replaced wholesale by the capitalist system. No one anticipated the rapidity of this metamorphosis, since socialism seemed so unchangeable and capitalism seemed anchored in a long history, not easily reproducible in such a brief period of time. Around 1990, those who dreamed of capitalism—almost to the same extent as those who wished for market socialism—thought that leaving Communism behind would take a generation. At the time, the notion was invoked of a *homo sovieticus*—a person whose character had been forged by Communism—who would require a long adjustment to liberty and personal responsibility. This pessimism proved unfounded because the Communist system was abnormal and because liberal democracy better reflects human nature. *Homo sovieticus* behaved like a free man from the moment he escaped his chains.

Another prophecy of the times, a cousin of *homo sovieticus,* also turned out to be false. Would it not take years, people asked in 1990, for Eastern Europeans to overcome their passivity and become active entrepreneurs? Here again, the power of normality was underestimated. As soon as people got their rights, they went about catching up—eager to participate as soon as possible in the lifestyle and materialism of Western Europe. Neither Sovietized in their heads nor passive in their economic behavior nor guinea pigs of some imaginary third way, Eastern Europeans spontaneously returned to their previous condition, that of Europeans like any others. The Communist system had been a horrible historical accident, in no way the crucible of a new humanity.

It is also notable that the poorest of these Eastern Europeans have been the most determined to make up for lost time: The growth rate in Poland, Slovakia, and the Baltic states (8 percent, on average, since 2001) is much higher than that of Hungary (around 4 percent over the same period) or the Czech Republic, because the former were starting from further back, whereas the economies of the latter were more mature. It is hard to read without smiling the economic literature of the 1990s, which condemned Poland in particular to prolonged poverty because it was

"Catholic, peasant, and socialist." Since 1990, per-capita income in Poland has doubled. Recall that the same culturalist school of thought condemned Korea during the 1950s to poverty because it was Confucian. Culture certainly makes a difference, but the economic system in place determines nations' material destiny more than their beliefs.

A Kind of Disappointment

The great transition that, from the West's viewpoint, appears as a historic miracle evokes, strangely, a kind of disappointment in the East. Kornai himself confesses disappointment in the Hungarians because they are frustrated by capitalism; his compatriots talk about missing the past, though without wishing to return to it. This contradiction is evident in most former socialist countries, but it is most obvious in Hungary. No doubt Hungarian disaffection is a consequence of its less-dramatic transition from the "goulash socialism" of the 1980s to the pure capitalism that took off in the 1990s. There were already a private sector and a certain degree of political freedom in Hungary. For a Romanian or a Bulgarian, for whom things were worse, it is rarer to hear people express longing for the old dictatorship and poverty.

It isn't surprising that in the new system, the losers make more noise than the winners. Those who are prospering, traveling, expressing themselves—all forbidden under socialism—do not boast of their good fortune. Those who have lost their bureaucratic power or who are unemployed, on the other hand, can be counted on to let us know. Another criticism laments the conversion of the Communist nomenklatura into a new capitalist class. Though the assertion is little contested, Kornai believes it has no real foundation. In Hungary, a third of the new economic elites—the big bosses and the nouveaux riches—indeed belonged to the nomenklatura before 1990. But most of them held modest positions. It is reasonable to suppose that this third of reconverted bureaucrats possessed some talent well adapted to the capitalist system. Moreover, two-thirds of the former Communist bureaucrats, including the most powerful, did not make themselves over into triumphant capitalists. This state of affairs generally obtains in all the formerly Communist countries. There was thus no Communist plot that deliberately facilitated the conversion of the nomenklatura. It is simply the case that in all ages, great upheavals produce great fortunes, including in Eastern Europe.

Another theme of disenchantment surprises Kornai: People are disappointed in the European Union. Doubtless many had idealized it, as they did capitalism and democracy. In addition, the European Union was presented, at the time of the referenda on joining it, as a source of subsidies more than as a framework of freedom. Consequently, the freedom is enjoyed as a matter of course, whereas the very significant subsidies are considered insufficient. The Hungarian standard of living remains only one-third that of its Austrian neighbors, with whom Hungarians can now easily compare themselves. Despite European aid, it will probably take a generation for Hungary to make up this difference. The distribution of the European subsidies has also become a source of corruption that adds acrimony to the political climate, especially in Hungary.

Acrimony, corruption, disenchantment: Are these not also the paradoxical proof that Eastern Europe has become normal, riven by the banal contradictions that characterize every Western democracy and every capitalist economy? When I hear that economic controversies in Hungary have to do with the budget deficit and those in Poland with upcoming privatizations, I conclude that everything is working for the least bad possible conditions within the capitalist system. Not everyone in the East remembers what János Kornai remembers. The child with the yellow star who took a position of intellectual resistance has forgotten nothing and rejoices in every second of freedom. For most others, political and economic freedom already seems as natural as the air they breathe. Freedom is most valued when people are deprived of it.

CHAPTER FOURTEEN

The Russian Addiction

THOSE WHO KNEW the Soviet Union before 1991 agree that Moscow is a happier place today. In the old days, the city wore a dark, brooding look. People were poor and afraid, and the ruble was worthless—though there was nothing to buy, anyway. Imperial Moscow boasted two, perhaps three, restaurants, offering meager fare. The only ones to ply a trade were watchmakers, who made their living repairing old watches—a telling sign of the low level of consumption and innovation. Soviet Russia manufactured weapons, and little else.

In just fifteen years, Moscow has been completely transformed. Restaurants, bars, and hotels overflow with people, day and night. Gilded youth and *nouveaux riches* flaunt their wealth and expensive cars. French and Italian luxury goods adorn the shops on Pushkin Square and Tverskaya Street. The roads, once empty save for the occasional official limousine, surge with traffic. The money from oil, gas, and raw materials is flowing freely, driving this revolution. The biggest gainers, those at the top of the pyramid, are the officials, bureaucrats, and merchants who are part of the export network. Prosperity has trickled down, though, and many Russians have benefited. In 2007, median wages rose by more than 25 percent, and the country posted 7-percent growth. Only those living in smaller towns and in the countryside, which still has not recovered from the trauma of agricultural privatization during the 1990s, have been left out, Yegor Gaidar informs me.

Gaidar, Boris Yeltsin's prime minister in 1992 and the architect of Russian privatization, insists that soaring oil and gas prices are not the sole reasons for Russia's economic recovery—indeed, he points out, the recovery began before the long-term trend toward higher oil prices, thanks to the Russian spirit of enterprise and the introduction of the free market. Gaidar famously went in for shock therapy, lightning-swift privatization, rather than gradual change. Russians hold him responsible for the disruptions and poverty of the 1990s, though it is unfair to paint him as a villain. He was just the doctor, summoned to do something for an economy in its death throes. His sale of state assets was an attempt at a cure, not the illness.

People tend to forget that Yeltsin inherited an economy almost wholly dependent on oil. Gaidar reminds me that Russia could feed its people only by importing food in exchange for oil, a choice made in the 1920s after Stalin's collectivization destroyed the country's agriculture. As energy prices plummeted in the 1980s, Mikhail Gorbachev drove the country deep into debt to maintain food-subsistence levels. When Yeltsin came to power in 1991, Russia stood on the brink of famine, in no position to repay its debts. The economy had ground to a halt, and oil production was dwindling. It was only after Gaidar's privatization that production picked up. True, the so-called oligarchs—the well-connected elites of Russia—made a killing, buying state enterprises for a song. Yet they also put the economy back on track. "Their enterprise saved Russia," Gaidar says.

So is Russia truly a market economy? "We're almost there," says Arkady Dvorkovitch, Vladimir Putin's economic advisor. Trained in the United States, Dvorkovitch has become the icon of the new generation in power. "We still do not have an independent judiciary," he admits, "nor do we have genuine rule of law and officials who apply the rules rather than embezzle funds." Suddenly, "almost there" seems quite far off.

No business can function in Russia without official protection, or having a "roof," in local parlance. The protection comes at a price, yet foreign investment has poured in, proof that profits are healthy, corruption notwithstanding. Like Gaidar, Dvorkovitch praises the Russian spirit of enterprise. But once you look beyond restaurants, shops, and real estate, I remark, there's little investment—just 20 percent of national wealth. "It will come. Things are happening very fast," responds Dvorkovitch. The Russians, he claims, are just beginning to have faith in the stability of the new economy; credit based on predictable rules have only just begun. But there is no going back, he maintains: No one wants a return to socialism. As in the West, the debate is about the role of the state in the market system.

Dvorkovitch would like to see greater market autonomy in investment decisions, rather than the state's making so many major investments. Despite all the privatizing of the 1990s, the state is still heavily involved in the economy—and in the energy sector, it has been retaking control from private companies, both Russian and international. The national ventures are hardly role models when it comes to investment strategy. State-run energy giant Gazprom, for instance, finds it more lucrative to invest its money in the financial market than to explore for new reserves or improve its technology. "It will happen," asserts Dvorkovitch yet again. "Putin is keen on investing in new sectors like petrochemicals, food processing, biotechnology, and IT," he adds, doing his best to sound convincing.

Putin may decree, but nothing happens on the ground, according to former finance minister Yevgeny Yasin. The Russian prime minister, he tells me, thought that it was enough to allocate public money for a sector to develop, as if by magic. Putin had yet to realize that in a market economy, development requires an institutional framework. "There can be no major innovation,"

Yasin explains, "as long as there is no rule of law and when entrepreneurs who refuse to kowtow to the establishment risk being put behind bars." Yasin calls the surfeit of oil and gas "the resource curse"; it exonerates both the Russian leadership and the people from thinking about needed reforms.

How long will the oil boom last? There are wild fluctuations in market prices, but the long-term trend will continue to ascend—or that's what the current Russian leadership seems to think. The growth potential of China and India has convinced them that oil prices can only rise further, to Russia's great benefit. When I raise the specter of global warming and the policy response to it, which could result in lower oil and gas consumption, my Russian interlocutors laugh. This is a debate fabricated in the United States, they explain, and it is not taken very seriously by the Indians and Chinese—and in any case, Russian climatologists do not subscribe to the global warming theory. "Hasn't Russia ratified the Kyoto Protocol on the limiting of greenhouse gases?" I ask. Dvorkovitch is dismissive: It was merely a political gesture.

Economist Vladimir Milov belongs to the same generation as Dvorkovitch, but he chose to leave the government on moral grounds. Unable to accept the high-oil-price way of thinking, Milov spoke his mind, a heroic feat under a regime intolerant of criticism. He succeeded in setting up an energy consultancy, which initiates foreign clients into the mysteries of Russian politics. "Marxism is very useful in understanding the political life and ideological development of Russia," Milov observes, aware of the irony. According to Marxism, the economic base determines the ideological superstructures. When Putin took office in 1999, Milov points out, energy prices were low, and the president happily adopted a liberal line and left things to civil society. But as soon as energy prices began to rise, and it appeared that they would continue rising for a long time, Putin started renationalizing parts of the economy, taking over the media, and restoring to the bureaucracy and the FSB (formerly the KGB) all their old powers.

Oil may have propped up the Russian economy, but no market can stay on a rising curve forever, Milov concludes. Eventually, prices fall. As things stand, Russia will not be able to cope. The sale of oil and gas brings in $150 billion every year; arms sales, a mere $6 billion. Is the oil boom a new Russian curse, or a restoration of national sovereignty? Moscow's youth lives it up. But some Russians believe that the KGB has never really left the dreaded Lubyanka, the city's dark heart.

In 1991, the people pulled down the statue of Felix Djerzhinsky, the founder of the KGB. Since then, it has lain on its side in the courtyard of Moscow's Museum of Modern Art, corroded and covered with weeds. In the same museum, a retrospective is devoted to Oleg Kulik, a video artist who epitomizes the new Russian art. Kulik became famous after he walked naked on the streets of Moscow, wearing only a necklace, barking or jumping on passersby to lick or bite them. "Today," Kulik says, "Russian artists have complete freedom to do what they want—provided that they don't criticize Putin or the Orthodox Church."

Thus Moscow today: newly prosperous, but only partly free—and completely addicted to oil and gas.

CHAPTER FIFTEEN

The Truth about China

THERE ARE AT LEAST TWO Chinas: one real, one mythical. First the Jesuit pioneers in the seventeenth century, then the Enlightenment philosophers, and now our contemporary businessmen—Western travelers have continually idealized China, imagined the Chinese as essentially different from themselves, and believed that nothing in China is similar to anything in the West. The Chinese do not aspire to freedom as we do, in this view. The tyranny exercised in an earlier day by the mandarins, or today by the Communist Party, is the regime most naturally adapted to the desires of the Chinese. These are so many platitudes, perpetuated in Europe and in the United States. In reality, the Chinese have revolted both against their emperors (in a republican revolution in 1911) and against the Communist Party (in Tiananmen Square in 1989). Unconditional Sinophiles in the West should be worried.

Real China and Mythical China

The growth rate of the Chinese economy, measured at 10–11 percent since 1990 and at 8 percent in 2008, has reinforced the

Sinophiles' prejudice, as if Japan, Korea, and Taiwan, when they took off, had not achieved comparable, or even superior, results. In 2008, India also achieved 9 percent growth without evoking the same amazement. How should we view this Western captivation with the Chinese economy? No doubt it is part of a long history of fascination with enlightened despotism. The Chinese model of capitalism without democracy does not displease Western investors, some heads of state, and even certain intellectuals. And apart from this willing Sinophilia, we should recognize the great talent of the Chinese authorities in dealing with the simple-minded, whether by seduction or corruption.

Still, there is the real China, which is harder to reach than the official statistics, the victory bulletins of the Communist Party, and the dazzling hotels of Beijing and Shanghai. It is all the harder to find trustworthy interlocutors in China, since most qualified economists work for the government. Any critical intellectuals are likely to wind up in prison or in exile—and in exile, an economist can quickly lose contact with an on-the-ground reality that changes rapidly.

Luckily, there is Mao Yushi, an independent economist, a lover of truth, and the founder of the only research institute in Beijing not linked to the Communist Party; he is old enough to be indifferent to police harassment. Mao Yushi does not hide his preference for a market economy, since, as he says, it is the only one that works. The observations that follow are essentially the result of our long conversations in Beijing over the last few years, as well as my extended stays in China from the time of Mao Zedong's rule to the present. Beyond Mao Yushi, it is a remarkable historical event that the largest country in the world, under the guidance of a Party that tried to reinvent economics from scratch in the 1960s, has admitted that, after all, there is only one economic system that works: the market economy.

A Success, Not a Miracle

As he approaches his eightieth birthday, it seems doubtful that Mao Yushi, who lives modestly in a dilapidated apartment in the center of Beijing, could shake the powerful Chinese government. Yet he is surprised to be under surveillance by government security agents; like a good economist, he has calculated the absurdly high cost of the surveillance, a complete waste of public spending. The officers in civilian clothing, who sometimes forbid him to leave his apartment for weeks at a time and take photos of his visitors, seem themselves to have no illusions about the usefulness of their assignment. But Mao Yushi does not think correctly—that is, as everyone in China is supposed to think. He is thus treated as what the jailed democrat Hu Jia of Beijing called a VIT: a Very Important Troublemaker.

Mao Yushi's main activity is consulting the official statistics of the Chinese government. This seems innocent enough, since the statistics are published and accessible to everyone. But Mao Yushi enjoys comparing and analyzing the numbers to expose their contradictions and inconsistencies. This is an old tradition. During the 1960s, the Party published absurd production numbers that proclaimed the victories of the regime over the most elementary laws of economics. Though the days of the "great leap forward" have passed and the government has become more rational, it retains habits from the old days. Mao Yushi notes, for example, that China announces its yearly unemployment rate at the *beginning* of the year. A ridiculously low rate, typically about 3 percent, it is a hope rather than a result. The figure takes no account of rural underemployment, or of the millions of migrants who wander from one construction site to another, or of the graduates of mediocre universities who wait several years before finding a job that matches their education. The growing number of Chinese graduates leaves many China-watchers in awe. But they tend not to look too closely at the quality of the degrees granted by

Chinese universities, or at the mismatch between this new army of lumpen intelligentsia and Chinese employers, who are in greater need of manual workers than (fairly) well-educated students.

The published growth rate is just as debatable. Until recently, it seems to have hovered at around 10–11 percent a year; but every country that is moving from an unproductive rural economy to rapid industrialization attains that level of growth. Moreover, since China is a latecomer to industrialization, it can take shortcuts, benefiting from production and management techniques that the rest of the world has already tested. Finally, China is lucky. Since the global growth rate has been about 5 percent since the beginning of the twenty-first century, at least until the 2008 downturn, Chinese industries have astutely tapped into heightened worldwide demand.

Mao Yushi also believes that it makes sense to deduct the costs of irremediable environmental destruction—that destroyed forests, polluted waters, and the unbreathable atmosphere should figure as a deduction from the growth rate, which he estimates at a more reasonable 8 percent. This growth is still healthy, but much of it is due to a period of catching up after an earlier phase, namely Maoism, when growth was zero or negative. When you start from zero, you progress faster.

The growth rate is thus satisfactory without being spectacular, but it is not enough to lift China out of poverty. In volume, owing to its population, China is the third-largest producer in the world, but per capita, it is only the 101st. We need to consider the content of this Chinese production as well as its volume. The economy functions mainly as a workshop for assembling and finishing. It imports in order to reexport, and its value-added is a matter only of intermediate manufacturing. In the circuit of globalization, China furnishes cheap labor; its advantage derives essentially from the exploitation of a bottomless reservoir of almost a billion peasants.

This is not to deny the quality of Chinese businesses. The workmanship, though poorly paid, is expert, and management is generally effective. But most of the businesses that make up the great Chinese workshop could not function without what is brought from the outside by an outstanding network of intermediaries. Initially, these were overseas Chinese, often based in Hong Kong; now they are everywhere in mainland China as well. The intermediaries provide foreign investors with anything they require to manufacture in China, from land to workers, from energy to help cutting through bureaucratic red tape. Without this mediation—a decisive advantage for China over India in attracting massive foreign investments—the Chinese model of development would not work. From outside China come orders, techniques, capital, and often management: Chinese from overseas, from Hong Kong and from Taiwan, followed by Koreans, Japanese, and Westerners.

The reason for China's relative success is thus no mystery and by no means miraculous: China is a skillful subcontractor, to its own great advantage and to that of those whose orders it takes. What comes to us labeled "Made in China" is only rarely invented in China. Often, the product is conceived in the United States, Europe, or Japan, improved in South Korea or Taiwan, and then merely finished in China, which reexports it. As Columbia University economist Shang-Jin Wei has demonstrated, assembling high-tech products does require a reliable workforce. But it does not transform China into a high-tech economy. The innovation still comes from abroad.

The ubiquitous iPod is a perfect illustration of China's role in the distribution of tasks through the global economy. When the average retail price of an iPod on the global market hovers around $150, the Chinese contribution to that price is around $4, mostly in assembling and packaging. Such an amount may look trivial, but multiplied by millions of units, it is not trivial, at least for the Chinese economy. With lower-technology products, like textiles, the Chinese input can reach 80 percent of the world price. Economic journals in the U.S. frequently mention that the value of Chinese exports is steadily growing; this is undeniable, but the value-added needs to be compared with the higher value of imports.

Further, a large portion of Chinese exports, perhaps as much as one-third, is produced by foreign businesses set up in China.

The trade imbalance between China and the West, if one deducts the profits of these foreign businesses, is less significant than it seems. The American economist Marc Chandler estimates that if one took into account the amount that American businesses import into China only in order to reexport after assembly, the United States' trade deficit with China would in reality be two-thirds smaller than it looks. China did not invent a new economy, argues Mao Yushi. If it is working well, it is because the times have been, until recently, favorable. Good economics is also a matter of good luck. China's remaining a low-tech subcontractor will pose no threat to the American economy.

Thanks to the Party?

To what extent is the Chinese government, the Communist Party, the author of this economic model? Does it deserve credit? The Chinese generally thank the Party for China's economic successes, and non-Chinese are even more sycophantic. It is true that the Party, after ruining China between 1949 and 1979, has reestablished the conditions of a normal economic life. Order was the first of these conditions. Without the civil peace that the Party enforces in China with a strong hand, there would be no development. After banishing the pursuit of wealth for fifty years, moreover, the Party now encourages it. It is once again permissible in China to work in order to make money. Indeed, this is the only authorized and encouraged activity. We see that the Chinese have the same aspirations as other peoples. From the poor peasant to the dynamic entrepreneur, everyone wants to improve his lot and that of his children. The *homo economicus* is a universal being, found in all civilizations.

The Party has also admitted one of the fundamental tenets of free-market theory: Rational investment is impossible without private property. How to reconcile Marxist ideology with respect for private property? This uneasy shift has been implemented in the most pragmatic manner, not by legalizing private property but rather by not confiscating private firms. During the early 1980s, private entrepreneurs, whether they were well connected with party officials or party officials themselves, started small businesses geared toward exports, mostly in the remote provinces far from Beijing. The Party turned a blind eye as the entrepreneurs drew some private profits out of these new firms. By not reacting, it encouraged larger companies to follow suit. Industrial and commercial property have therefore become a fact of life, in circumvention of the ideological contradiction between Marxism and capitalism.

Let us therefore praise the Party for letting the Chinese work, and for understanding the simple mechanisms of the market economy. We should also give it credit for rigorously managing the money supply after decades of inflation. This rigor encourages the creation of businesses and commercial transactions. (At this level, it is as if the Chinese Communists had fully adopted the teachings of Milton Friedman—in fact, with more rigor than the U.S. Federal Reserve.) Massive public investments, sometimes excessively concentrated in infrastructure—roads, ports, airports, energy—have contributed to the effectiveness of Chinese production.

But then there are all the things that do not work, and about which one hears little, such as the gigantic public sector that employs half the industrial labor force. This relic of socialism survives thanks to bank loans that are never reimbursed and that mask the failure of obsolete businesses. And the Party has carried to an extreme an abuse for which capitalism was always blamed: the exploitation of manual workers.

Exploited Peasants

As Karl Marx and Friedrich Engels explained in their day, the Industrial Revolution in the West was accompanied by the reduction of the peasantry to a proletariat. However, in Europe, as in the United States, Japan, and Korea, this exploitation of manual labor, however brutal, was tempered by certain social shock absorbers: Charities, churches, unions, newspapers, and parties restrained the voracity of capitalist industries and preserved certain social goods amid the Industrial Revolution. Nothing like this holds true in China. In order to escape his condition of extreme poverty, the Chinese peasant has hardly any choice but to turn himself over to the bosses of either public or private enterprises. These bosses are not sensitive souls, and they pay as little as possible. Sometimes they do not pay at all, and they give no rights to their workers. In China, the only unions are the official ones, strikes are taboo, and workers' rights are minimal. From time to time, the foreign press, and even sometimes the Chinese press, denounces the brutal treatment of workers, which is close to slavery. The government then displays its indignation and promises the strict application of social legislation—which already exists on paper, mostly for the benefit of softhearted foreigners. The Chinese government reacts only to threats of Western boycotts; otherwise, it is immovable. Chinese workers' real protectors are in the West. Beijing cannot allow foreign orders and foreign capital to get away.

On the worksites where itinerants build the infrastructure that the world admires, the fate of migrants is more lamentable than in the factories. This exploitation, in the Marxist sense, of Chinese peasants is facilitated by demography—the reserve army of the proletariat is inexhaustible. Legislation encourages exploitation, for peasants do not have the same rights as city dwellers. Their origin dictates their fate—an origin stamped in the identity papers *(hukou)* that make them totally dependent on their employers. Their *hukou* forbid them from finding lodging in a city without authorization, from securing medical care, and from sending their children to school.

Occasionally, the Party announces the suppression of the *hukou,* but without effect, because power relations in China play to the advantage of the exploiters, not the exploited. The latter have no right to expression, nor do they have political influence. Their protests may be constant, but they wind up brutally repressed. It is, paradoxically, their number that is their weakness: About 20 million industrial jobs get created each year, but there remain some 700 to 800 million poor peasants in China, of whom 300 million make less than $1 a day, the threshold of poverty as the World Bank defines it. The reserve army of the proletariat is thus not close to drying up. Wages will remain low, and the pressure on the unskilled workers who turn the wheels of Chinese production will remain extreme. Mao Yushi observes that there are a few bottlenecks where labor is scarce and wages can suddenly increase. But this increase is always in the province of Canton, where the density of factories motivates bosses to bid for workers who are already qualified. This is an exception in China and will long remain so. The size of China's reservoir of workers slows its progress from being a cheap labor–based economy to being a more knowledge-based one. Entrepreneurs have little incentive to innovate, since they feel no pressure from rising wages or other worker-related demands. The current global downturn has revealed how fragile the Chinese model is. As it totally depends on cheap labor and exporting the goods produced by that labor to the West, the slightest decrease in Western basic consumption brings Chinese factories to their knees.

Winners and Losers

Who has gained from China's high growth rate? How, Mao Yushi asks, can China be so rich (the state holds $1 trillion in reserve) and the Chinese so poor?

At the top of the country is a prosperous ruling oligarchy made up, essentially, of the leaders of the Communist Party, the military, and their families. Some have become heads of businesses, either through their connections or by taking over businesses that once belonged to the state. More often than entrepreneurship, the sources of their wealth are sinecures and extortion. One can do very little in China without obtaining administrative authorization, which requires payments to officials up and down the party ladder. Since China does not respect the rule of law, Mao Yushi observes, and since property rights aren't clearly established, law becomes "personalized"—an expression of servility toward the Party. The proof of the great productivity of Chinese businesses, Mao Yushi observes with irony, is that despite this general regime of extortion, Chinese and foreigners continue to invest there. For the victims of this corruption are, ultimately, not so much the bosses who are shaken down as the wage earners at the bottom of the ladder and the world consumers to whom these costs are passed on.

China's so-called middle class—some 200 million people whose standard of living and aspirations converge with those of Westerners—does not constitute a true middle class, maintains Mao Yushi. Its prosperity derives not from its work but from its strategic situation and the system of extortion. Most are Party members who maintain family or client relations with political power. The name "society of parvenus" would suit them better than "middle class." Notwithstanding the illusions of Western political scientists, we should not expect this pseudo–middle class to demand the democratization of the regime, since if the Party lost power or China evolved toward the rule of law, it would be the first victim. In a democracy, the peasants and the workers would claim their due. (There is, adds Mao Yushi, an authentic middle class in China, according to Western criteria of professional qualification and economic autonomy, of some 30 million people: professionals, tradesmen, and entrepreneurs.)

To this critique, let me add a few nuances based on personal observation. The relative losers in the new Chinese economy are indeed the peasants, but a few crumbs of growth nonetheless reach the most remote villages. The prosperous urban population's demand for food products has raised agricultural prices; certain conveniences—televisions, electricity, telephones—are penetrating deep into China; and roads facilitate agricultural producers' capacity to reach urban markets, which pay more than the traditional local intermediaries. It is expected that at least one member of each family will leave to work on a construction site or, better still, get a steady job in industry. The portion of wages that these migrants send back to their villages represents a considerable monetary increase for these communities, which otherwise remain in a subsistence economy.

It is also true that the Communist Party has recently reduced the fiscal burdens on rural regions, which, since the time of Mao Zedong, had financed the forced march of industrialization on the Stalinist model. Still, crushing rural poverty remains, with emigration the only hope. The frequent absence of elementary schools, the complete absence of medical clinics, and still more, the lack of income, lock the villages into a hopelessness that one seldom finds in other poor countries, such as India. The tyranny of the Party makes it impossible for the peasants to express grievances. Mutiny remains the only outlet when the extortion of apparatchiks becomes unbearable. No surprise, then, that during the 1980s, millions of peasants were reduced to selling their blood—a business that lasted into the present decade, even as the AIDS epidemic was decimating whole villages, especially in the poor province of Henan.

This poverty, rarely perceived by foreigners who do not venture far into the countryside, is also underestimated by the residents of the cities; urbanites do not visit the country, or are indifferent to the "provincials." But the central government knows. For the Communist Party, it has become a ritual to bemoan the poverty of peasants and to wish for a more just and "harmonious" society. This rhetoric has had little concrete effect. The Party Congress of 2007 announced prominently that the government would support the creation of rural elementary schools—a fine plan that implicitly acknowledged that, until then, few existed. (Before this Seventeenth Congress, official propaganda had declared that all Chinese children were schooled.)

The Necessary Exodus

One might propose a Marxist explanation for this abandonment of the countryside: Economic interests dictate the Party's attitude. From top to bottom, public funds are siphoned off by manufacturing interests and directed as far as possible toward exports, for this course is in the interest of Party members. Why would one invest in schools or clinics when that would bring no immediate profit and risk raising the consciousness of the masses? The Party isn't elected and does not owe its power to the people. It only fears the people's anger.

For this subject, Mao Yushi proposes a different analysis, which borrows from development theory. He thinks that the real remedy for rural poverty is an exodus from the countryside and that this is progressing too slowly. Some 100 million peasants have left the countryside over the last ten years, which, for a population the size of China's, is insufficient. The creation of 20 million urban jobs a year is also insufficient, since it would take forty years to bring the rural population down to a level commensurate with the labor supply required by agriculture.

This necessary rural exodus is impeded by the absence of property rights for land. Local governments grant a lease for life to the peasant families that work the land—but they can neither buy nor sell it. This public appropriation of land freezes all progress in agricultural productivity: One cannot invest in land that one does not own, since no bank will give credit without a mortgage. And what is the point of investing in something that the Party grants and can take back, as it has done in the past? For the migrant who leaves for the city, this land is a safe harbor; it serves as his social insurance, and it discourages him from definitively adopting the urban life. But, Mao Yushi reminds us, a rural exodus is an inevitable stage in economic progress—an iron law of development. Such an exodus would require the privatization of land holdings, which would allow for their more rational consolidation and exploitation. For the Party, however, this would mean renouncing its ultimate dogma and its main means of putting pressure on 800 million Chinese. The Party is thus caught in a dilemma: If land is privatized, peasant exploitation will cease and the Party's profit will diminish; if land is not privatized, the income gap between the rural areas and the cities will increase, generating more unrest.

Looking for a third way, the Chinese government is now inclined to grant peasants the right to lease their land and to use it as collateral for mortgage credit. The Party therefore understands the root of the peasant's poverty. Will it go as far as to embrace privatization, acknowledging the necessity for private property as a condition for further development? A reform of the political system, improbable at present, would be the necessary precondition for such a modernization.

Rising Dangers

Is political reform conceivable? Is the current Chinese model durable? In economic terms, it is unlikely that Chinese growth can continue if China limits itself to being the world's workshop. This unsophisticated economic activity will eventually meet competition from other countries where costs are lower still, especially India. Thus the future modernization of China will only be made possible by following the Korean or Taiwanese model, that is, by incorporating a greater value-added than manual labor alone. Some Sinophiles believe that we are witnessing this evolution, noting that Chinese industry is moving into automobile manufacturing and biotechnology. But large-scale innovation has been slow in coming because the conditions for it are absent.

If Japan and Korea made the transition from the workshop to the postindustrial economy, it was because manual labor began to be scarce. China seems far from that situation. But Shang-Jin Wei is more upbeat than Mao Yushi on this subject. Wei thinks that the number of peasants is much smaller than official statistics indicate because of the industrialization of the countryside. Small factories are cropping up everywhere in China, even in the most remote rural areas. Despite their remoteness, they link to the global market via the network of intermediaries mentioned earlier. Perhaps the industrialization of inner China has advanced further than we think and the pressure for higher wages, which in turn will spur more innovation, could exert itself sooner than Mao Yushi predicts. This remains an open debate.

But right now, the absence of true legal property rights (apart from lodging, which the middle class greatly appreciates) discourages risk-taking industrial ventures. Chinese citizens prefer foreign investment or investment in real estate. Long-term investment in China is mainly the work of foreigners. The lack of protection for intellectual property produces an incentive for piracy, which might be profitable in the short term but does not encourage Chinese creativity. Is this a passing phase? Japan and Korea went through the copying stage and got past it. However, in China, the dominant sentiment in the press and the universities is that intellectual property is a form of Western imperialism, intended to prevent China's rise.

For Mao Yushi, the major risks are the underemployment of college graduates and the fragility of banks. Much is made of the number of Chinese students, an impressive quantity of gray matter, but Mao Yushi, an iconoclast on the subject, believes that the increase in the number of students and universities reflects a decrease in their quality. Nor is the buying of diplomas by the children of the new bourgeoisie any proof of their quality. In any case, the underemployment of graduates is characteristic of the new urban China, reflecting the mediocrity of degrees and the nonexistence of businesses sufficiently innovative to recruit educated personnel.

In the near term, Mao Yushi fears financial bankruptcy more than he fears a failure to innovate. The banks, which remain state-controlled, make loans as a function of their clients' political influence rather than on the basis of the quality of their projects or their capacity to repay. A number of public enterprises—still the biggest Chinese employers—hang on thanks to loans that hide their virtual failure. Those whose profits would allow them to repay choose not to, preferring to invest the money in real estate or outside China. Chinese banks survive despite these bad debts only because of the abundance of savings. Since the yuan is not convertible, investment possibilities are rare outside real estate and a risky stock market, so the Chinese put their funds in banks, where they earn only mediocre returns. If savers were to withdraw their funds, the banks could not replace them; this has happened regularly in the province of Canton, provoking riots. The Chinese, Mao Yushi observes, may tolerate the deprivation of their freedom, but they would not forgive the Communist Party for losing their savings.

But Mao Yushi does not fear a global crisis provoked by China withdrawing its funds from the United States, or a general slowdown of trade that would affect China. The Chinese economy appears to him too integrated into the global system for the world to withdraw from China or for China to withdraw from the world. Nations have become interdependent, in an international division of labor profitable to all partners. Nor is Mao Yushi betting on a destabilization of the Chinese regime by the frequent riots reported in Western media. Spontaneous and unorganized, without leadership, program, or coordination, these rebellions testify to the malaise of Chinese society, but they do not threaten the Party's dictatorship.

It is true that information now circulates freely in China, especially via the Internet; that the Chinese travel in their country and abroad; and that a civil society is emerging and making more demands. But the Party is in control of the situation through the force that it never hesitates to abuse, and it controls things even more by exploiting the fear of disorder that haunts Chinese memory. After a century of civil wars, the population accommodates itself to injustices as long as the Party appears to be the guardian of order. Better injustice than disorder—this could be the motto of Chinese Communism. But for how long? In 2008, thousands of children died in the Sichuan earthquake, the victims of corrupt Party officials who used shoddy materials in school buildings, which instantly collapsed. Parents who intended to sue the government received hush money. The same year, thousands of babies were poisoned by a milk powder deliberately laced with melamine to increase its apparent protein content and generate more profit. This lack of ethical standards, probably a consequence of the Maoist Cultural Revolution combined with the insatiable greed of Party officials, could someday provoke a spontaneous revolution in the name of justice and morality.

Demographic Uncertainty

There is one final risk that is hard to measure because it is without historical precedent: the demographic, economic, and social effects of China's one-child policy. Since the 1970s, the government has mandated the ferocious repression of parents on the pretext that there were too many Chinese. This demographic tyranny is perplexing. What are the true motives behind it? Thirty or forty years ago, certain economists, echoing the Malthusian theories of the early nineteenth century, believed that people were poor when they were too numerous and that reducing the birthrate was a precondition of development. But this theory proved incorrect; thanks to innovation, agricultural production has grown continually over the last century, more rapidly than the world's population. Moreover, all developing countries have undergone a spontaneous demographic transition from large to small families. History has shown that this demographic transition is not a precondition of development but its consequence. But that well-known fact has not dissuaded the Chinese government from pursuing its repressive policy.

Mao Yushi believes that the reasons behind the policy are more political and financial than economic. The agents of family planning profit by controlling the population; to have a second child, one has only to pay them. If one does not pay, these apparatchiks are capable of extreme violence—kidnapping women, sterilizing them, forcing them to undergo abortions. Though prohibited by law, this is a common practice that the government never punishes.

Even though, in reality, the average number of children per family is not one but close to two, the Chinese population is destined to age and to decrease. Certain harmful consequences of the one-child policy are already evident. In a country where familial community is the only form of social solidarity, aged parents are now abandoned to their own devices. There are neither retirement homes nor pensions, apart from rare exceptions in public enterprises. How will old age henceforth be experienced in China? Probably very badly. In the longer term, how will the Chinese economy manage with a scarce and aging labor force? It is impossible to know, but there is reason to worry.

The End of Despotism

The most uncertain future is that of the Party itself. It is less and less representative of Chinese society. Made up almost exclusively of educated men, without peasants or workers, without women in responsible positions, this party of technocrats is cut off from the people. It does not hear public demands. The muzzled media reflect the desires of the Party and do not mirror—or barely mirror—public opinion. Many conflicts occur among the factions of this party of 16 million members, but in the absence of any democratic procedure within or outside it, factions prevail only by the force of money or with the support of the military. This makes the evolution of the Party and its economic and foreign policy unpredictable. Sinophiles overlook the instability inherent in all despotism because China has benefited from fortunate circumstances since 1979. Mao Zedong's four successors have been fairly rational and relatively enlightened leaders (without forgetting the Tiananmen massacre of 1989). But in a despotic regime, no procedure can guarantee that the next leader will be the same. No one can say that a consensus exists within the Party for the pursuit of economic liberalization or for a peace-loving foreign policy. We can only hope for it, for the sake of the Chinese and for the sake of the rest of the world, which has a great interest in China's prosperity. Anything is conceivable, including the happy evolution of China toward democratic normality.

Mao Yushi, for his part, hopes for it. Though there is a Chinese experience, he does not believe that there is a Chinese model, distinct from the free-market model, that could endure. The alliance between Communist tyranny and unfettered capitalism since 1979 is not a durable model, nor can it be exported to the rest of the world. If we posit that this model corresponds to a certain stage of development, we can say that as long as growth is based on the mobilization of an available supply of unskilled labor for textile and computer factories, the despotism of the Party and of the boss can be effective. It can be effective, for instance, at organizing an Olympic Games or sending an astronaut into space—the Soviet Union could achieve such things as well. By mobilizing public resources and manpower, a military regime can successfully carry out military-style operations—even impoverished North Korea can do that. But to move beyond this stage, toward innovation and personal initiative, seems less likely in the absence of a rule of law guaranteeing property, the security of contracts, and entrepreneurial freedom. The absence of any world-recognized Chinese brands or patents is proof of the current lack of innovative spirit in the country.

The Chinese experience is thus provisional, a moment in Chinese history, not an alternative model to liberal democracy. China is not a challenge to the West as long as it does not provide new economic, behavioral, or ethical norms that could become universal.

CHAPTER SIXTEEN

The Turkish March

ACCORDING TO EVKET PAMUK, understanding Islam is of no use in understanding the economic backwardness of the Ottoman Empire. And it is hardly more useful for interpreting the dynamism of contemporary Turkey. From the University of the Bosporus (Istanbul Strait), where he teaches, Pamuk contemplates Istanbul's two shores, which are called European and Asian. But the names are only symbolic, for this stretch of sea has never separated two continents or two civilizations. For twenty centuries, it has been the site of an intense circulation of men and merchandise, once in boats, now along the great suspension bridges that link the two banks into a single world. Yesterday's Ottoman Empire, like today's Turkey, was never half in Europe and half in Asia, but at once in Europe and in Asia. By choosing what was then called Constantinople as its capital, the Ottomans long ago presented themselves as successors to the Eastern Roman Empire, not to the caliphate of Baghdad; their administration borrowed more from the Roman and Byzantine traditions than from the mythical times of the Prophet.

In any case, it was for convenience, no doubt to control the Middle East better, that the Turks converted to Islam—a conversion that the Arabs of an earlier time, like Arabs today, greeted with little enthusiasm. Turkish Islam has always been distinct from the practices of other Muslim cultures; in particular, it gives a greater role to women than one usually finds in the Arab Muslim world, and it distinguishes between private religion and the public space. The Ottomans erected a state in which the religious authorities were subordinated to the sultan, and modern Turkey, founded in 1921 by Mustafa Kemal, followed the same principle: The state is not officially Muslim but rather was inspired by the French model, with a strong Jacobin overtone. In Turkey, as in France, the secular order prohibits interference from religious authorities. This distinction between the state and Islam, which remained strong from the founding of Turkey until the last years of the twentieth century, has recently blurred, beginning with the demonstration of a certain public piety by the Democratic-Muslim Party (AKP), which came to power in 2002. But Pamuk, himself of a militantly secular tradition and culturally but not religiously Muslim, believes that the Turkish state is no more on its way to Islamization today than it was previously. The dominant character of the state, first Ottoman and then Turkish, has always been more bureaucratic than religious. It is bureaucratic excesses, claims Pamuk, that have been the obstacles to development; it is bureaucratic inertia, not Islam, that explains the Ottomans' lagging behind Western Europe.

Since the fourteenth century, the levels of wealth of these two civilizations have diverged, with wages (or the equivalent) progressing in Western Europe (more notably in the northwest than in the southeast) but stagnating in the East. The reasons have to do with the organization of Ottoman society.

Islam Exonerated

When Max Weber attempted to explain the divergence of nations, in the case of the Ottomans, he incriminated Islam. But

Weber and his disciples keep getting it wrong; their idealist school has used religion to explain, one after the other, the incapacity of Catholics, Confucians, and Buddhists for progress. Southern Europe, Korea, China, and India keep proving them wrong and invalidating their theory. There remains Islam, the last bastion of this culturalist version of economics. But is it not paradoxical to link Islam with poverty and Christianity with prosperity? The Koran praises commerce and the pursuit of wealth, whereas the Gospels extol poverty. We would do better, argues Pamuk, to investigate the institutions and social structures of the Europeans and the Ottomans.

In the West, sovereigns have traditionally accorded social space to merchants, who have always had an influence on institutions. The most important cities of the West over the last thousand years have been those in which merchants have exercised the greatest influence: Genoa, Venice, Lyon, Amsterdam, and London. A city-by-city comparison makes it possible to measure the direct relation between the autonomy of the bourgeoisie and economic prosperity. This analysis of institutions is now beyond dispute in the case of Europe. For what obscure reasons, then, would it not apply to the East? Why would it make sense to explain everything in the West by institutions and in the East by Islam—especially considering that the Ottomans were concerned only with the exercise of political power, not with religious proselytizing?

The big gap between East and West is a matter of politics. The Ottomans' bureaucratic inclination and Roman heritage led them to keep at a distance any group that might offend them—in particular, merchants. For the same reason, in the Ottoman Empire, the state kept control of land, to prevent the emergence of a landed aristocracy. This authoritarian passion was only reinforced in the nineteenth century, when the Ottomans undertook Europe-inspired reforms in the period known as Tanzimat; this modernization touched only the state. Concerned for his empire, the sultan borrowed administrative and military institutions from the West, but not economic principles.

This preference for the state was reflected in the status that the Ottomans gave to commerce: It was indispensable to the empire but best entrusted to foreigners, Italian or Greek. These groups benefited from a special juridical status and were granted certain exemptions or privileges denied to other subjects of the empire. The Ottoman economy, one might say, was subcontracted to nonresidents.

A State Bourgeoisie

Did everything change with the creation of modern Turkey and the dispersion of the Ottomans? At the outset, no. Mustafa Kemal, infatuated with French culture, borrowed especially its emphasis on the majesty of the state. He took account of the economic backwardness of his country; he knew that Western prosperity was the work of an entrepreneurial bourgeoisie, and it seemed to him that Turkey had no comparable social class. How could such a class possibly have emerged after centuries of marginalization?

Kemal, who was no free-marketer but no socialist either, preferred to create a state bourgeoisie from the top down, a new class of entrepreneurs that he would so designate. This concept was not specific to Turkey during the 1920s; it partly justified the Soviet model, and shows up again in Korea in the 1950s and in China and certain African states today. The idea that it is preferable not to select entrepreneurs but rather to create conditions favorable to their spontaneous emergence has become a universally accepted theory only since the 1980s. Kemal was influenced by the dominant ideas of his time, but he nevertheless introduced a revolutionary rupture in the Middle East. He was the first to recognize that development could not be the work of the state— that only a group distinct from the state could create prosperity. The realization that the state could not do everything brought Turkey into the modern world and separated it from traditional

Middle Eastern societies. For the first time in Turkish history, a truly private economic sector appeared. Under the aegis of these new state entrepreneurs, Turkey industrialized. But it industrialized badly. Until the 1980s, its crony capitalism did not provide incentives for the new Turkish entrepreneurs to make the most judicious choices.

Why was the state bourgeoisie more effective in Korea during the same period? Comparing Asian industrialization with Turkish, Pamuk believes that the gap between the two experiences has to do with distinct administrative cultures. In Asia, we find a certain Confucian rigor and concern for the long term; in Turkey, we find refined corruption and a lack of strategy. Turkish administration is culturally continuous with the Ottoman bureaucracy. Between 1930 and 1980, sheltered by closed borders, Turkish entrepreneurs took no risks and exported nothing. To prosper, it was enough to satisfy current local demand for consumer products. Luckily for these entrepreneurs, domestic consumption progressed rapidly, thanks to Turkish emigrants in the West, who sent most of their income back to their families.

Still, in 1979, Turkey exported only 3 percent of its production. By 2007, that number had jumped to 25 percent! How can a nation go from 3 percent to 25 percent, from archaic industrialization to export-driven dynamism, and from Third World status to being an economic tiger, all in just twenty-eight years?

Free Market, à la Turk

As Pamuk explains, Turkey leaped from one status to the other because it embraced the free-market revolution in 1980. This was the work of the head of government at that time, Turgut Özal. Özal's American experience had shaped him, first as a student and then as an official at the World Bank. Was he akin to Ronald Reagan or Margaret Thatcher? Indeed, Pamuk says, but à la Turk.

To leave the Third World behind, Özal understood that it was necessary to move from protectionism to globalization. But since Turkey was not yet in the West, Özal had recourse to local practices. He subsidized businesses that exported, and he employed the military to control rising salaries, even to break strikes. Faithful to the Turkish-Ottoman tradition of personal power, he neglected to create financial institutions independent of the government. Public spending, clientelism, vote-buying, and subsidies finally ruined the state and plunged the country into inflation to the point of bankruptcy. In 2001, when the IMF responded to the emergency with help for the Turkish state, it forced an end to the public mismanagement and political clientelism of Kemal's economic system.

These troubles finally brought to power the supposedly more rigorous and non-corrupt AKP, but Özal's essential legacy has nevertheless survived. Turkey has become a major economic actor in the global market. What comes next is most surprising: the emergence of "Anatolian Tigers."

The Tigers of Anatolia

The top stratum of Turkish businessmen, which sprang from its closeness to the Kemalist state, is mostly based in the western region of Turkey, near the Sea of Marmara. It is a secular and Westernized class. In the recent flourishing of Turkish exports, this old business class, with the advantage of a solid head start in finance and industry, remains a major factor. It is no longer alone, however. In all the provincial capitals of Anatolia, some dozen cities, there is a new wave of industrialists who have turned to exports. Their comparative advantage over already established businesses in the global market derives essentially from the Anatolian backcountry's low salaries and lack of social rights. Industrial techniques remain primitive and products unsophisticated. In textiles and household appliances, most of these enterprises are in competition with Chinese producers. However, rather than confronting the Chinese head-on, the Anatolians select niches and specialize in jobs that others have failed to master. These midsize businesses are also more flexible than the large Chinese manufacturers. The Anatolians are more similar to Western consumers and can respond more rapidly to their changing demands.

The success of these entrepreneurs—called the "Anatolian Tigers," by allusion to the "Asian Tigers" (Korea, Taiwan, Hong Kong, and Singapore)—remains a mystery. How did they arise from these sleepy cities? Pamuk mentions an unconvincing explanation that is popular in Anatolia but that he considers folklore: These cities recovered ancient traditions of craftsmanship and commerce from the Ottoman era, when the Turks exported goods to Syria and Egypt. Another common sociological explanation sees in the new class of entrepreneurs the heirs of the "farmers-general" who raised taxes for the sultan's treasury. These families supposedly have preserved important resources from those bygone days, including capital and a certain readiness to exploit the people, with the army's support. Meanwhile, the militant Muslim entrepreneurs, who are closest to the ascendant AKP, invoke religion as an explanation: The "Anatolian Tigers" are pious Muslims, they claim, and the Koran encourages business and the seeking of wealth. The Anatolian entrepreneurs are affiliated with employer associations that are openly Muslim and distinct from the secular associations of Istanbul; these Muslim groups support the AKP, which is largely a political expression of the Anatolian renaissance.

This Islam, Pamuk observes, is traditional and conservative rather than radical; it is far from the political Islam of the Arab world. Should we worry, along with many in Istanbul and in Western Europe, about a sudden re-Islamization of Anatolia? But Anatolia was never secularized, as Istanbul was, by the Republican regime. Kemalism, with its anticlerical program, was confined to the west of Turkey and never reached the deeper recesses of Anatolia. In any case, is this a question of religion? In listening to the Anatolian businessmen, it is clear how much their entrepreneurial spirit expresses local pride and a desire to get back at the Kemalist bourgeoisie of Istanbul; it's the revenge of the province against the capital, and the local population participates with enthusiasm. Sharing this economic and patriotic enthusiasm are millions of Anatolian émigrés who invest their savings in the new businesses, often without contracts, based on shared trust in Islam—but a local Islam, rooted in Anatolian customs and as far as can be from radicalism.

None of these factors is sufficient by itself to explain the phenomenon. Taken together, though, they account for the emergence of this new power: a meeting of culture, tradition, religion—and good strategy.

Turkey in Europe

And then there is Europe. Modern Turkey's takeoff owes much to the opening of European markets, which are now closed only to Turkey's raw agricultural products and, in principle, to its immigrants.

Could Turkish development continue without Europe? In theory, Pamuk admits, joining the European Union is not absolutely essential; whatever the outcome of the negotiations, the common market with Europe will not disappear. Moreover, Turkish exports are increasingly globalized. The Euro-skeptics—a growing camp in Turkey—conclude that they can do without the EU. Yet Europe remains indispensable to the consolidation of Turkish institutions, Pamuk believes. Without solid political, judicial, and financial institutions, the Turkish economy will not necessarily secure a framework for lasting development. If Europe rejects them, there is no guarantee that the Turks will remain on an upward trajectory, and if Turkey returns to stagnation, emigration to Western Europe will probably accelerate. European opponents of allowing Turkey to join the EU invoke, among other fears, the risk of a massive immigration of Turks to the West. This is possible, but the opponents fail to consider that a Turkey in Europe would probably develop faster than a Turkey outside Europe, creating more jobs in Turkey. Instead of leaving the country, Turks would stay home or return home, just like the Spaniards and Portuguese, whose migratory patterns reversed themselves after their countries joined Europe.

There is another threat to Turkish development. The AKP, with its commitment to the free market, democratic politics, and religious moderation, has tied its destiny to membership in Europe; if it should fail, there is the chance that the Turks would turn to radical Islam, currently represented by a minuscule political party that wins only 1 percent of voters. For the moment, the Turks have clearly chosen moderation, Europe, and the market. Would rejection by Europe be good news for radical Islam? The possibility cannot be dismissed. Islam, which until now has not been a major factor in Turkey's rise, could suddenly become one. What is at stake in the relation between Turkey and Europe is thus not a conflict between the West and the Muslims; it is a more profound confrontation, the outcome of which is unknown, between a moderate Islam and one that is radical and anti-Western. Turkey's gaining membership in Europe would strike a damaging blow to radical Islam. Turkey's exclusion from Europe would be a major boon to Islamist propaganda against the West.

Growth in Islam

Beyond the Turkish example, too little is said about the strong economic growth that Muslim countries have recently enjoyed. There has been an average annual growth rate of 5.9 percent during the period from 2004 to 2008 for thirty-two Muslim countries, excluding Iraq, Somalia, and the Palestinian territories because of conditions of war. (I consider a country Muslim if at least 80 percent of its population is Muslim.) Does this new prosperity come from oil? Oil is a factor, but if one excludes the oil-producing countries from the sample, the growth rate of the others stands at 5.5 percent, still above the worldwide average.

Economies long anesthetized, even moribund, such as Morocco, Bangladesh, and Egypt, have reached annual rates of 6 percent; Pakistan and Indonesia figure in this same category of emerging economies. It is therefore not Islam that prevents economic development, as claimed by the old pseudo-culturalist thesis. All these "Muslim" economies were in reality paralyzed by counterproductive strategies generally inherited from socialism: middle classes expelled or dispossessed, protectionism, and central planning. But since the 1980s, under the influence of free-market economics, with the advice of the International Monetary Fund, and thanks to the globalization of trade, the governments in question have all pursued market-friendly policies, which bring positive results in all climates and all civilizations. The route is the correct one, but the governments of Muslim countries still have far to go, as is evident in their inflation rate, which remains above the global average: 7.6 percent in Muslim countries, compared with 3.6 percent worldwide. This discrepancy reveals a still-mediocre public administration and states that are too spendthrift. When they have mastered their public spending, these countries will be able to look forward to joining the BRIC economies (Brazil, Russia, India, and China) with 7–10 percent annual growth potential.

Islam does not discourage economic growth. It is even conceivable that Islam favors growth, since the "Anatolian Tigers" are not isolated cases in the Muslim world. The Koran is the only fundamental sacred text that praises worldly riches, and Mohammed was the only prophet who was an entrepreneur and married to a trader. Material success can therefore be, as it would later become among Calvinists, a sign of election. This explains why the political parties that call themselves Islamic, such as the AKP, always favor a market economy.

The various explanations for the failure of Muslim countries in the modern era include colonization, Arab socialism, despotism, and wars. Religion is a less convincing explanation than any of these. Nasser, who nationalized Egyptian businesses in 1954, expelled the bourgeoisie and the minority entrepreneurial class, and embraced the Soviet model, is infinitely more responsible for the misery of his people than is Mohammed. In the twentieth century, Muslims sank into poverty under authoritarian and socialist regimes; now they are progressing toward well-being, thanks to regimes that are less repressive and that have converted to a market economy. The rise of Turkey—and with it, thirty-two other Muslim countries—proves that development is a matter not of religious belief but of good economic choices. Antimarket ideas are always a catastrophe. The free market is a verifiable source of progress, with or without Islam. This is the good news from Turkey and elsewhere. There is no need to fear Islam when it is modern.

PART 5

Cases of Decline

From the end of World War II until the beginning of the 1980s, Western Europe's and Japan's economies were catching up to America's, and their convergence appeared imminent. Since then, continental Europe and Japan have faltered, surrendering leadership in growth and innovation to the Americans, a trend that the 2008 downturn has not modified. This loss of "dynamism," to use Edmund Phelps's expression, holds no mystery for economists. As the Italian Alberto Alesina explains for Europe, and Fumio Hayashi for Japan, the shortening of the workweek, at the very time that the American workweek was increasing, was an essential cause. With technologies similar to America's, the French and Japanese work less, produce less, and earn less.

Furthermore, the engines of the new growth seem to have been poorly understood in the stagnant states. The first of these engines is the innovation that derives from close connections among cutting-edge universities, research centers, and businesses. The other engine is "creative destruction"—the rapid abandonment of retrograde activities to make room for new entries into the market, as the Austrian Joseph Schumpeter explained.

In the declining European economies, it is evident that the rules of economics are misapplied. The legal rights of workers and of businesses, as well as taxation and credit policies, protect existing businesses rather than those that might be born. So this decline, unlike former economic crises, has its beneficiaries: The acquired advantages of insiders are preserved, while the victims of the status quo are the youngest, the least educated, and the outsiders. True reform thus requires the reestablishment of positive and durable incentives in the labor and education markets.

258

Any other economic policy amounts to short-term tinkering for short-term political effect.

Decline is not inevitable, as surges in 2007 by Japan and Germany and certain initiatives of the European Commission demonstrate. The lengthening of the workweek and the introduction of competition brought about almost immediate gains, showing how all nations respond similarly to the same incentives. Nor is it still necessary to copy an American model to benefit from growth. Olivier Blanchard and Jean Tirole, both French, propose labor laws that reconcile economic efficiency with the social policies typical of "Old Europe capitalism."

Is the free-market model of growth threatened by global warming? British economist Nicholas Stern calls for an immediate reorientation to avoid a catastrophe in the year 2100; the more skeptical Bjørn Lomborg, a Dane, trusts technical innovation to contain any future warming; and the Frenchman Roger Guesnerie—in the name of scientific uncertainty—suggests acting, but with moderation, so as not to disrupt market mechanisms. Bad economic policies could prove more dangerous for humanity than the greenhouse effect.

Finally, will the global economic downturn that began in 2008 destroy American economic leadership or change the fundamental rules of development? Probably not, as the dominance of the United States goes back to 1820 and has survived many cycles. Neither an alternative model nor a challenger has appeared on the horizon.

CHAPTER SEVENTEEN

Europe Versus the United States

A THIRD OF HARVARD'S ECONOMISTS are Europeans. Among them is Alberto Alesina, an Italian who would like to return home—if only Europe would wake up. During the 1980s, Alesina says, there was an economic revolution in the relation between the United States and Western Europe. Europe broke down, but except for the British, its inhabitants never took account of their problems. Was the relative decline of Europe predictable?

At the end of World War II, Western European per-capita income was only 42 percent of the American figure; by the beginning of the 1980s, it had made up most of that gap, reaching 80 percent of the U.S. standard of living. During this period, the European model was considered exemplary for its productivity and for the social cohesion established by its welfare states, while the United States, by contrast, was progressing only in cycles, from crisis to crisis, and was shaken by violent social problems. Over the last twenty years, however, this relation has been reversed (Great Britain aside). After reaching 80 percent of the American standard, the Europeans have since fallen back to 70 percent—the same gap as in 1970. Italy is the worst off: In 1950, it was at 30 percent of American per-capita income; in 1990, it had attained 80 percent; but since then, it has fallen back to 64 percent, the level of the mid-1960s. France and Germany are descending the same slope.

This is not to say that Europeans have become poor. Their standard of living is still comfortable, but they have stopped progressing. Compared with the United States, Alesina believes, it makes sense to speak of Europe's "decline." This decline is relative, true, but it is still a decline, and every year it is becoming more marked.

Europeans put up with this decline because it is only relative. But will they remain content for long with their children's lack of prospects, their own loss of influence in world affairs, and seeing themselves surpassed by the Koreans or the Chinese? This lack of development could give rise to a morbid culture of stagnation, of which Argentina offers an example. Beyond these psychological consequences, stagnation makes it impossible to eliminate poverty, which has not totally disappeared in Europe; the integration of immigrants also becomes more complicated.

Alesina, who knows the differences between the two continents, does not conclude that catching up with the American standard of living is as simple as applying the American model to Europe. Moreover, the 2008 financial crisis has made the American model much less convincing to Europeans. Alesina's research deals only with the reasons for the gap between the two continents. His proposed explanations are more historical and cultural than those of Edward Prescott, whose more theoretical model explains variations solely by the amount of labor. Assuming that Europeans wish to avoid decline, Alesina proposes tools that they could adopt without giving up their distinctiveness.

The Former European Model

How is it that between 1945 and 1980, Europeans nearly managed to catch up with the United States economically while at the same time shortening their workweek? This conjunction gave rise to the belief in a European economic model that was superior to the American model. In industrial economies, Alesina explains, it is easier to imitate than to innovate. Europeans were content to replicate American ideas, whether those were methods of production or management techniques. Moreover, since labor costs and benefits are higher in Europe than in America, European businesses had a greater interest in automating than Americans did. Consequently, the service sector is smaller in Europe than in the United States; Europe is more automated and, in a certain sense, more modern, but unemployment has become endemic for unskilled workers. During the catch-up phase, a period called the Thirty Glorious Years (an expression of Jean Fourastié's), European governments were able to play a more decisive role because industrialization and the creation of major infrastructure facilitated public centralization. In the end, precisely by catching up, Europe saw its relative advantages disappear. When one can no longer imitate, one must innovate. But the European model proved ineffective when it came to innovation. While the United States was creating a new economy based on innovation and information, Europe was walking in place.

Does this European slippage go back only to the 1980s? Another good observer of Europe, Edmund Phelps (who won the Nobel Prize in 2005), believes that the gap is cultural and that it came about in the 1920s, when American capitalism took a key turn that still defines it today; at the same time, Europe chose the welfare state, which condemned it to the status of economic follower, both in product development and in management. The loss of European "dynamism," a concept dear to Phelps, is thus part of a long history, and therefore all the more difficult to overcome.

Two Cultures, Separated by an Ocean

The founding principle of American dynamism is well-known: "creative destruction." Entrepreneurs and stockholders abandon, close, or relocate old enterprises without misgivings, moving around in search of higher profits and better salaries. Universities and research centers produce ideas that turn into profits for global capitalist businesses.

The enthusiasm for creative destruction in the United States is not unanimous, of course, especially during a recession. The disappearance of factories provokes local uprisings and nostalgia, as illustrated, to take one example, by Michael Moore's films. Nor is the big capitalist boss a universally respected figure in the United States; a certain American Left has never ceased, since the nineteenth century, to denounce the "robber barons." Bill Gates, the emblem of the "new economy," has never escaped this criticism. His reputation as the richest man in the world made him so unpopular in the media that he conveniently reinvented himself as a humanitarian. Now the foundation that he runs with his wife to fight epidemic diseases in Africa wins him compliments that he never received when, as head of Microsoft, he created millions of new jobs and accelerated the economic growth of the planet. On the whole, though, the U.S. does enjoy a consensus on innovation.

To speed the transition from an industrial to an information economy, the role of the American government is therefore not to protect existing businesses but to facilitate the arrival of newcomers into the marketplace. Detroit's lobbies would disagree, but in the long run, they will be overcome. To establish a business in the United States, Alesina observes, one must go through four formalities that take four days and cost $166. The same process in France requires fifteen formalities that take fifty-three days and cost the equivalent of $3,963. In Italy, the sum would be $5,012, and in Greece, $10,218! In Sweden, which has become the most "flexible" of European countries, such a process would still cost $664. In a similar vein, Alesina points out, if one wants to recover the loss on an unpaid check in the United States, one must wait five weeks to get a judgment and then wait two weeks for it to be executed. In Italy, it is necessary to wait twice, for a year each time; in France, twice for three months each time. These processes reflect the priority that a society accords to the logic of capitalism.

In the United States, monopolies, barriers to entry, and acquired advantages are likely targets for the state and the courts. Economic policy makes sharpening competition a priority. The deregulation of transportation and telecommunications during the 1980s has done more for the dynamism of the American economy and the world economy, Alesina argues, than the tax reductions loudly boosted by conservative and liberal politicians alike, which have more to do with reelection than with economics. Without deregulation, air transportation would have remained an elite way of traveling, and cell phones and the Internet would not have reached the masses. American financial institutions also adapt to creative destruction by placing their bets on innovation; in Europe, they prefer to stick with the going concerns. Sometimes the innovations work, and sometimes they do not. The cost of risk-taking can be high. In 2008, poorly managed securitization brought down the world banking system. Yet this does not mean that securitization is entirely bad. In the future, it needs to be much better managed, but to forbid or overregulate securitization could kill investment and stop growth.

For continental Europeans, it is almost impossible to favor the "brutal" American economic model. While Americans prioritize the opportunity to get rich, Europeans are preoccupied with poverty and inequality. A European citizen hardly tolerates the shrinking of social programs; an American tends to refuse any tax increase. Conservative and liberal politicians know this and take it into account. Europeans, according to Alesina, should not be perceived as partisans of the market economy taken hostage by interventionist politicians. Their collective preferences explain why tax rates in Europe have gone from 30 percent on average during the 1960s to 50 percent during the present decade. In the absence of sufficient growth, public spending and debt have necessarily risen to the level necessary to maintain the advantages of the welfare state. Stagnation results in debt, which aggravates stagnation.

Anticapitalist Traditions in Europe

Socially rather than economically conscious, Europeans follow priorities dictated, Alesina says, by two traditions: Christianity and Marxism. Neither is favorable to profit; both consider social justice an imperative that trumps productivity. Even Europeans who are neither Catholic nor Marxist are imbued to varying degrees with these spiritual and intellectual principles. By contrast, because the dominant ethic in the United States is Calvinist, and Marxism has never had great popular influence there, many Americans accept poverty and inequality as natural.

A poor person in the United States draws the suspicion that he has not worked hard enough to escape his condition. The obligation to work, that is, trumps public solidarity. In Europe, a poor person is perceived as a victim of the economic system. In the United States, inequality is more tolerated than in Europe, even by the least advantaged; it is considered a kind of fate for the individual to rise through work. In the United States, taxation will favor the entrepreneur in order to incentivize creativity, whereas in Europe fiscal policy will be redistributive. Even American liberals avoid the term "redistribution," as it smacks of socialism. They prefer to "spread" the wealth around, to use an expression made popular by President Obama.

The importance in Europe of aid to the poor is well-known, but its efficiency is not evaluated. Is it not surprising, Alesina asks, that European poverty does not disappear, despite massive public expenditures? The reason is that compassion trumps efficiency; processes take on greater importance than results. In the United States, it is results that matter.

Edmund Phelps, who sits on the liberal side of the American political spectrum and who is as dismayed as Alesina by the lack of recognition of the efficiency of capitalism, proposed that the Italian government (which had hired him as a consultant) establish a holiday to celebrate bosses—a "Boss Day." Phelps thought that in Italy, where all the saints' days are celebrated, it would make sense to recognize symbolically the saving role of business leaders. His proposal wasn't implemented.

The Tyranny of Interests

Are the cultural differences between the two continents sufficient to explain their economic divergence? Alesina says that Europe's stagnation has as much to do with organized interests as it does with cultural factors. The tyranny of the status quo, as Milton Friedman described it, dominates in Europe: Groups of workers who have an interest in blocking change have a great capacity to hinder innovation.

The inequity of these vested interests isn't always well understood, as European agricultural policy demonstrates. As owners of agricultural concerns, the Queen of England receives €600,000 in subsidies every year, and the Prince of Monaco €300,000! In the United States, this would be a scandal. In Europe, agricultural subsidies remain untouched. Because information is confidential in this area, Europeans have no idea that the great beneficiaries of European aid are large globalized industries. In the Netherlands, for instance, the two top aid recipients are the industrial concerns Philip Morris (€1.5 million annually) and Royal Dutch Shell. In Great Britain, Nestlé received €11.3 million in 2004! And in France? Alesina was not able to obtain this information, but he would be surprised if the small farmers were well positioned (assuming that the farmers deserve special treatment). Agriculture is the only activity in Europe for which 77 percent of revenues come from subsidies! And what of those who would benefit from change—the young entrepreneurs, the creative innovators? They are dispersed, unorganized, and unaware of the possibilities that would open up in an unfettered society.

How did Great Britain escape decline? The free-market convictions of Margaret Thatcher, so exceptional among the European political class, were essential, but there were also certain paradoxically favorable conditions: The economic crisis of the 1970s was deeper there than in the rest of Europe. For change to be acceptable, it is necessary either to achieve rapid growth, as in the United States, which allows for the immediate reemployment of wage earners from archaic sectors, or to stagnate so obviously that the need for major change is generally recognized. Continental Europe vegetates in between, experiencing neither rapid growth nor recession, which results in the passivity of political leaders and of public opinion. This in-between state explains why the European economic decline, so evident statistically, does not provoke a major call for change. French president Nicolas Sarkozy, elected in 2007, showed signs of being the exception, but his reforms so far have been cosmetic, so as not to disrupt the social consensus. Sarkozy also has made himself popular by lashing out against "wild" capitalism versus good capitalism—an easy line, but a bad omen for meaningful reforms.

Laissez-Faire: Let the Market Do What Markets Do

What reforms would Alesina suggest if the psychological and political conditions were favorable? He does not envision applying an American model to European societies or a European model to American society, but hopes instead for an intellectual evolution, an understanding that the market works and that individuals everywhere respond to incentives. In Europe, however, the market is perceived as an ideology. Europeans believe, on the whole, that the state is more efficient than the market, even though the science of economics has disproved this belief. Economics teaches that economic actors always respond to market signals and that the state should never intervene, unless the market has been shown to be ineffective and it has been demonstrated that state intervention will not make things worse.

The choice that Europe faces is not, Alesina says, between the market and social solidarity. If European governments let the market work, more businesses will disappear, yes, but still more will be created. Employees will rapidly find new jobs, and these will pay better than their old ones, since there is no hope for progress in an obsolete economic sector. Further, the evidence shows that wherever it is easier to fire workers—the Netherlands, Denmark—the unemployment rate is lower than where it is hard, as in France, Italy, or Germany. In a more flexible market, the role of the state does not disappear, but it changes. It manages the transition of workers rather than propping up businesses.

To reconcile market efficiency with the stress on compassion characteristic of "Rhineland capitalism," as French economist Michel Albert calls it, Europeans could also show a little imagination. Alesina suggests two mechanisms that presently exist only in economic theory. The first is in the area of employment. Olivier Blanchard, the IMF's chief economist, and Jean Tirole have proposed the creation in France of a "tax on layoff," which would restore to firms the right to fire employees. The present legislation authorizes firing only for economic reasons, a vague criterion that nearly always must be validated by a labor judge, who rarely accepts the employer's analysis. The usual outcome is to prohibit the firing and to fine the employer. Employers thus fire rarely—and recruit even less. The result is a freeze on employment that hinders innovation and increases unemployment.

Blanchard and Tirole acknowledge that a layoff also can impose a social and financial burden on society as a whole. The laid-off worker, if he does not find another job, will become the responsibility of state relief agencies. It would thus make sense for businesses to enjoy the right to fire, but also to pay a tax corresponding to the burden shifted to society. This tax would be calculated as a function of the actual length of the period of unemployment of the fired worker; in some American states, where this system has been in place since 1930, the tax is usually capped at six months' salary. The proceeds would go toward the financing of unemployment aid, so employers would benefit from a corresponding decrease in their contributions to unemployment insurance. Courts would no longer have reason to intervene in firings except in cases of outright malfeasance, such as, say, the firing of a pregnant woman because of her condition. Since the employer knows that the tax on firing will be proportional to the time necessary for the fired worker to find another job, he will be motivated to help his personnel find work—for example, by facilitating their ongoing training. The tax would also motivate recruitment because the employer would know the cost of firing in advance, whereas now he is subject to a general prohibition or at the mercy of the courts. A tax on layoffs would thus have many virtues, while restoring economic freedom. Nevertheless, no European government and no association of employers or workers has yet taken a position in favor of Blanchard and Tirole's proposal, so fearful is Europe of authentic reform.

Another ingenious mechanism, conceived in 1984 by Thomas Moore of the Hoover Institution, offers a way to overturn the regime of public subsidies: Government could trade one lump sum for all future payments expected over, say, the next ten years from all government-subsidized occupations (farmers, in particular). From the moment of this buyout, market mechanisms would reestablish themselves, eliminating some jobs and motivating other economic actors to innovate. But should we pay for reform? The economists Jacques Delpla and Charles Wyplosz have calculated that, in the case of France, a state buyout of vested interests (from taxi licenses to lifetime public employment) would be compensated for by a recovery of dynamism, while avoiding protests by these interests. In the case of taxis, the replacement of licenses by entrepreneurial freedom would increase the number of cabs (by attracting more entrepreneurs), thus lowering rates and increasing the number of clients. The wager would be costly (several billion euros just for taxis). But this sum reveals the actual cost of these protections and the extent to which they block economic growth.

The experience of the United States, and of Europe, too, illustrates that in modern economies, the positive effects of unleashing the market kick in rapidly. In sectors deregulated by the European Commission in Brussels, such as airlines and telephone companies, it took just a few years to see the creation of many new jobs in new services widely available at low prices. The market solution works perfectly well—provided it is adopted.

The German Proof

Germany has tested the speed of market solutions with some success since 2004. The Social Democratic government, by negotiating with the unions, obtained a stabilization of salaries, a raising of the retirement age, a requirement that those receiving unemployment benefits return to work more rapidly, and a decrease in the taxation on work. The subsequent government, called the Great Coalition and led by Angela Merkel, held this line. The budgets of the central states as well as those of the *länder* have been balanced, thanks to a reduction in the number of public employees and the privatization of local public services. The Great Coalition also announced the phasing out by 2018 of subsidies to all mines, railroads, culture, and agriculture. These measures are hardly revolutionary. None upsets legitimate expectations much, and their delayed implementation eliminates any shock to society. But all have the same tendency: They reduce costs and increase the quantity of labor. The signals that they send may not be spectacular, but they are clear, pointing to a more flexible, more competitive, and less protected market.

German leaders know that capitalism has no better reputation in Germany than in the rest of Europe. The free-market tradition that gave rise, after World War II and under the influence of

Ludwig Erhard, to the German miracle was diluted by reassuring talk about a "social-market economy." Reunification has strengthened the taste for public benefits, for the East Germans made a seamless transition from Communism to the shelter of their new welfare state. The earlier market tradition had to take refuge in the marginalized Free Democratic Party. But the Social Democratic government, and then the Great Coalition, knew to base their reforms on another, more durable national tradition: the horror of budget deficits and the specter of inflation. Gerhard Schröder, as chancellor, made reference only to a return to balanced budgets; he never mentioned economic flexibility or market competition.

But the result since 2006 has been an almost instantaneous improvement in competitiveness. The modest reduction of taxes on labor and the faster return of the unemployed to the workplace have allowed for an increase in production at a minimal cost in wages. This new comparative advantage is evident in the increased activity of small and midsize businesses and in the expansion of exports. This recovery is unspectacular but in the right direction, and it has been favored by a lucky coincidence: The growing need for equipment in Eastern Europe and in emerging countries such as China, India, and Brazil plays to Germany's industrial tradition and the strengths of its businesses. The decentralization of German industry is also a traditional comparative advantage. But these advantages do not explain the upward turn of 2006 and 2007 by themselves, since they did not prevent the stagnation of the 1990s. It was necessary that positive signals revive the market for entrepreneurs to return to the sources of growth. Let us call this the German proof.

Ambiguous Europe

Could the European Union contribute to the dynamism of continental economies? Alesina believes that it has, and that it will continue to, when the European Commission in Brussels opposes monopolies, imposes deregulation, and heightens competition. But when national governments formulate common European policies, they are disastrous, as agricultural policy illustrates. Common policies give rise only to bureaucracies and vested interests, never to innovation. Governments favor such policies only for short-term political benefits and publicity. Even more surprising, viewed from the United States, is the style of these European projects. In their plans, studies, and declarations of intention, the Brussels bureaucrats give the impression of a perfect mastery of the future. Everything suggests that the economy is a piece of machinery and that it suffices to push the right button to ensure a predictable result. Alesina sees in this the influence of French technocracy and voluntarism on European authorities. This influence is diminishing, however. Luckily, the diversity of a Europe of twenty-seven countries renders any attempt to impose new common policies futile, Alesina says.

But isn't the success of Airbus versus Boeing proof that states can create national and transnational champions? Alesina has a nuanced view of this success. We will never know what Airbus has cost taxpayers; no one has calculated what other businesses would have emerged, or what other jobs would have been created, if Airbus had not monopolized public spending. In any case, the example of Airbus is unique and hardly reproducible, since aeronautics, in Europe as in the United States, is the only industry where the economies of scale are so considerable that there is room for only one builder per continent. Finally, Airbus does not represent a technological advance. Aeronautics is a mature industry in which Europeans follow on the heels of Americans but do not replace them.

The Price to Pay? Inequality in America

The American experience can be a useful example, but Europeans stigmatize it for the undeniable inequalities that it produces.

Kevin Murphy demonstrates that they are becoming deeper. This young economist, known for the baseball cap that he never removes, teaches at the business school of the University of Chicago, the most free market–oriented university in the United States, which was shaped by the ideas of Gary Becker and Milton Friedman. Murphy is not an enemy of capitalism, but he does not idealize American society. Every economy, he comments, represents a choice, never really satisfactory, among priorities. In Western Europe, the preference is for stability at the expense of employment; in the United States the premium is on growth and full employment at the expense of certainty and equality.

These features, evident in the distribution of incomes, have become more marked since the United States entered the information economy. American anticapitalists denounce the existence of the superrich at one extreme and of great poverty at the other. These realities, Murphy says, are incontestable, but there is a deeper concern: Gaps are growing all along the income scale. This new inequality derives from the nature of the new economy. Businesses are looking for ever more qualified workers, and high salaries appear as a response to demand that America has not found a way to meet. Sophisticated occupations thus put an astronomical premium on university degrees. Twenty years ago, a college graduate could generally expect a salary 40 percent higher than that of a high school graduate; today, the average gap is 80 percent. The premium for a university degree, in other words, has doubled. This gap should not be interpreted as bad news but as a sign of how investment in higher education is proving increasingly profitable. Parents and children are aware of this reality, so there is ever-greater pressure on college admissions. Unfortunately, Murphy notes, the proportion of those who fail to complete their studies is also growing because mediocre primary and secondary education does not equip the mass of students to succeed in college—and so the premium on university degrees increases all the faster.

As Murphy explains, the labor market works according to rules no different from any other market's: Salaries are determined at the intersection of the supply and demand curves. The right way to increase wages is thus to reduce the supply of unqualified workers. In the fight against poverty, education is a more effective mechanism than regulations like the minimum wage. In the United States, Congress sets the minimum wage, but it is only a symbol reflecting the good intentions of the political class. The American minimum wage is always set at a level beneath real wages in order not to interfere with the market. No one in the United States sees this as a way to eliminate poverty. In Europe, by contrast, the legal minimum wage represents the real income of many workers. In Europe, an increase in the minimum wage really influences the job market by reducing the demand for unskilled workers—which boosts unemployment.

This perverse effect of the minimum wage is well understood by economists in Europe and the United States. But governments never increase the minimum wage to create jobs or to fight poverty. An increase is always a political decision designed to satisfy insiders, those who have jobs and are in the political majority, rather than outsiders, the unemployed. Outsiders are marginalized, without political influence or union organization. Whenever the minimum wage rises, the question we should ask is: How many additional unemployed people are we ready to accept, in particular among disadvantaged and uneducated minorities? Obviously, the question never gets asked—not in the U.S. or in Europe.

To explain the growing inequalities, should we blame immigration or globalization? These are accessory factors, according to Murphy. Imported workers or products reflect a global economic trend toward innovation. Commerce and migration speed this tendency, but they do not create it. But it is easier to criticize Latino immigrants and exports than to question innovation. In economics, Murphy concludes, the win-win situation does not exist; there are winners and there are losers, and every game has its downside. The fatal temptation would be to destroy the engine of progress to eliminate its undesirable consequences. The best solution is to invest in education to moderate the perverse effects of innovation, since these are inevitable. This moderation requires collective action, which can be either private (nonprofit) or public.

Where Is Life the Best?

How do we decide between a more dynamic economy and a more just one, conceptions that one might call American and European, respectively? A good economy, Edmund Phelps replies, is one that satisfies our aspiration to a good life. And what is a good life? Expectations are not different on the two sides of the Atlantic, Phelps says. On both sides, people hope for self-realization. Theory as well as experience, Phelps adds, shows that this self-realization is more achievable in an economy that generates change. The fact is that what is called capitalism produces more innovation than any other system; it has also been demonstrated that entrepreneurs and financiers produce innovations from the moment that they must compete with one another. To support these contentions, Phelps produces a 2006 Organization for Economic Cooperation and Development (OECD) study that shows a higher level of satisfaction, both at work and outside work, in the United States than in Western Europe. The more satisfied people are at work, moreover, the more satisfied they are in life. Phelps concludes that we must include a larger part of the population in business. In the United States, 85 percent of people of working age are usually employed, as opposed to 76 percent in France. In a recession, these percentages go down, but the gap remains. Phelps adds that the vitality of businesses is the best means, coordinated with education, to increase this inclusion in the working world: "Capitalism, far from hurting the weak, includes the weak." It is the weak who suffer most from a capitalism without dynamism. There is thus no contradiction between social inclusion and economic dynamism. In fact, the contrary is true.

How can an economy be both more dynamic and more inclusive? Without taking sides, Phelps notes that in Europe and the U.S., two opposing schools seek the same goal of economic growth. The neo-Keynesians (to whom he is close) propose investing more resources; the state could take on this responsibility with increased tax revenues. Meanwhile, advocates of the free market count on a less regulated labor market and a smaller state to encourage entrepreneurs' creativity. If an economy is not dynamic enough to include everyone, Phelps says, social assistance can be justified because the existence of too many excluded individuals threatens the legitimacy of capitalism. Capitalism must be preserved by any means necessary, including public intervention. We can call this Phelps's paradox; it was also Keynes's. Following the 2008 financial meltdown, all governments have chosen to save capitalism through public intervention. None has suggested getting rid of the free market and free trade, which is truly remarkable—and a huge difference from former crises. Would nonintervention—letting the market clean up its own mess, letting the banks follow the path of creative destruction—have been more efficient, if crueler? The theory cannot be tested by actual experimentation. Nonintervention would have received scant public support, and politicians are not supposed *not* to act. The best we can hope for is that their interventions not be too harmful.

America at Work

Europe usually responds to bad news from the United States with a mixture of outward sorrow and hidden jubilation; the Germans call it *schadenfreude*. This ambivalence made an appearance after 9/11, and it has reemerged with the 2008 financial crisis. Few European media and political leaders have failed to wonder whether this is, at last, the end of arrogant Anglo-Saxon capitalism; the Continent could then return smugly to its preferred statist stagnation. By thus overreacting, the Europeans overlook the fundamentals of any growing economy: It is cyclical, growth requires innovation, and there can be no innovation without trial and error. Further, today's error will not change America's economic leadership of the world. An economy that takes no risks will have no accidents, true, but in the long run, it will not grow.

In 1820, about ten years before Alexis de Tocqueville made his famous visit to America, a spectacular event took place, though no one could have known it at the time: U.S. per-capita income overtook that of Western Europe. This stunning fact was revealed only in 2007, in a new study by the OECD. The study, conducted by Angus Maddison, also showed that the U.S. economy has remained the world leader ever since 1820. (Though some small European countries, like Norway, rank ahead of the United States in per-capita terms, the OECD compares areas of similar size—the U.S. as a whole versus Western Europe as a whole.) Prior to the study, American economic preeminence was widely believed to date to 1904, the year the World's Fair was held in St. Louis. We now know that St. Louis represented not the moment when the U.S. overtook Europe economically but the moment when large European business delegations discovered that Europe trailed America in mechanization and innovation.

How did a then rather small nation, which had no more natural resources than Europe and little in the way of trading activity, overtake Europe economically? Was it through slave labor? No: The economy of the Northern states was performing better than that of the Southern states, where only the local aristocracy attained a decent standard of living. The true reason for the American economy's takeoff was the very focus of Tocqueville's visit soon thereafter: democracy itself. In early-nineteenth-century Western Europe, still dominated by the nobility, aristocratic consumers set the tone for the whole economy, and they wanted beautifully handcrafted (and expensive) goods. In the United States, by contrast, egalitarian-minded citizens wanted access to cheap goods—and mechanization and standardization fulfilled their wishes, leading to the Industrial Revolution and the world's first mass market. To a degree unknown in Europe, standardization became the economic manifestation of the Jacksonian age. Nearly two centuries later, the same practical rationale—standardizing products to meet popular demand—underpins the U.S.'s continued economic leadership. Despite much talk about American decline and the recent Wall Street crisis, the U.S. economy continues to set the pace for the world.

To better understand this sustained American leadership, in the midst of the financial crisis—the autumn of 2008—I visited with executives from three representative firms: Google, in Mountain View, California; IBM, in Yorktown Heights, New York; and Nanodynamics, in Buffalo. Though different in many respects, these three companies share an adherence to democratic principles, a dedication to collaborative relationships with universities, an understanding of the economic phenomenon of creative destruction, and a commitment to cultural diversity. Those are the fundamentals of American capitalism.

Google's Internet search engine and its other innovations, like the Chrome web browser, target the masses, not the elites. Google's innovations are based on a uniquely American and democratic belief in the wisdom of the crowd, as opposed to the European conviction that experts always know better. Google ranks results based on popularity; in Western Europe, experts would give the grades. True, Alan Eustace, Google's vice president, prefers the term "enlightened popularity," since websites' rankings are determined not only by the number of visits they receive but also by many other criteria, such as the number of links to them or the number of quotations from them in related websites and in published articles. But ultimately, he admits, "the web decides, not the experts." He adds that "Google's criteria are now accepted by the whole world." Whether the world is becoming Americanized or the U.S. is an advanced laboratory for mankind is an open question.

"The American entrepreneur has a passion for the market," says Keith Blakely, founder and CEO of Nanodynamics, a pioneer in the revolutionary field of nanotechnology. While European fundamental research can sometimes be superior, American innovations are usually the first to market. In the American vision, an idea is good only when the market buys it. Again, it's a democratic view of the purpose of innovation. This explains the unique relationship in the United States between universities and business. In Western Europe, professors and entrepreneurs seldom talk to one another; in fact, to do so is often regarded as a breach of etiquette. In America, Nanodynamics uses university equipment, consults university professors, and shares its discoveries with universities.

Beyond the democratic principle, another engine is at work within these companies, one that existed on a much smaller scale in the early nineteenth century: Schumpeter's principle of creative destruction. Schumpeter, as we have seen, meant that the new constantly replaces the old and that the market reallocates resources accordingly. Nanodynamics has offices in a former Ford plant in Buffalo, in the heart of the Rust Belt. In this building, low-skill jobs have been replaced with high-skill, better-paying ones. In Yorktown Heights, IBM survived several waves of creative destruction and now prospers by following Schumpeter's principle internally: The company sold its hardware-manufacturing operation to a Chinese firm and now focuses on customer service and the development of sophisticated systems.

Finally, there is American cultural diversity (which was not as important a factor in Jacksonian or Tocquevillian America). Wherever you come from, if you have the "fire in the belly," you go to the U.S., says Ajay Royyuru, who left India and eventually became manager of IBM's computational biology center. Does Suvankar Sengupta of Nanodynamics feel nostalgic about Bengal?

"As a land of opportunities," he says, "the U.S. remains unchallenged, while you are never criticized for taking risks. Moreover, when you are good at what you do, nobody in America asks you where you come from."

"A German company is ahead of us in the market," admits Caine Finnerty, a Nanodynamics fuel-cell expert and transplanted Englishman. "But we'll eventually take over while we tackle the subject from all cultural angles with our cosmopolitan team." As Milton Friedman loved to say: only in America.

CHAPTER EIGHTEEN

Setting Sun

FASHION AFFECTS EVEN ECONOMICS. During the 1980s, a whole literary industry grew up around the subject of Japan. In Europe and in the United States, journalists, politicians, and commentators prophesied that Japan would soon surpass America. One heard about nothing but the "Japanese model" and the "Japanese challenge"; economists and entrepreneurs flocked to Tokyo to penetrate the mystery and get hold of the secret. This frenzy lasted some ten years—until 1990, when the Japanese economy entered a phase of stagnation from which it still has not recovered. That Nippophilia was not unlike the current Sinophilia. Both cases involve an infatuation with societies that are little known and preferably far away. These economic speculations respond to the same drives as political ideologies: The Persians (so dear to Montesquieu), the Soviets, the Cubans, and the Chinese never hold any interest for their worshipers except inasmuch as they contest Western society. The Japanese of yesterday, like the Chinese today, only serve to criticize our economy, our laws, and our ways.

Regarding Japan, we have gone from one extreme to the other: Once praised to the skies, it is now neglected. Today, it is barely covered in the economic press. We forget that Japan remains the second-greatest economic power in the world, the second-largest exporter after the United States, with a per-capita income of $40,000, higher than that of Europe, no significant unemployment, and few social problems comparable to those that rend Western societies. The great power of Asia is still Japan, not China: 150 million Japanese produce more than the 2.5 billion inhabitants of China and India combined. To be sure, the irresistible growth of the two decades from 1960 to 1980 is past. Japan has stalled in the same manner as continental Europe. But this stagnation can be explained without appealing to national fatigue or to cultural notions like the "impenetrable Orient": The Japanese, like the French and the Germans, work when it pays to work. When pay goes down, so does commitment. Japan has slowed down since the Japanese started to work less; and they started to work less because the incentives to work were diminished. The gap between the glorious period and the "lost decade" (as the economist Fumio Hayashi calls it) that followed can be explained by economic analysis. The same science that applies to Europe applies to Japan.

The Legend of the Japanese Challenge

Behind the title *Japan as Number One*—a book by the American Ezra Vogel, prefaced by Jean-Jacques Servan-Schreiber, himself the author in 1967 of the well-known *The American Challenge* —is there some earthshaking economic formula? No, it was never more than a legend, says Hayashi. Educated at Harvard, a disciple of Edward Prescott, Hayashi shook up the academic gerontocracy in his country by introducing a scientific rigor into the University of Tokyo that is far indeed from orientalism, with its reassuring stories about Japanese "difference." Economics, Hayashi says, has its myths; Japan was the myth of the 1980s, as China is the myth of the present decade. Legend always draws on the surprise of the exotic—the German miracle in 1960, the

American challenge in 1970. Japan and China have the surprise factor because they arise from elsewhere, from an East that is supposedly passive, contemplative. No doubt India will be the next marvel, or perhaps Turkey.

In the period from 1960 to 1980, Japan was simply catching up with the West. During such a catch-up period, the growth rate can be spectacular, but it results from the low starting point and new access to Western techniques, which make it possible to leap over economic stages. The legend gathers mystique from the penetration of the world market. Today, the West is being invaded by products made in China, as it was during the 1970s by electronics and automobiles made in Japan. At that time, American industries were shaken by the appearance in their domestic market of cars that cost less and performed better than those made in Detroit. The United States found itself seized by protectionist panic and at the same time by a fascination with Japanese methods. Recall that this protectionism fortunately did not take hold, thanks to consumer demand. Japanese competition actually woke up American and European industry, whose leaders had long believed that Asians would never manage to manufacture a popular automobile. Similar scenarios happen repeatedly in electronics, textiles, and machine tools. Soon, we can expect them in medications from India, while we await Chinese aircraft.

The singularity of the Japanese legend, Hayashi argues, has to do with management methods. Westerners marvel that Japanese businesses function like communities of value in which harmony and social peace reign: no strikes or company unions; no excessive salary demands; lifetime employment for all; promotion with seniority; and harmonious relations among businesses, the state, banks, and subcontractors. Perceived from the outside, and without having inquired too much among the Japanese themselves (especially not the young and women), did this not seem a miraculous elixir? Would it not be a fine thing to import some of this oriental harmony into the conflict-ridden capitalism that is so characteristic of Europe and United States?

The same Western commentators now explain Japanese stagnation with the same tools that they used to describe the miracle. Is it not excessive harmony that destroys Japanese dynamism? Is it not lifetime employment that encourages laziness, seniority-based promotion that paralyzes management, and cohabitation with the state that prolongs the life of obsolete businesses? The fact that the same cultural factors have been adduced to explain first Japan's success and then its failure proves that the truth is elsewhere. But it is also possible that certain assets in 1980 became hindrances in 2000 because the world changed faster than a Japan that had become complacent.

The Empire of Laissez-Faire

Over the last century, Hayashi points out, Westerners have always been astounded, and sometimes frightened, by the Japanese capacity for moneymaking. But from the Japanese point of view, the perspective is inverted: In the nineteenth century, the Japanese wondered why they were poorer than Westerners. Today, they ask why Americans remain richer than they are. They're all the more perplexed because they were certain that they had adopted the winning formula as early as the 1870s: a good state with good technologies. After studying the material success of the West attentively, Japanese leaders concluded that what they lacked was the rule of law, which was promptly established by the Meiji emperor. But as for technologies, traditional Japan mastered none, even the steam engine. It imported everything.

Fortunately, a third pillar indispensable to development had been there forever: an entrepreneurial class. The merchants of Osaka, still Japan's economic capital today, have always been masters of commerce and finance. Japanese political leaders never considered taking the place of these private entrepreneurs, or favoring state capitalists, as in Korea. Thus Japan escaped economic statism as it did the poison of protectionism; both were foreign to its civilization. And there was never any question of socializing the Japanese economy. It is true that immediately after World War II, the Communist Party mobilized crowds, but this was a reaction to the fascism of earlier years, or to the American occupation. Japanese Marxists, a species bound for extinction, showed little interest in the economy. Hayashi says that Japan has always been the country of laissez-faire economics. If there is no socialist tradition, it is no doubt because there is no intellectual, political, or religious elite in Japan that claims to know how to make people happy. It is notable that in the West, socialism appeared only in continuity with enlightened despotism; such circumstances existed neither in Japan nor in the United States.

Laissez-faire, Hayashi explains, has hit only one snag—but it was a major one, following the crisis of 1930. To contain recession and deflation, the government thought it wise to invite businesses to form cartels, the *zaibatsu*. These zaibatsu fixed prices and production limits and prohibited all competition, so the crisis grew worse. But where did the idea of cartelization come from, if not the United States? The crisis of the 1930s was aggravated in Japan, as it was in the United States, by the adoption of the misguided protectionism of the New Deal. The Japanese recession of the 1930s, Hayashi says, was made in the U.S.; it interrupted Japan's rise and stymied its efforts to catch up with the West.

To this imported crisis was added another obstacle to catching up, this one made in Japan: the prevention of a rural exodus. Rural exodus is an iron law, a necessary precondition of development. *Homo economicus* increases his productivity by moving from the country to the city. But in Japan—from the Meiji period until 1950, a phase of rapid urbanization and industrialization— the number of rural households remained constant, at about 3 million. It was only thanks to demographic growth that industries could recruit the necessary labor force. Heads of households remained on their farms, and this rural stability considerably slowed development. The absence of a rural exodus, says Hayashi, explains why Japan languished behind the West until 1945 and only began to catch up later.

Farmers stayed in the countryside because they had to do so. Until its abolition in 1945, the old civil code required the eldest son to continue his father's cultivation of the land. This customary and legal restraint made no economic sense. Farmers who weren't landowners worked the land only for the benefit of an urbanized landed aristocracy. When the government of the American occupation redistributed landownership in 1945 and gave the property to the farmers, most resold their land and left for the cities. The rural exodus, which had been restrained by law, followed from people's desire to improve their lots, in Japan as elsewhere; it was only at this point that growth accelerated (by 12 percent a year in the fifties) in such a way as to astonish the world. Japan, Hayashi says, had lost fifty years; laissez-faire principles would have made it possible to catch up with the West as early as 1930, but cartelization and the lack of rural mobility prevented it. It is possible that Japanese fascism and the war against the West were consequences of this paralysis of growth.

The Lost Decade

How did Japan go from being the legend of the 1970s to slumping during the 1990s? The country's stagnation generates intense debates among Japanese economists. Before two of them, Hayashi and Heizo Takenaka (who was also the finance minister in the government of Junichiro Koizumi from 2000 to 2004), reversed the tendency, the dominant explanation was Keynesian. It was believed that production stagnated because the Japanese spent too little and saved too much. In fact, on the basis of this hypothesis of insufficient demand, Japanese governments during the 1980s encouraged wage increases, created vacation days to promote consumption, and lowered interest rates to facilitate credit purchases. The state went into debt and invested massively in public-works projects of doubtful utility—all with little result. This Keynesian policy, Hayashi says, could only fail, because the Keynesian analysis of the stagnation was false. Japanese bureaucrats, like those in the West, embraced Keynesianism only because it gave them a feeling of power; Keynesian theory lets one believe that it is the state that commands the economy.

In 2000, Hayashi and Takenaka succeeded in rebutting this analysis and then modifying Japan's economic policy. Stagnation, they said, had nothing to do with inadequate demand; its cause was rather a lack of supply. In simple terms, it was not the consumers not consuming enough but the entrepreneurs ceasing to innovate.

But how had the entrepreneurial spirit disappeared from Japan? Capital invested in Japanese businesses had changed little since the 1980s and the technologies employed there were the same as in the West, so what factor would explain the slowing of production and innovation? The difference in working hours, Hayashi says, suffices as an explanation. From 1988 to 1993, the legal workweek in Japan fell from forty-four to forty hours—that is, 10 percent—in response to a government initiative (not the demands of the population). The reduction began in 1988, when the government closed its offices on Saturdays and encouraged banks to do the same. It seems that the Americans, feeling invaded by Japanese imports, had asked the Japanese to restrain themselves or else face retributive measures. Japanese automakers acquiesced, before a later phase in which they established plants in the United States as a substitute for their exports.

Also during the 1980s, the American press ridiculed the Japanese as workaholics who didn't know how to enjoy life: Were they really civilized? In the same period, a French prime minister, Edith Cresson, compared Japanese workers with blue ants! Ever the good pupils of the West, the Japanese were finally convinced by these campaigns that they were working too much. Heeding their Western teachers, they undertook to work less and drove their businesses into stagnation. Hayashi acknowledges that other explanations may exist, but his view is that the reduction of the workweek is enough to explain Japanese stagnation. In any case, it coincides exactly with the beginning of the crisis.

The Choice for Slow Growth

There are other reasons for the stagnation that are more specific to Japan. The same factors that contributed to the miracle of the 1980s later contributed to the freezing of the economy by restraining creative destruction. Lifetime employment is an example: It is difficult for a business faced with global competition and a decrease in the workweek to adapt to a new environment when it must retain all its personnel. Attempts to lay off or reassign workers in Japan generally result only in the employer's conviction for violating customary practices, for lifetime employment is more a tradition than a law; but Japanese judges, Hayashi observes, have no love for entrepreneurs or for profits. Another cultural trait of Japanese business, once celebrated, is the promotion of managers by seniority, with a marked preference for conformism and collegiality. This practice is inhospitable to original minds. These selection criteria for leaders were tolerable during the 1970s, when competition was weak and profits considerable, but they became counterproductive after 2000, when global competition was eroding profits.

And then there is China, which is not popular in Japan. Might China be the cause of Japanese failure? This is a frequent accusation, but it's hard to understand how China would inhibit Japan's growth while it speeds up Taiwan's and in no way harms South Korea's. Moreover, Japanese businesses are prominent among those that subcontract with China to lower their production costs. But a Korean business that subcontracts with China can dismiss its workforce, whereas a Japanese business that produces in China must retain its workforce for life! In this case,

China indeed harms Japan, but only because of the rigidity of Japanese business.

Another guilty party in Japanese stagnation is the banks. Little exposed to international competition, they maintain relations with their clients that are more familial than objective. This has long led them to stand by troubled businesses and to renew indefinitely lines of credit that are never reimbursed; the main beneficiaries of these automatic extensions are firms in public works and construction. This sector also maintains incestuous relations with the political parties; indefinite lines of credit thus fill the parties' coffers while the nation is covered with roads that lead nowhere, useless airports, and vacant offices. This real-estate bubble has shifted savings away from more innovative and productive investments. But these days are coming to an end. Thanks to Hayashi's work and Takenaka's action, the practice of extending credit indefinitely has ended, and the government has reimbursed banks for their bad loans on condition that they stop financing what the Japanese call "zombie businesses." These businesses are then reorganized so as to be productive; creative destruction has been restarted and so has growth, if at a slow pace, notwithstanding the 2008 global recession.

Hayashi blames one local factor for this slow pace, a factor that may be seen as either cultural or economic: Local mom-and-pop shops and services in Japan are the least productive in the developed world. These shops and services employ considerable numbers, and their productivity is 25 percent below that of comparable businesses in Europe or the U.S. This inefficiency is a choice: It restrains growth, but this sector helps absorb the shock of economic change. If Japanese stagnation has never been reflected in an appreciable unemployment rate, it is because local shops and services have absorbed workers. In pure economic theory, it would be better for unproductive sectors to let their excess workforce go, leaving these workers temporarily unemployed, so that they might then be retrained and directed toward more modernized activities. This would certainly increase Japan's rate of growth, and creative destruction would bring the country closer to its American competitor. But this does not happen. It is as if the Japanese implicitly wish both to surpass the United States and to retain the habits that prevent them from catching up. Behind this implicit non-choice, one senses that the price to be paid—transitional unemployment—would be collectively unacceptable.

Since 2004, Japan's economy has risen out of stagnation and growth has resumed at a slow rate. Compared with America, it has settled into an income shortfall of 20 percent per capita. This makes it impossible to catch up—a situation that resembles that of continental Europe. Is slow growth a choice? It is conceivably the choice, if not an explicit one, of the older population, which is a distinct majority. This preference for slow growth is no more acknowledged in Japan than it is in Europe; in both societies it is expressed in terms of cultural considerations (such as the protection of the national identity against globalization) and equality. It is true that after a few privatizations and the halting of unprofitable loans by the Koizumi government (2001–06), inequalities have grown—reason enough, in Japan, to freeze any additional initiative that might speed growth but that would perhaps engender new presumed injustices.

In reality, the inequality argument—which is not only used in Japan—is biased. If inequalities as measured by the Gini coefficient (the gap between the richest 10 percent and the poorest 10 percent) appear pronounced, it is largely because of the aging of a population: Gaps in income obviously increase with age. But that is a difficult point to make in a public debate. Public opinion attends only to the inequality, and elderly persons are the most sensitive to it. Thus, in the name of identity, stability, and solidarity, Japan will probably stay on its current trajectory, in pace with global growth, but hardly better. Those who pay the bill for its defense of identity ignore its cost and have no voice. The decline of nations is never a consensual choice but is always the preference of those whose personal interests it suits (the rich, the comfortably retired, and vested interests) to the detriment of outsiders (the young, women, and those unheard). However, we should not count Japan out yet: It still ranks second in innovation, just behind the United States and ahead of the whole European Union, measured by number of yearly patents. The Asian future could still be more Japanese than Chinese.

CHAPTER NINETEEN

Will the Greenhouse Effect Leave Us Broke?

THE 1974 NOBEL PRIZE in Economics was jointly awarded to Friedrich Hayek and to Gunnar Myrdal, whose works contradicted each other on every point. The first, an advocate of economic freedom, swore by nothing but the spontaneous order of markets; the other, a social democrat, returned always to state intervention. They had nothing in common except that they were economists at a time when the socialist and capitalist systems were equally respected options that the Nobel committee did not dare decide between.

Similarly, in 2007, the Nobel Peace Prize was shared by Al Gore and the Intergovernmental Panel on Climate Change (IPCC), directed by the Indian physicist Rajendra Pachauri. Gore and Pachauri have global warming in common, just as Hayek and Myrdal shared the science of economics; but Gore and Pachauri only appear to be saying the same thing. Pachauri, a careful scientist, proposes hypotheses surrounded by numerous safeguards and conditionals; Gore exploits these hypotheses beyond all rigor and all moderation, transforming them into resounding speeches. One sees the possibility of global warming, and the other announces the end of the world. It goes without

295

saying that Pachauri's approach, in its complexity, is preferable to the televangelism of the ex–future president of the United States.

A Very Uncertain Climate

Supported by the findings of the scientists that the United Nations brought together to study global warming, Pachauri admits that though a future threat is probable, for the moment there is little or nothing happening. Global warming is primarily a hypothesis that follows from a theoretical model. This model, conceived by NASA during the 1980s, indicates that a greenhouse effect conditions the planet's ambient temperature. In this greenhouse effect, methane and carbon dioxide in the atmosphere play a decisive role. The greater their concentration, the higher the average temperature. Methane increases partly because of the expansion of rice fields and herds of livestock. The increase in carbon dioxide is a greater concern because it accumulates over centuries, unlike methane, which is reabsorbed within a few years. This accumulation of carbon dioxide goes back to the beginning of the industrial age during the 1850s and sped up considerably beginning in 1950.

All this is fairly certain; what follows becomes increasingly hypothetical. Since the increase of carbon dioxide coincides with industrialization, Pachauri and the IPCC infer—without any certainty—that industrialization is indeed the cause of the accumulation of carbon dioxide: The greenhouse effect, according to this hypothesis, is a result of economic development. Since the greenhouse effect has an impact on the climate, the theoretical model predicts that the atmosphere will grow warmer and that this warming will be partly irreversible, given the accumulation of carbon dioxide; it is possible to reduce additional outputs to stop the increase in the temperature, but not to restore past conditions, at least for many centuries hence. This predictive model makes it possible to foresee an average rise in temperatures of 2–5 degrees Celsius around the year 2100, depending on whether the output of carbon dioxide slows down or continues at the same rate. The effects of an increase of 2 degrees would be insignificant, a variation on the order of what humanity has often experienced since the dawn of civilization; an increase of 5 degrees, on the other hand, would create an unprecedented situation, with considerable risk of droughts, storms, and floods.

The theoretical model does not exclude other possible explanations of warming. But these are factors over which we have no control because they are difficult to measure or are not caused by human beings, such as sunspots or the displacement of the Earth's axis. The IPCC focus is on what human beings have doubtless brought about and what they can control. Its approach is therefore more operational than it is a matter of pure science.

Is this theoretical model verifiable? Uncertainty grows with experience. Certain measures of temperature indicate a slow warming of the atmosphere since the beginning of the twentieth century, but these measures aren't reliable before 1950; it is not absolutely demonstrable, in other words, that measurable warming results from the greenhouse effect. More audacious or more adventurous climatologists believe that they can discern symptoms of warming predicted by the model in certain exceptional events, such as the European heat wave of 2003. But are these really symptoms announcing a coming fever, or only random events like others that have happened in the past? Pachauri takes no position on such questions.

Taken as a whole, the scientific community knows that it does not know much beyond a minimal consensus. Some climatologists are of the view that Pachauri is too cautious, but others contest the very notion of consensus and of a scientific community. In fact, great scientific breakthroughs rarely result from consensus or community; they arise instead at the margins, in the form of dissidence. Excluded from the IPCC are the dissident climatologists who contest the model of global warming by the accumulation of carbon dioxide, such as Professor Marcel Leroux of Jean Moulin University in Lyon, who believes that warming can be explained by displacement in the Earth's axis of rotation.

To sum up: Warming seems certain, and causality by carbon dioxide of human origin probable, but it is possible that the temperature increases are random. The greatest uncertainty surrounds those climatic variations that have indeed been observed but that are presently impossible to attribute to some future warming. This is what Pachauri says. What Gore says is another matter.

Apocalypse Now

Hurricane Katrina destroyed New Orleans in 2005. To listen to Al Gore, it's hard to know whether this was an anticipatory consequence of global warming, a divine punishment against George W. Bush's America, or a sign of the last days. No doubt all three! According to Gore, we have now witnessed the rising waters foretold by climatologists and a particularly violent hurricane, both consistent with the model of global warming. Global warming is also to blame, apparently, for the war in Darfur. It was a drought brought about by warming that led to the displacement of populations and to inevitable clashes between "climatic refugees"—the nomads versus sedentary farmers.

In both examples, of which he makes extensive use, Gore misleads. The IPCC climatologists who talk most about catastrophe, such as Hervé Le Treut, believe that the Katrina and Darfur disasters merely prefigure events that could multiply if the climate became warmer. Thus Katrina and Darfur are at most parables, not effects of the accumulation of carbon dioxide. The views of the insurance industry should also be heard, for its job is to discern and measure risks over many centuries. By historical standards, Katrina was nothing but a hurricane of ordinary force that occurred in a region vulnerable to floods. Katrina's staggering cost—$65 billion—was out of the ordinary only because of the wealth accumulated in the area and the inadequate protection of real property. Contemporary natural catastrophes are more costly in human life and monetary values than in the past only because of the concentration of populations in areas that were formerly uninhabitable (seashores, valleys) and because of the wealth of these populations. Despite its force, Katrina did not catch the insurance industry off guard; if it was able to reimburse clients for $65 billion, that was because it foresaw the risk. The same insurers recuperated their stake in the following years, 2006 and 2007, because there was no comparable crisis during that period, which was statistically predictable. Insurers have learned that Nature is as destructive in our day as in the past—no more, no less. Global warming has as yet caused no catastrophe to add to that of New Orleans. Nor has it visited Darfur: The conflict between nomads and farmers was foreshadowed long ago by Cain and Abel.

The risk, if indeed there is one, lies in the future; it has not yet been verified. Then why does Gore deceive? Perhaps he thinks that it is his duty to capture worldwide opinion well in advance of a disaster. Perhaps he wishes to give humanity a cause that transcends national borders—a globalization guided not by economics but by ecology. Public choice theory offers another analysis. According to the school of public choice founded by the economists James Buchanan and Gordon Tullock, politicians are entrepreneurs like any others; they seek to maximize their votes, their popularity, and their power because of the business they are in. Gore and, more generally, all the politicians who have embraced the cause of global warming undoubtedly see their prestige enhanced. The subject lifts them above tired ideological quarrels. It gives them new legitimacy (for their commitment to save the planet) and restores to them the authority which economic globalization has deprived them of, since there is no near-term market solution to global warming. The long time frame and the global nature of the risk tend to return authority to states and to superstates in the form of international organizations.

Beyond the particular case of Gore, the global warming hypothesis is thus a boon for political leaders, NGO ecologists, and the United Nations: a rejuvenating bath in a warm spring. This is perhaps why Gore speaks untruths, deliberately or unconsciously. At best, we can conclude that he has reason to do so.

Nicholas Stern Saves the World

In attempting to restrain global warming, is there not a risk of destroying our economies and saving the planet only at a devastating cost to humanity? The British economist Nicholas Stern, who was an advisor to Tony Blair, has succeeded in bringing economic calculation to a controversy that had been merely ideological. Since its publication in 2006, the *Stern Review on the Economics of Climate Change,* whether one accepts it or not, has become the foundation of all serious debates over global-warming risks and possible countermeasures.

On the basis of the IPCC conclusions, which he considers certain, Stern estimated the loss of wealth that uncontrolled warming would result in by around the year 2100. According to his analysis, if we do nothing, continuing to develop at the current rate with present methods, the increase of carbon dioxide in the atmosphere will bring about an avalanche of natural catastrophes (floods, hurricanes, epidemics, migrations). These catastrophes would reduce global wealth by some amount between 3 percent, the minimum hypothesis, and 90 percent, the maximum; Stern predicts about 30 percent. India and China would by then have significantly surpassed the United States and Europe in carbon dioxide emissions, owing to their population, their industrialization, and their dependence on polluting energy sources like coal. If mankind does not wish to lose 30 percent of its wealth (not its current wealth, but its potential future wealth) or to suffer the ecological consequences that warming would cause, it would make sense, according to Stern, to begin investing in alternative means of production immediately; given the accumulation of carbon dioxide in the atmosphere and the length of time it takes for it to dissipate, only efforts that begin now will bring tangible results in 2100 and beyond. A reduction of emissions beginning now would, in principle, allow for the stabilization of the climate around 2050 and the containment of the temperature increase at a level of 2 percent in 2100: The planet would be saved.

At what price? It would suffice to devote 1 percent of global wealth per year to the task of modifying our economy, Stern says, so as to avoid losing 30 percent in 2100. At first glance, the wager seems rational. But 1 percent less growth worldwide implies a more considerable effort at reduction by rich countries than by poor ones. There is no question of asking Bangladesh to reduce its standard of living—the rich should pay for the poor. They should also pay for future generations that will be the beneficiaries of our current efforts. Stern's economic calculations are thus based on two ethical postulates: First, solidarity exists between rich and poor because we live on one planet and global warming is universal; and second, there exists or should exist solidarity among generations, for we are all but transitory occupants of a world that will be left to our descendants (an idea found originally in English moralists of the eighteenth century, such as Edmund Burke and Adam Smith).

The postulate of solidarity between rich and poor is hard to contest, but that of solidarity among generations is more debatable. One might object to Stern that our descendants in 2100 will be richer than we are and that they will inherit the production equipment that we leave to them. Would it not be advantageous for them as well as for us to continue growth rather than slowing it down? Thanks to development, we would leave them additional means of fighting possible warming. Stern refutes this objection by citing the gravity and the immediacy of the risk—an unknown risk, he argues, and one that traditional economic calculations cannot estimate. In this debate among economists,

Stern himself sometimes slips from a more rigorous register into Gore's prophetic style: Global warming seems to heat minds as well and to make calm discussion almost impossible, even among experts.

Following Stern's logic, where should we act, and how? Deforestation and energy production are two essential sources of warming. Therefore, to stop deforestation and to produce energy (nuclear, solar, or wind-driven) with less carbon dioxide would be rational investments in terms of risk avoided. But how is this risk avoided to be measured? Economists less politically engaged than Stern criticize him for overestimating the value of the risk avoided and for underestimating the investment necessary to move, for example, from fossil fuels to solar energy. Moreover, the benefit would go to humanity in general, while the investment would be the responsibility of a given category of nations, probably the rich nations; global benefits might be paid for by local impoverishment.

Even if we accept Stern's reasoning, his methods of calculating, and his ethic of solidarity across space and time, it remains to be seen what the incentives for action will be. Since he remains more an economist than a prophet, Stern sticks with classical mechanisms of proven effectiveness: the market and taxation. A tax on carbon emissions would motivate consumers to change their behavior by buying more non-carbon products. By making carbon dioxide–producing energy more expensive, this tax would make the production of energy without carbon dioxide profitable: This would be a formidable encouragement to innovation. And who would be the victims of this tax on carbon dioxide? The oil-producing countries, first of all: Their profits would be reduced and transferred to countries that consume. The other mechanism that Stern supports is a market in pollution rights, as is already provided for in the Kyoto Protocol on global warming: Countries that do not use their pollution rights could sell their quotas to countries that produce too much pollution. The general equilibrium that would follow would remain under the ceiling determined by Kyoto. And here is a little fact to consider: The country that would now have the most warm air to sell would be Russia, because its quota was fixed before the collapse of its industry.

Ecologists do not like the idea of a pollution market; they are offended that one could pay to get around set limits. But if we look past their punitive impulses and anticapitalist hysteria, it is clear that the market strategy would give better results than prohibition would. Using a market in pollution rights, the United States got rid of its sulfur dioxide, the main cause of "acid rain," in ten years.

But a strategy that worked in a single country, the United States, has so far produced no results for carbon dioxide at a global level. The carbon dioxide fund provided for in the Kyoto Protocol does not work, even within Europe. A market cannot be created by decree. Despite all the urgent declarations, nothing has stemmed the production of carbon dioxide since the signing of the Kyoto Protocol in 1992. Stern is thus something of a Jeremiah: We listen to him, we acclaim him, and everyone goes about making his daily contribution to warming. Is this because of skepticism? No doubt. Is it because the effort is too costly, in view of its invisible results? Definitely. Even more important, economies are national, whereas carbon dioxide is global. Centers of decision do not coincide with places of pollution; local prices do not reflect the cost of emissions that affect the rest of the world.

Ecologists of the World, Unite!

Roger Guesnerie is a French economist with an international audience; he is the author of, among other works, the essay "Will the Greenhouse Effect Leave Us Broke?" To reduce one's personal consumption of carbon in Paris, Guesnerie reminds us, has no influence on carbon dioxide emitted in Beijing or in Los

Angeles. Europeans are committed to a significant reduction in the production of carbon dioxide (a 75 percent reduction by 2050, in France's case), but their gesture will have no concrete value where global climate is concerned. Any country that instituted a carbon tax by itself—that ventured alone along the path traced by Stern—would be committing economic suicide: The carbon tax would drive producers to untaxed countries, and consumers would buy less expensive imports from those untaxed countries. In theory, Guesnerie says, one could impose the equivalent of a value-added tax on carbon, where exports would be exempt and imports would be taxed in such a way as to incorporate the cost of imported carbon. But how would we calculate the carbon involved in the production and circulation of an imported object? A national carbon tax and a carbon value-added tax may be theoretically possible, but they would be difficult to administer, besides being dangerous for the national economy. There is still the possibility of setting up a carbon tax at a very low rate, but such a low rate would not provide enough of an incentive to modify behavior; the only expected result would be pedagogical, along with resources for the state if the carbon tax were not offset by a reduction in other taxes. Guesnerie concludes that one cannot be virtuous all by oneself.

But why don't other governments, non-European governments in particular, desire to be virtuous? Are their reasons cultural? Not all societies give the same priority to nature, or to the future, for reasons both spiritual and economic. Europeans, since the Romantic era, have worshiped nature and natural landscapes. As for Americans, their relation to nature is more Promethean: Sites that are called natural in the United States are organized to be visited. Moving now to another continent, we notice that the Chinese do not have an acute sense of the future, perhaps because they believe neither in paradise nor in resurrection. In China, the business of improving one's lot here and now trumps nostalgia for a paradise lost.

These cultural generalizations illuminate—without completely determining—the differences that exist among national behaviors. Economic logic can be more convincing. Europeans are inclined to ecological virtue for cultural reasons, but at a standard of living comparable with that of the United States, they produce ten tons of carbon per capita, as opposed to twenty tons for an American. A Chinese person produces, on average, two tons, and an Indian one ton. To stabilize the temperature in 2100, it would be necessary to bring global production down to three tons per capita. Such an effort would wipe out the American economy and halt Chinese growth, but it might be attainable for Europeans. Only the Indians and the Africans would benefit from this norm; perhaps it is not an accident that an Indian leads the IPCC. And perhaps now it is clear why the U.S. Senate, under President Bill Clinton as well as George W. Bush, has refused to ratify the Kyoto Protocol.

Sometime before 2012, China and India will emit more carbon dioxide than Europe and the United States combined. But neither the Chinese nor the Indians have any intention of slowing their development to save the planet. When they aren't expressing doubts about the IPCC's conclusions (is this not an imperialist plot of the rich against poor?), the leaders of poor countries get around the carbon dioxide obstacle by introducing the notion of an "ecological debt." The argument is that Westerners, who have been industrializing since the beginning of the nineteenth century, have exhausted their right to pollute. By warming up the atmosphere, which belongs to us all, have they not incurred a debt to the rest of humanity? We cannot ask the poor countries to refrain from developing on the pretext that the accumulation of carbon dioxide caused by Western countries must not be exceeded. According to this view, it is up to rich countries alone to reduce the flow of carbon dioxide so that poor countries can take their turn in producing it. The calculation of this ecological debt, the principle of which the Stern report admits, is complex.

It is hard to ask present generations to pay for acts that past generations committed at a time when no one knew that industrialization would warm up the planet in 2100.

To Save the Planet or to Save Humanity?

Will the negotiations for a Kyoto II treaty, initiated at Bali in 2007, overcome the contradictions between planetary visions and immediate interests? Bjørn Lomborg suggests that we should expect no such thing and that we should begin to reason differently. Lomborg, a Danish economist, is the anti-Stern, an internationally recognized troublemaker on the subject of global warming. Lomborg does not doubt the reality of global warming, but he judges Stern's conclusions, ecologists' proposals, and the Kyoto Protocol's repressive logic to be ineffective. If the climate is warming, Lomborg asks, is it more effective and viable to struggle against the greenhouse effect or to try to counter its harmful consequences for mankind? What matters to us: mankind or nature? For mankind, not all consequences of warming are harmful. Every year, Lomborg reminds us, 200,000 people in Europe die from excessive heat, and 1.5 million from excessive cold, when extreme temperatures provoke cardiovascular incidents. If the climate warms up, the number of victims of heat will increase, but that of victims of cold will decrease. The balance sheet for human beings thus improves, even without taking into account the foreseeable progress in air conditioning.

Starting with this example, Lomborg faults Stern for never presenting a global balance sheet—positive and negative—for global warming, one which would show, for example, that certain agricultural regions—like Canada and Siberia—would benefit from these changes. Stern also fails to consider the human capacity for adaptation, Lomborg charges. Thus, the average temperature in cities is now 4 degrees Celsius higher than that in surrounding rural areas, and yet city dwellers do not suffer; they have adapted, with air conditioning more widespread in cities than in the countryside. And 4 degrees is at the high end of the warming that the IPCC predicts.

Lomborg is equally skeptical concerning certain catastrophic effects predicted by the IPCC, such as the possible elevation of sea levels. Ecologists often cite Miami as the most threatened city in the United States; if it were swamped by the ocean, losses could amount to $23 billion. But the construction of a dike around Miami would cost $5 billion. The advantage of such a dike is so obvious that it would certainly be built. Lomborg also considers malaria, a disease that heat favors. By investing $3 billion between now and 2050 in fighting malaria directly, we could reduce the number of cases by 28 billion. The same sum devoted to reducing the amount of carbon dioxide would prevent only 70 million cases of infection.

The real choice for political leaders comes down to three possibilities: Do nothing because one does not believe in global warming, at the risk of great losses; act against the effects of global warming by evaluating the costs and benefits of protective measures (Lomborg's approach); or fight the warming itself (the Stern method), insofar as this is possible. Does it make more sense to fight the poorly understood causes of a hypothetical warming (thus running the risk of economic ruin), or to contain the more measurable effects of that warming? Lomborg does not deny global warming; he does not deny that it will produce losses and that we must invest to contain the risks. What he contests is the allocation of these investments and their economic rationality. To invest in the reduction of carbon dioxide emissions would lead to an economic recession without changing the climate, given the previous accumulation of carbon dioxide.

Lomborg thus arrives at a conclusion apparently opposed to Stern's, based on the same numbers. This paradox can be explained largely by the choice of different time periods: Stern is looking at 2100 and Lomborg at 2050. From now until 2050, Lomborg is doubtless right, since whatever we do, the temperature will not go down. For this period, it makes sense to protect against risks, including taking actions requiring solidarity between rich and poor countries. The West could, for example, build a dike in southern Bangladesh, since the Bangladeshis do not have the means to do so.

Stern might be right about 2100: If we do not reduce carbon dioxide emissions immediately, by then we might no longer be able to control natural catastrophes. But in Lomborg's view, we do not have to pose the question in these terms because, by 2050, we will probably have discovered new means of production that are both economically viable and non-polluting: hydrogen, photoelectric, the capture of carbon emissions. Though Danish, Lomborg shares the American Promethean vision, not the European skepticism. Innovation is always the solution.

European governments that denounce Lomborg do not avoid hypocrisy on this subject. Research funding for energy production has gone down consistently in Europe since 1980. Is Europe so virtuous? While Europeans worry about the extinction of species that warming would cause, all the governments of maritime Europe subsidize the saltwater fishing that destroys the very biodiversity that they claim otherwise to defend! When interests are at stake, ecological virtue is forgotten. Lomborg suspects European leaders as well as NGO ecologists of preferring posturing over action, feeling good over doing good.

How to arbitrate between Stern and Lomborg, between 2050 and 2100? Since few of us will still be around to proclaim a winner, it is tempting to adopt the middle way recommended by Guesnerie. The fact that we live with uncertainty, Guesnerie says, does not justify inaction. On the contrary, it is because of this very uncertainty that we must act—but with moderation. Between renouncing all action on the climate, as Lomborg recommends, and betting everything on the fight against carbon dioxide, as Stern proposes, Guesnerie favors doing all we can against carbon dioxide and against its consequences, a middle way, as long as we do not endanger the mechanics of development—the market economy and the progress that it brings about.

This moderation has immediate implications—for example, concerning the calculation of a possible tax on carbon emissions. If we set this tax at a level suggested by the Stern report—about $30 a ton—it would, in effect, compensate for the long-term cost of this additional ton; but any state that acted alone would be committing economic suicide, and at the global level such a tax would block growth. At $30, for example, this tax would double the price of cement and increase the price of steel by 50 percent. Lomborg proposes a tax of $3 a ton, sufficient to motivate innovation. The right tax rate, no doubt somewhere between these two, would induce a gradual change in modes of production without destroying them.

A Political Conclusion

Economic models cannot supply a solution to the enigma of global warming: The risk is too indefinite and too remote for markets and insurers to manage. In the final analysis, as both Stern and Guesnerie emphasize, the choice is an ethical one: Are we in solidarity with those peoples whom warming would most affect, and also with distant generations? Since no one authority in the contemporary world has the legitimacy to dictate a global response, it will be up to voters to decide. It is they, at least in the democracies (China remains the only significant exception), who will elect governments that are either favorable or unfavorable to global and intergenerational solidarity. It will be the task of these governments, constantly under the eye of public opinion, to apportion the necessary sacrifices, to run the risk of an economic slowdown, and to decide whether to abdicate some of their national powers to world organizations whose legitimacy is still in question.

What is at stake in the controversies surrounding global warming is not only warming itself but also political power. If warming turns out to be real and threatening, as the models predict, the authority that would flow from that situation would be global and without precedent; it might be at once a subject of rejoicing and an object of grave concern, for under the cover of ecology a new, green totalitarianism could emerge. The role of economists in this human adventure is to clarify the decisions, in the hope that they will be rational, and to provide tools consistent with the ends sought.

CONCLUSION

In Search of a Consensus

If economics is finally a science, what, exactly, does it teach? With the help of Columbia University economist Pierre-André Chiappori, I have synthesized its findings into ten propositions. Almost all top economists—those who are recognized as such by their peers and who publish in leading scientific journals—would endorse these propositions. (There are exceptions, whose public pronouncements are more political than scientific.) The more the public understands and embraces these propositions, the more prosperous the world will become.

1. The market economy is the most efficient of all economic systems. Adam Smith's eighteenth-century take on market efficiency was metaphorical, nearly metaphysical: He said that it seemed guided by an "invisible hand" that produced outcomes beneficial to society. In the mid-twentieth century, Friedrich Hayek observed that no central-planning institution could possibly manage the huge quantity of information that the market organized automatically and spontaneously by pricing resources. More recently, Berkeley economist Gérard Debreu used models to demonstrate that the spontaneous order that Hayek postulated does exist in a mathematical world.

Market mechanisms are so efficient that they can manage threats to long-term development, such as the exhaustion of natural resources, far better than states can. If global warming does become a real problem, for example, price mechanisms or a carbon tax would easily encourage a more efficient use of energy. It is worth recalling that during the 1970s, when an excess of sulfur in the atmosphere was sometimes producing acid rain harmful to North American forests, the U.S. government did not ban sulfur emissions outright. Instead, it created a market in which companies could buy and sell the right to pollute above a certain amount or "cap," pricing emissions so that factories had a financial incentive to turn to non-sulfurous technology, which was already available. Over time, companies shifted to cleaner technology, and the acid rain disappeared—to the dismay of many green activists, who tend to prefer doomsday discourse to efficient market solutions.

Some economists favor free markets not only for their efficiency in allocating resources but for political reasons as well, fearing that central planning or excessive bureaucratic controls could, in the guise of rationality, stifle individual freedom. They think that markets leave us "free to choose," in the words of Rose and Milton Friedman, and that society is the better off for it—though not all economists embrace their libertarian political vision.

2. Free trade helps economic development. As Smith observed when his native Scotland began to benefit from free trade, it is through access to the world market that poor nations become rich. They never do so by trying to become self-sufficient. Free trade also makes rich countries richer, economists agree. By importing less expensive goods made in low-wage nations like China, wealthy nations effectively increase their own citizens' income—and the main beneficiaries are poor and middle-class people, who can buy cheaper clothes, electronics, and myriad other goods. In addition, importing cheaper components—computer chips, say—lowers the cost of equipment in wealthier economies. In fact, economists have long understood the law of comparative advantage: Whenever differences in the cost of producing goods exist between two countries, both will benefit from free trade, a mechanism that allocates their resources most effectively.

Free trade not only generates the greatest possible growth; it tends to distribute it widely—though not universally—both within nations and among them. As evidence, consider the emergence of vast middle classes in all free-market societies, as well as the economic convergence among nations that have embraced capitalist economics. After less than twenty years of market-driven growth, Brazil, China, and India—whatever their injustices—are closer to the Western level of development than they were before that growth got underway.

This does not mean, as some observers fret and others gleefully predict, that the United States is about to stop leading the world economically. Other nations may draw closer to it, but the American economy has remained the world's most vigorous for over a century because of its superior efficiency, demographic dynamism, and innovation (today, for example, the U.S. is the world leader in the hugely promising fields of nanotechnology and biotechnology). One might add that no globalization, with all its economic benefits, could take place without a global security framework to protect shipping from piracy and to contain border conflicts. Today, the U.S. military provides that security, just as the British navy once did.

3. **Good institutions help development.** The research of Stanford University economist Avner Greif makes a forceful case for this proposition, as we've seen. Back in the twelfth century, to repeat the story, Genoese merchants competed fiercely with the Maghrebis, Jews from north Africa. The Maghrebis relied entirely on family and tribal connections to raise funds for their business ventures; powerful as they were, this tribalism limited their resources and hence the reach of their commercial expeditions. The Genoese, on the other hand, built institutions to bol-

ster good economic practices, such as private contracts, insurance firms, bills of trade, bank credit, courts of appeal to handle disputes, and a financial market from which they could raise capital to finance far-flung journeys. The Genoese also founded a city-state, probably the first state to follow the rule of law. Over time, they won the competition, and the Maghrebis faded away. Familial trust proved no match for reliable, neutral institutions.

All economists acknowledge today that economic development requires an independent and reliable legal system to enforce contracts and ensure fair competition. Institutions that improve market transparency are particularly important, since they counter what Nobel laureate George Akerlof calls "asymmetric information." Economic actors do not all have the same information at their disposal. Without institutions to improve transparency, insiders can easily manipulate markets, provoking outside investors to lose faith in the system and withdraw their funds. This is why the government bans insider trading.

In complex free economies, private informational intermediaries, such as ratings agencies, also spring up, helping economic actors make relatively well-informed decisions in the labyrinth of global finance. These intermediaries aren't perfect, of course, as financial crises like the collapse of Enron in 2001 or the 2008 credit meltdown have shown: Investors, relying on the intermediaries, believed for far too long that Enron was a healthy company and that bonds backed by subprime mortgages carried virtually no risk. But in general, the intermediaries have improved the operation of modern markets.

Some argue that neuro-economics, a new field of research inaugurated by the psychologist Daniel Kahneman, demonstrates the need for greater activity by the most powerful institution of all: government. This field shows that economic actors tend to behave both rationally and irrationally. Laboratory work has demonstrated that one part of our brain can be blamed for many of our economically mistaken short-term decisions, while another part is responsible for decisions that make better economic sense, usually taking a longer view. Just as the state protects us from Akerlof's asymmetry by forbidding insider trading, should it also protect us from our own irrational impulses? To a certain extent, it already does—for example, by giving borrowers a grace period in which they may decide not to take out a loan after all. Jean Tirole suggests that knowing about our irrationality should compel the private sector to inform consumers better about the consequences of their actions—again, the mortgage crisis comes to mind—but that it would be preposterous to use behavioral economics to justify restoring excessive state regulations. After all, the state is no more rational than the individual, and its actions can have enormously destructive consequences. Neuro-economics should encourage us to make markets more transparent, not more regulated.

There is less agreement among economists on which other institutions may be essential for development, and less still on how to create them. Democracy, for example: Its relation to economic development resists any unequivocal description, as each seems to evolve on its own plane. (There are cases of capitalism without democracy—such as China—but none of democracy without market capitalism.) Analyses also diverge, but these days only marginally, on the roles of culture, history, and religion in creating the institutional conditions for prosperity. Until the 1960s, many sociologists, embracing Weber's cultural determinism, believed that culture was the cornerstone of economic development. According to Weber, for example, Confucianism was incompatible with economic growth. But the rise of South Korea and Taiwan has put paid to that theory. Some today say that Islam impedes development, but both Turkey and Indonesia are growing at a fast clip.

4. The best measure of a good economy is its growth. Unlike other proposed measures (happiness, for example), economic growth can be determined objectively: It is the rate of increase in a country's GDP over a given period. Yes, some economists believe it necessary to temper that purely quantitative measurement with such factors as quality of life and efficient management of resources, and there is wide agreement that GDP omits important aspects of economic activity, such as home production. But all economists agree on growth's importance. While a high rate of growth doesn't solve every problem, its absence doesn't solve any.

Economic science also distinguishes between long- and short-term growth. As Nobel Prize winner Edward Prescott has shown, long-term growth results from capital accumulation and, above all, technological innovation, which makes labor ever more productive. States have few ways to promote this long-term trend—in the West, productivity has increased by about 2 percent per capita per year over the last 100 years—but the ways they do have are key: improving the rule of law, securing property, developing infrastructure, and enhancing the quality of education.

Governments also have the capacity to intervene and create seemingly positive outcomes when it comes to short-term growth, which is subject to incessant fluctuation. Whether such interventions can significantly boost economic activity in the short run is a hotly debated topic. For instance, several economists (including Nobel laureate Paul Krugman) have argued that a huge increase in public spending is needed to alleviate the current recession, but others (including Nobel laureate Ed Prescott) disagree. At any rate, any short-term benefit must be traded off against its long-term costs. If public expenditures are funded by money creation, the result is higher (and possibly hyper-) inflation, as in the Weimar Republic of the 1920s or in Zimbabwe more recently. Funding the expenditures by increasing the government's deficit, on the other hand, adds to the nation's debt, which eventually increases long-term interest rates and harms investment. An additional concern is that both the magnitude and the structure of such interventions are more likely to be motivated by politics than economics, so that we end up with "bridges to nowhere." Economists agree that even when public interventions are necessary, they must not result in wasted resources—a trap that may be hard to avoid, especially when huge amounts of money must be spent in a short period of time.

The Anglo-Bengali economist Amartya Sen has distinguished—usefully, to my mind—between growth that takes place under democratic conditions and growth that occurs under tyranny. In China, the Communist Party channels the country's newly generated wealth less to benefit the people than to build a powerful state with imperial ambitions. But in a democracy like India, where popular demands cannot be ignored, wealth trickles down to the people, improving the daily lives of most Indians. Over time, Sen argues, democratic institutions provide a more stable basis for development, since they are predictable, whereas authoritarian rule is not.

5. **Creative destruction is the engine of economic growth.** As Schumpeter argued, capitalism unleashes a "gale" of innovation that "incessantly revolutionizes the economic structure from within, incessantly destroying the old one, incessantly creating a new one." This ceaseless replacement of the old with the new—driven by technical innovation and entrepreneurialism, itself encouraged by good economic policies—brings prosperity, though those displaced by the process, who find their jobs made redundant, might understandably object to it. The long-term answer should be better education, as higher education has proven to be the best way for individuals to overcome crises and evade the trap of low-skill jobs and low wages.

6. **Monetary stability, too, is necessary for growth; inflation is always harmful.** No reputable economist today would deny that a stable money supply encourages investment and bolsters social cohesion, since it helps people save for the future. Inflation, on the other hand—always caused by governments spending more money than they have, and then printing extra money or borrowing to finance the expenditure—destroys entrepreneurship, slows growth, and generates social inequality. Those with less money fall victim as wages and pensions lag behind prices. It's no surprise that hyperinflation often leads to revolution. Milton

Friedman's advocacy of monetary stability, "monetarism," considered revolutionary when first proposed during the 1960s, is now common wisdom.

The best way to restrain inflation, economists now understand, is to transfer money management from governments to independent central banks like the Federal Reserve and the European Central Bank, whose directors—monetarists all, these days—try to create only enough credit to provide liquidity and prevent the financial panics that often accompany credit crunches, while resisting vocal politicians who believe that printing more money would generate new jobs. Even in a downturn, the banks must keep money stable to stimulate investment.

7. Unemployment among unskilled workers is largely determined by how much labor costs Regulating the labor market (with a minimum wage, for example) adds to labor costs, economists say, and increases unemployment. No solution to excessive unemployment is conceivable without reducing such regulations. The rigidity of European labor markets—in France, as we've seen, firing an employee requires paying him a large indemnity and obtaining a judge's consent—is likely one reason that the unemployment rate in European countries remains much higher than in the United States.

8. While the welfare state is necessary in some form, it isn't always effective. Economists recognize that government assistance always produces incentives that may affect, for good or ill, recipients' behavior and well-being. The key is to avoid making individuals and groups dependent on state assistance, locking them into sustained semi-poverty. This economic truth is now better accepted in the U.S., where welfare reform triumphed during the 1990s, than in statist Western Europe. Eastern European countries, because of their experience of socialism, are more attuned to the dangers of welfare dependency.

9. The creation of complex financial markets, despite excesses, has brought about economic progress. These sophisticated instruments, like securitization and derivatives, have facilitated risk-sharing on a global scale, boosting innovation and hence prosperity. There is no economic rationale for distinguishing this "virtual capitalism" from "real capitalism": Nothing real has ever been produced without first being financed. The new instruments are not free of problems, of course—even major ones, as seen in the subprime failure. Financial enterprises are enterprises like any other; they think up new ideas, try them out, too often underestimate the risks, and sometimes crash. This trial-and-error process is not without costs, but mankind learns from its errors, and excessive regulation would only stifle innovation. Even in a time of bursting bubbles and economic instability, the global benefits of the new financial markets have surpassed their costs. The debate among economists today concerns the degree of transparency, risk assessment, and regulation that is necessary for their most effective functioning.

10. **Competition is usually desirable.** Beyond that, there is no unanimity: Some economists believe that under certain circumstances, a private or public monopoly may contribute to innovation or progress. The kind of protection to extend to intellectual property is also disputed. Economists remember that a British patent protected James Watt's steam engine from competitors from 1769 through 1790, stalling the Industrial Revolution. To what extent do patents for computer software or drugs slow or enhance progress? The most creative period in Silicon Valley's history took place before the patenting of software, as noted earlier. Stanford University's Paul Romer, the leading U.S. economist in this field, suggests that the answer may be "soft property"— short-term property rights that make research worthwhile without unduly hindering competition.

None of these ten propositions would have been accepted so unanimously thirty years ago. Some were under consideration (such as the positive role of new financial markets); others existed only at the margin (such as the dire effects of inflation).

We can say, then, that economics has recently undergone a scientific revolution. Neither economic policymaking nor public opinion has yet registered all the lessons of this revolution—but a time lag is characteristic of every paradigm change.

Acknowledgments

The author would like to thank Michael Berstam and Romain Wacziarg for help in selecting the economists interviewed in this book, Pierre-André Chiappori for verifying the scientific data, and *City Journal*'s Brian Anderson, Ben Plotinsky, and Janice Scheindlin for their editorial work on the final version.

Index